C000253286

MUSIC TO EAT CAKE BY

BY THE SAME AUTHOR

Into the Tangled Bank
Why Do Birds Suddenly Disappear?
Waving, Not Drowning

MUSIC TO EAT CAKE BY

Essays on Birds,
Words and
Everything in Between

Lev Parikian

First published in 2020

Unbound
Level 1, Devonshire House, One Mayfair Place, London W1J 8AJ
www.unbound.com

Text design by Ellipsis, Glasgow

A CIP record for this book is available from the British Library

ISBN 978-1-78352-874-5 (hardback)
ISBN 978-1-78352-875-2 (ebook)

Printed in Great Britain by CPI Group (UK)

1 3 5 7 9 8 6 4 2

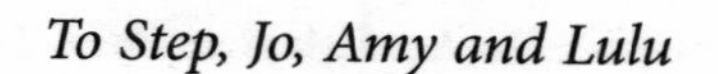

To Step, Jo, Amy and Lulu

CONTENTS

INTRODUCTION

800

This book is a kind of experiment. Taking as my starting point the idea that Unbound's unique publishing model offers writers an opportunity to shrink the gap between them and their readers, I started to think about how best to exploit that opportunity. In one of those moments of utter clarity that come all too rarely, and usually at 3.26 a.m., I found the answer: as well as appealing to readers to fund the book, why not let them choose what it would be about? After a little more maths than I was ready for at that time of night, I surmised that forty pieces of writing, starting at a hundred words and going up in increments of one hundred words, would just about fit the bill.

Naturally I had no idea what subjects I would get – but that was all part of the fun. I'm happy to say that the forty people who provided me with those subjects rose to the challenge magnificently. They are mostly known to me, either in real life or as fragrant exceptions rising to the top of the cesspool we know as social media, and they will, I hope, now be sitting back in their comfy chairs knowing that without their contribution, both financial and creative, this book would not exist.

Some of the subjects have caused hair-tearing, head-pummelling, perturbation, despair and angst. How can I possibly choose the 'best' music? Why make a decision about the 'greatest' batsman? Who the hell is Derek Brockway? The approaches taken by those forty generous sadists when choosing the subjects seem to have fallen into some broad categories: stuff they know I love and know something about (music, cricket, birds, food), stuff they know I don't know anything about (space travel, ice hockey, numbers), stuff that is close to their own hearts (steam railways, Jack Hargreaves, guide-dog puppies), and stuff they've cruelly thought up just to torment me. But I can honestly say that I greeted each and every contribution with gratitude and excitement. In a few cases these emotions were tempered with varying amounts of trepidation and a bit of swearing – while I admire the Wombles as much as the next person, linking them to chocolate and musical theatre was always going to be a stretch. But at least it enabled a few research trips to Wimbledon Common, so some good came out of the bewildered fug through which I tried to concoct spurious connections between those widely disparate subjects.

As well as the subjects, I invited contributions of individual words for me to shoehorn into the text. This task again seems to have brought out the mischievous in people – in a few cases I had to resort to the dictionary, and have taken the liberty of including definitions of some words for the benefit of those, like me, to whom they might be unfamiliar.

In the subjects themselves there is, inevitably, a bit of overlap. I have banged on about my love of cricket for so long and to so many people that it would have been amazing if a few of the pieces hadn't touched on it. I know it divides people – to those who hate it or know nothing about it I can only apologise. Feel free to skip those sections. In fact, that applies to all the subjects – dammit, why not stop reading now and jump to the very last piece, which at least has the advantage of being extremely short? Or perhaps those who are used to reading nothing longer than a tweet might just dip in and out as they please – it's a book, I think, well suited to dipping, but I'd also hope that those who read it from beginning to end will be rewarded with a sense of its wholeness, and will be able to discern that it's not just a randomly assembled compendium of essays of varying lengths on varying subjects.

After much thought I decided to arrange the pieces in descending order of length, so if you choose to read it in strict order you'll find yourself accelerating eagerly through its pages before hurtling impetuously to the conclusion.

With any luck.

Any journalist will be familiar with the tyranny of the word count. The little challenge I set myself to hit the precise number of words for each piece is entirely irrelevant, but I'm hoping it will give a pleasing, if subliminal, symmetry to proceedings, as well as reminding me of the importance of editing. And if the word count of this introduction (including my signature at the bottom) also happens to equal the number of wickets taken by the great Muttiah Muralitharan in Test matches, as well as being a pleasingly round number, then I can only describe that as a gratifying coincidence.

Lev Parikian

GETTING THE BEST OUT OF ENTHUSIASTIC AMATEUR MUSICIANS

4,000

Subject provided by Sharon Curtis

You are, let us say, standing in a room. Around you, for the sake of argument, sit fifty-two musicians, faces turned towards you. You sense in the air the sweet savour of expectation, and it's only with the greatest reluctance and foreboding that you realise the inescapable truth: the expectation is directed towards you.

They have their instruments ready, but they do not play. They're waiting for something, some kind of leadership, and they're looking to you to provide it. Your task, should you wish to accept it (and at this stage you have little choice), is to unite these disparate individuals; to draw out of them something cohesive, convincing, even uplifting; to help them coalesce into an entity that is more than the sum of its parts, while still allowing them room for individual flair; to enthuse, cajole, exhort, nurture, tease, praise, energise and inspire them towards heights hitherto unimagined, manufacturing from the instruments in their hands and the conglomeration of dots on the page a sound to provide balm for the weary soul.

In short, to make music.

There flashes into your head a memory of a cartoon – *The Far Side*. Gary Larson, purveyor of talking cows, bewildered butterflies and laconic deer, at his most surreal. In this image, an elephant dressed in a tailcoat sits at a piano, a rictus of fearful realisation on its face. It gazes blindly at the audience, a thought bubble springing from its head in the traditional way.

'What the hell am I doing? I'm a flautist!'

You're not a flautist. You're not anything. An elephant would almost certainly be better musically qualified than you, possessing as it does an impressive-sounding trumpet.

A cold lump of dread forms in the pit of your stomach. The silence grows. Someone needs to do something, and that someone is you.

Another cartoon pops into your head. A conductor, standing in front of a music stand, the instructions on the music written in easy-to-read block capitals. 'WAVE YOUR ARMS AROUND UNTIL THE MUSIC STOPS, THEN TURN AND BOW.'

If only it were that simple.

Some people might agree with George Bernard Shaw's assertion that 'Hell is full of musical amateurs.' I am, I'm proud to say, not one of them. Musical amateurs have not only provided me with a decent portion of my livelihood for twenty-five years – they've entertained, educated and enlightened me too. I say this not in a desperate attempt to curry favour with a group whose approval I must win over and over again on a daily basis,* but because it is true. All too often the word 'amateur' is bandied around to denote incompetence ('amateur hour', for example). I prefer, as a fan of morphology,† to bear in mind its Latin root: *amare* – to love. Harness that love, and channel it into a collective effort to lay bare and communicate the music's soul to instrumentalists and audience alike, and you won't go far wrong.

Amateur music flourishes in Britain like nowhere else. You can't heave a brick in London without hitting a musical group of some kind and a perusal of amateurorchestras.org.uk reveals the rest of the country to be much the same. On that redoubtable website – the first stop for any enthusiastic amateur musician in search of like-minded companions – are listed nearly 1,500 groups of various kinds, from orchestras to wind bands to saxophone septets to steel-pan bands to ukulele choirs and every stop in between. These groups are in many ways the lifeblood of British musical activity – more so, I dare suggest, than in any other country.‡ Add an even larger number of choirs, and you have a wealth of people engaged in non-professional music-making. And, for better or for worse, you are now standing in front of a mini-pile of them, and wishing you weren't.

---

* Well, maybe it's a tidge desperate.

† Word provided by Stephanie Bretherton.

‡ In Germany, for example, you could cite the local *Stadttheater* as the backbone of the country's music-making – an enviable system of professional opera companies that remains the ultimate training ground for many a singer and conductor. We have no such thing in Britain. Cue rant about public funding for the arts – a subject, you can be sure, for another essay in a different book.

For these fifty-two people looking towards you for guidance and inspiration are not the BBC Symphony Orchestra or the Berlin Philharmonic or any of those magnificent and daunting institutions. They are the —— ———— Symphony Orchestra, and this is their first rehearsal of the new season.

And here, as you might guess from my enforced redaction of the orchestra's name, I already find myself in treacherous waters. It's difficult to address the difference between amateurs and professionals without potentially arousing wrath on both sides. But I'll have a crack.

Let us compare the top professional orchestras to a Maserati or Aston Martin (or maybe that continuing signifier of German reliability, the BMW). Using those terms, the average amateur orchestra might more suitably be compared to a ———— (brand name removed on legal advice).

This is not to belittle them. But we have to be realistic. Playing a musical instrument is hard. It requires talent, dedication and perseverance. And while there are a lot of exceptionally talented amateur musicians out there, they're not, for a variety of reasons, professionals. Perhaps they didn't have what it takes; or perhaps they did, but preferred a job offering such mundanities as security of employment, a pension, sociable working hours and the possibility of earning enough money not to have to subsist on pasta and Doritos for the rest of their lives. Whatever the reasons, they have pursued other careers, reserving music as a hobby, a refreshing counterpoint to the rigours of their working lives. And they bring to that hobby an enthusiasm and freshness you might not always encounter in the world-weary, worn-down professional musician (not overtly, at any rate). In fact, with reference to the subject at hand, you might even say that the words 'enthusiastic amateur' are a tautology – the enthusiasm is, or should be, implicit.

Nonetheless, zeal isn't enough. It takes more than keenness to come in to a rehearsal after a hard day's actuarising or veterinarianing or assistant-laboratory-technicianing or whatever it might be, and to sit down and play a Rachmaninov symphony.

Whatever the whys and wherefores, we have to accept that the beast before us – that magnificent, frustrating, awe-inspiring, infuriating, life-enhancing beast, the amateur symphony orchestra – is flawed. And if you're aware of its flaws, you can be sure its members are too. But if those limitations are painfully obvious to all present, compensation can be found in the energy coursing through the room. It's this enthusiasm, this will to be as good as they can be, that drives the amateur group to such success as they achieve. They want to play as well as they can. Sometimes they don't make it – but they're not going to die wondering. And it's worth remembering that, except in the most unusual of circumstances, nobody was harmed in the making of an amateur music performance.

So we return to our opening scenario. There you are, in front of these eager musicians. How can you help them?

At this point it would be easy to trot out a checklist of advice, all of it valid, that might be offered to aspiring conductors: arm yourself with the most thorough musical education possible, developing a profound understanding of music of different styles and genres, a facility on at least one instrument, and a solid grounding in harmony, counterpoint and especially aural skills; acquire a knowledge of all the instruments and their capabilities; study your scores in depth and over time, absorbing their nuances and honing your inner ear so you can hear the music in your head; make informed decisions about speed, phrasing, balance, style and character; when conducting, make and maintain eye contact with your players; develop the art of attentive listening so you can pick up on mistakes and discrepancies; develop a repertoire of gestures designed to convey the tempo, volume and character of the music and communicate your wishes to the players with utmost clarity and expressiveness, so that your interpretation of the composer's intentions is not in the slightest doubt to anyone observing; ensure your conducting is relevant to and connected with the music, engaging and drawing in the players so they have no choice but to respond to the subtleties of your carefully crafted gestures; don't forget to wake up the trombones before a big entry. That kind of thing.*

All of that, and much more, is true. But a conductor can obey everything to the letter and still come a cropper, for reasons apparently unknown and unknowable. Because what it comes down to is a mixture of an understanding of, on the one hand, the complex dynamics at play in a group of musicians, and on the other, what Jeeves would call 'the psychology of the individual'.

And if all that sounds daunting, then good. It's supposed to. You wouldn't want any old hobbledehoy in possession of a tailcoat and a pointed stick standing in front of these musicians ~~nicking my gigs~~ making a mess of things.

* I told you it would be easy.

Does the fact that these are amateurs rather than professionals make your task any less daunting? Beethoven, after all, is Beethoven, Sibelius Sibelius, and Ippolitov-Ivanov Ippolitov-Ivanov. Your first duty, we are so often told, is to the music, and, looking around, you find yourself somehow lacking in confidence that the people around you are up to the task. Perhaps it's the sound some of them are making as they warm up, or the awkward body language others display with relation to their instruments. Maybe it's just something in the air. You're not preternaturally disposed to quailing; nevertheless you quail.

But let's temper the enormity of the task with some good news. It's a truth not often acknowledged, or at least not out loud, but understanding of it is essential to a grasp of the art of conducting. It is this: most of the time, most groups of musicians manage fine without a conductor. Just ask any change-ringing group how they manage to coordinate a Stedman Cinques.*

It's what you suspected all along, isn't it? The conductor is no more than a puffed-up egotist indulging their monomaniacal fantasies at the expense of others.

Yes and no.

It's true that with the wind behind them, a decent knowledge of the piece in question, and an absence of potentially disruptive factors (speed changes, stops and starts and such like, as well as the sheer complexity of the music), any orchestra of reasonable experience and ability can keep a piece of music going and give it some sort of coherence. In

* Word provided by Chris Gould, a keen bell-ringer. The Stedman Cinques is a specific method using eleven bells. This, I'm afraid to say, is the full extent of my knowledge.

general, the bigger the group and the more complex the music, the harder this is. But the conductor's job, having listened to an orchestra play a piece without their help, is to know what they can add, and – crucially – how. The bare minimum is to stand there and not make things worse; the utopian ideal is to achieve some sort of transcendence whereby the whole is very much greater than the sum of the parts. And if they can do it 'in the running', so to speak, and without subjecting the assembled company to a tedious litany of criticism, negativity, nitpicking, faux philosophy and leaden anecdotes, then so much the better.

Bearing all this in mind, knowing that the first job of the conductor is to start proceedings in a timely and orderly manner, and all too painfully aware of the gaze of the orchestra upon you, you raise your arms. The players adopt a position of readiness. You give a gesture that you hope conveys both the speed and character of the music, as well as affording all the players, whatever instrument they play, a chance to take the breath without which the music can't exist. We call it, in the trade, an upbeat, and it is the quality of this upbeat, and its corresponding downbeat,* that will set the tone for what follows. A good upbeat imbues the musicians with zest and confidence; a bad one bestrews uncertainty and foreboding.

On this occasion the sound that emerges from your gestures is the musical equivalent of a picture of a giraffe drawn by a child who once spoke to a man who'd read a book about a woman who went to a zoo where there had

* Although this is very much the undervalued supporting character in the partnership, the Wise to the upbeat's Morecambe, if you will.

been a giraffe the week before. The best that can be said for it is that it's a noise not entirely dissimilar to music. The worst, that it sounds – how to put it delicately? – fucking atrocious.

Do not panic. This is the natural order of things. We have, believe me, all been there. The opening period of any amateur rehearsal is merely an opportunity for the players to find their feet, remember what it is they're supposed to be doing, get themselves 'into the room'. More often than not, all the most egregious disasters of the first play-through will resolve themselves on a second outing, so all that is needed at this point is to play the passage again, and then the rehearsal proper can begin.

But then what? How best to manage that rehearsal? And where to start? While the initial improvement may be encouraging, it will still leave you some way short of something that is presentable to a paying public – the last thing you want is for that public to stand up three minutes into the performance and plead for the torture to stop, please, oh God, make it stop, for pity's sake, will no one think of the children?

Luckily, you will normally have upwards of six rehearsals to hone the collective interpretation of the music; but in mitigation of that luxurious timeframe, those rehearsals are usually separated by a gap of a week, affording plenty of opportunities for those present to forget entirely what happened at the last one.

For now, you have to prioritise. Offer a brief assessment, maybe some encouragement, and some pointers as to how best to improve on what has gone before. Sometimes it pays to be honest, but kindness is a reasonable watchword. If the music sounds absolutely filthy, you can be sure everyone in the room will know it, so it's no use saying, 'Wow that was superb – my heart swells with pride and joy* at the glory and magnificence of your playing,' when the truth is that the string sound was rancid, the brass drowned out everyone else, the horns were between a beat and four bars behind, and the second oboe playing the wrong piece of music altogether. But by the same token, too much criticism can discourage – a cheery 'Let's have another go, shall we?' or 'You can have that one for free' can set the right tone while making it clear that not all was as it should have been.

'If you don't like what you hear, lower your standards' might have been said as a joke to an overly perfectionist conductor, but there is some truth in it. If you compare the sound you hear to your idealised recording, you risk harbouring unattainable ambitions and engendering frustration all round. Perhaps a wiser goal is to realise the potential in the room. It's usually greater than you might at first think. The trick is to know where to set the bar, and then, gradually, to raise it until the group has jumped a personal best without realising it. Accept what you're given with the forbearance of a well-behaved twelve-year-old receiving a pair of Christmas socks from a much-loved grandmother. But then coax them towards something more acceptable. And, of course, never neglect the possibility that you may yourself have contributed to the aforementioned rancidity. All too common is the conductor who blames the players for their own shortcomings. Remember the old

* Word provided by Rebekah Drury.

Italian proverb: if you want to know whether a fish is bad, look at its head.*

One thing that might help – as well as the patience of a saint – is if you can cobble together something serviceable by way of what's often called 'technique'. The trouble is that conducting technique is an extraordinarily nebulous thing. Teaching an instrument is difficult, but is at least grounded in demonstrable cause and effect. It's possible to show a violinist, say, just how their hand position, bow arm, posture and myriad other factors affect the quality of their playing – the connection between a conductor's gestures and the resulting sound is more elusive.

Here's the theory: the conductor, through gesture, facial expression, body language and general demeanour, represents the music to the players, imbuing them with irresistible and clear instructions on how to play. Speed, dynamics,† expression, the lot.

That's the theory. Would that it were so in practice.‡

The reality is that any musician, and particularly an amateur one, has a great deal to contend with without paying attention to the gurnings, thrashings and writhings of the loon on the podium. They have to read the music, for one thing. That will occupy a decent percentage of their attention – perhaps all of it. The more proficient players will have a lot of the mechanics of their instrument more or less under control, but the more difficult it gets, the less attention they can devote to extraneous distractions. And the

* Not that I would ever compare an orchestra to a rotten fish.

† That's louds and softs to you and me.

‡ Fans of the films of the Coen brothers might like to read this line in the manner of Ralph Fiennes in *Hail, Caesar!*. Repeatedly.

conductor definitely falls into that category. Much as we would love to have the adoring gaze of all musicians on us at all times, the practicalities of playing a musical instrument mean this is a pipe dream. And even if they are watching, there's a fighting chance that a lot of them won't be able to interpret your finely honed gesture to your satisfaction. Try to denote expression with a subtle quiver of your left elbow and the majority of players might assume (if they're watching at all) that you're having a funny turn. Antonia the second flautist doesn't know that when you rub the index finger and thumb of your left hand together it means you'd like her to play with more vibrato. Why the hell should she? She's a primary-school teacher – all she wants from her evening is to spend some time playing her flute without having to extricate half a ton of Play-Doh from her hair.

So while your artistic ideal might be a sort of musical telepathy, your intentions transmitting themselves wordlessly through your being to the group in front of you, the reality is more mundane and pragmatic, especially in the early rehearsals when the music is still unfamiliar. And the larger the group, the more the 'traffic cop' element of the conductor's job comes into play. Stan – French horn, fifty-three, GP, mildly traumatised by a patient who collapsed mid-examination earlier that day – might not be able to hear what Terri – back of the cellos, thirty-six, artist, stressed out by her exhibition that opens next week – is playing, and meanwhile Stef – second clarinet,* forty-eight, freelance proofreader, trying not to worry about the

* Word provided by James Holloway.

spiralling mental health problems of her teenage daughter – is having trouble with her reed and doesn't want to get in anyone's way, so is playing as quietly as possible. A reliable and rhythmic beat with a clearly defined ictus* will help them tune in to the prevailing speed and better understand their part in the whole shindig – a further improvement would be some kind of indication that the balance is somehow out of kilter and that Stef, Stan and Terri should play, respectively, louder, quieter and exactly as they're already doing.

Whatever your skills in the semaphore department, there will come a time when you have to address the players with words. At this point it is often tempting to bombard them with corrections, directions and instructions, all in the interest of saving time. This is often a mistake. Rather, it might be better to bear in mind the sage words of a viola player of my acquaintance, a wise and observant man who spent his working life teaching mathematics to teenagers: 'Orchestras are like classrooms full of schoolchildren – they can only take in one piece of information at a time.' It was a reasonable and tactful critique of my own scattergun rehearsal technique, all the more so for containing only one piece of information.

Whatever it is you end up saying – from 'Perhaps it might be better if we play together' to 'What the hell was that?' – your aim should be to make everyone in the room feel as if they've played their part in the collective endeavour. Sometimes this can be as simple as asking an underused

* Word, meaning in this context 'the point of arrival of a conductor's beat', provided by Hugh Lydon, who has, in his time, both suffered a number of my ictuses and delivered many of his own.

trumpeter what the score is in the football match they're so keenly watching on their iPhone while you zealously over-rehearse the first violins. If you can come out of a rehearsal knowing that everyone in the room has been given a relaxing end to the day to offset the stress of their working lives, that they have been stimulated to give their best, that each and every one of them is eager to return to the fray the following week, well, you will have done a rare and handsome job, and more power to your elbow.

And if they've got away with some blatant mistakes or dodgy tuning or playing in the wrong key throughout, there's always next week. It's not that you shouldn't care – on the contrary, you must care a great deal – it's that you shouldn't mind. The mistakes (and they'll be there, by the bucketload) are a necessary part of the process. And it's the ability to make the mistakes, to laugh them off and learn from them, that will earmark the ambitious amateur group for later success. Sometimes 'later' means 'much later', but that needn't matter – we have plenty of time, and while we're learning we're getting to know the music of some rather fine composers. And, as previously noted, doing nobody any harm whatsoever. Quite the reverse, in fact.

Once the rehearsal period is done, the time will come for the concert, and here's where all the players' hard work (often left till the last possible minute – it's wise to be prepared for this universal truth) will pay off.

There will be nerves – that's inevitable – but your task is to act as if the music simultaneously really doesn't matter all that much and is the most important thing in the world. Tip the balance one way or the other and you'll be rewarded either with sloppiness or tension.

On a good day, when every member of the group contributes all they can, when everyone from leader to tambourine player 'gets' it, and something in the air signals the creation of a performance that is better than it has any right to be, then you can take the satisfaction of your contribution away with you and bathe in it. And sometimes the performance takes off in a way that is hard to replicate or explain.

And if it all goes wrong, remember: unless you were recklessly irresponsible with your baton deployment, nobody died.

SOUP

3,900

Subject provided by Isabel Rogers

It was enough to make my heart sink.

'What's for lunch?'

'Soup.'

Oh.

It wasn't that I hated the taste. The soup might have contained things I would eat: chicken, peas, sweetcorn, potatoes, sometimes even pasta. But it was soup, so all bets were off. Honestly, what was the point of it? It wasn't food, and it wasn't a drink. If it didn't have chips or chocolate or jelly* or sugar or clotted cream, did it count as food? Put Frosties with extra sugar and top-of-the-milk in front of me and I'd eat three bowls; call it 'cereal soup' and I'd vomit. I was like Augustus Who Would Not Have Any Soup from *Struwwelpeter* – five days of soup and I would have died of starvation.

I gradually learned the trick. Soup was a vehicle for toast, and nothing was better than toast. Except butter. And that came with toast. So soup meant I could have toast and

* Hands up who ate cubes of Chivers jelly neat, torn off from the packet. ME.

butter. I even learned to appreciate the heady pleasure of dunking toast into soup. That way it was like messy jam saturating the toast, and I could accept that. The other advantage of toast with soup was that I didn't come away from a meal immediately wanting another one.

If this sounds like the confessions of an unadventurous eater, then that's about right. Family legend holds that until the age of thirteen I ate nothing but hard-boiled eggs and Grape-Nuts, but I know that can't be right, because I'm sure I had a packet of Rolos most days from 1972 onwards.

When did the breakthrough come? At what point did I transition from non-souper to souper? I don't remember a Damascene moment, no 'Holy wow, why didn't you tell me about THIS?' It just happened, and before you could blink I was souping with the best of them. Perhaps my gateway soup was, like many people's, the tin of Heinz Cream of Tomato – sweet, bland, comforting; or maybe, fancying myself a foodie in my early twenties, I sneered at tins and found the fledgling Covent Garden Soup Company, with their upmarket cartons and adventurous combinations more appealing to my snobbish taste buds (this was the late 1980s – nouvelle cuisine had infiltrated the consciousness of readers of the *Independent*, but putting carrot and coriander onto the supermarket shelves was very much pushing the outer limits of exoticism). It wasn't 'proper' cooking, but, for no good reason I can think of, opening a carton somehow felt closer to it than opening a tin – more grown-up, less bedsit-y.

If I don't remember the exact moment of enlightenment, I do remember the first soup I made by myself. It was a French onion soup, by far the most ambitious thing the twenty-three-year-old me had ever cooked. I'd decided, with no basis in fact, that I was a foodie, and this meant I should be able to cook the fancy stuff you might normally find in top restaurants. The palaver of the making of this soup cannot be overstated. It took me about a day and a half.

It was, predictably, awful – a honking atrocity of a soup, an insult to both recipe-writer and guests, whose silence as they forced it down was testament to its inadequacy.

The broth was insipid, lacking depth or flavour, its resemblance to dishwater more than superficial; the bread, intended to offer a layer of contrasting texture to a rich and deeply flavoured liquid, was like the grubby washing-up sponge in the bowl; the cheese – stringy, pointless, dismal – added nothing to a dish already wallowing in a quag* of its own ghastliness. It was an offering entirely lacking any of the qualities that might have made it palatable.

I haven't made it since.

TEN SOUPS

Cream of mushroom soup

A basic soup, yes. A standby, even. But not to be dismissed lightly. That combination of earth and silk, depth and smoothness – it can be a fine thing, a comforting pleasure.

My taste is for some ceps or morels to fend off blandness.

---

* Word provided by Jim Hall, who is clearly a keen Scrabble player, because 'quag' – preferable to its extension 'quagmire' because it has half the letters – is one of the classic uses of the letter 'q' in that game.

And of course I use the soaking liquid to help the flavour along. And garlic and parsley, or maybe thyme – yes, actually, thyme is good. Maybe both.

And I wouldn't thicken it with bread, as some recipes suggest. Much better to use the bread for some contrasting crunch in the form of croutons.

You can keep your chopped chives. And your truffle oil. Needless fancy-shmancy.

But are we going to give it a kick with some Marsala? We are.

So that's agreed, then.

Soupe au pistou

The kind of thing you try to recreate the week after you return from a Provençal holiday – always a mistake. Full high summer sun is required, soles-of-feet-burning-on-the-terrace heat. Otherwise you might as well pour it down the sink. The *pistou* is of course the same as *pesto*, but in the Niçois dialect – garlic, basil, Parmesan, olive oil. Without the *pistou*, it's 'just' your average vegetable soup – beans moderately prominent, thin pasta adding bulk – but it's the light kick of basil and garlic that lifts it. I use a lot of garlic, at least twice what the recipe says. But who doesn't?

Chilled avocado soup

You're sniggering, I can tell. 'How much more seventies can you get?' Well, unsnigger and try it. The avocado doesn't half get a bad press, and maybe the idea of pale green gloop doesn't immediately thrill the senses, but balance the bland smoothness with a zesty coriander, lime and chilli salsa, and kick your sinuses into action. Like all such soups, it's no use whacking it in the fridge half an hour before serving – it has to be properly chilled.

Leek and potato soup

Well, I mean yes, it's obvious, and yes, you could argue it's a bit bland, but let's not be sniffy – it's a classic for a reason, and it's cheap. Solid, dead easy, ripe for embellishment if you're so inclined. Get fancy with it, put it through a fine sieve, chill it and call it Vichyssoise if you want. Or just leave it hot and chunky. It won't let you down.

Fridge soup

Get it right, and this meeting of stock from the freezer and the floppy veg at the back of the fridge can be as good as anything. Get it wrong, and . . . well, at least you've used those vegetables up, and the resulting smug glow counteracts any disappointment about the soup's naffness.

Borscht

I grew up in the 1970s. To me, beetroot came vacuum-packed, limp and pointless. And when I started learning about food and cooking, the preparation of beetroot seemed to be an inexplicably complicated ritual designed to drive out the devil. You had to wrap it in things and bake it for a week just to get it to the point where you might consider handling it, and even then it felt as if you needed gloves, tongs and a three-inch layer of beetroot-resistant glass. We treated beetroot as if it was a witch in the Middle Ages. 'Kill it. Twice, if possible. Boil it to buggery – give it a month or so, just to be sure – then soak it in vinegar or seal it in plastic.'

This was, of course, all to do with the vegetable's notorious staining qualities,* but that hurdle once breached, and the staining treated as no more than a mark of honour, enlightenment was within my grasp. And the gateway to that enlightenment was borscht.

While most people think of borscht as Russia's national dish, Ukrainians, whose claim to its parenthood is arguably greater, might beg to differ. Whatever the provenance, borscht, in its almost infinite variety, is a cracking soup. Here's the ingredient list from a Russian cookery book in my possession: beef chuck, beef marrow bones, ham bones, carrots, onions, parsnips, celery, dill, parsley, bay leaves, black peppercorns and salt for the stock; beetroot, potatoes, tomatoes, onion, pepper, carrots, cabbage, lemon juice, tomato paste, prunes, sugar, garlic, bacon, parsley, dill, soured cream.

Now that's a soup.

Fruit soup

I suspect this is an alien concept anywhere outside Scandinavia and parts of northern Germany. In countries where preserving fruits is a handy way to mitigate the effects of harsh winters, dried fruits are staples, and fruit soups, with gelatinised broths acting as a medium for the fruit, an entirely logical choice.

---

* The deep red version, that is – other varieties are available, notably the radiantly attractive and non-staining Chioggia.

Pappa al pomodoro

The clue's in the name. A pappy Italian tomato and bread soup to be consumed warm in hot weather, with lashings of really good olive oil to embellish. Make it with the most tomatoey tomatoes you can find. They need to smell of sunshine.

Noodles in broth

Simplicity itself. A tub of stock from the freezer. Noodles. Whether you choose the slippery allure of ramen or satisfying little mounds of Italian stelline or even the childish pleasure of alphabet pasta is entirely a matter of personal taste.

Nourishing broth enhanced by noodly bulk.

Simple. Beautiful. Classic. Like Spinal Tap's 'black' album.

Split pea soup with ham hock

Now you're talking. We're getting to the nub of soups here. Because while a summer soup can be a fine thing – refreshing, light, not overwhelming – where soup, in my view, really gets going is in the autumn. Pour a glass of an inexpensive hearty red, fill an earthenware bowl with thick pea soup – the granular blandness of the peas given pep by the background umami* of the ham. Comfort in a bowl: the culinary equivalent of a thick woolly jumper and a roaring log fire.

---

* Known as 'the fifth taste', umami's existence was first mooted in 1908 by Japanese chemist Kikunae Ikeda, and since its official scientific recognition in 1985 it's been all the rage.

Soup is universal. From avgolemono to zuppa pavese, ajoblanco to zōsui, aguadito to zalewajka,* soup encompasses everything, contains multitudes.

Soup can be silver tureens and white-gloved waiters, lunch with friends at the kitchen table, supper in front of the telly, sustenance out of a thermos on a cold winter's day. Soup is thick or thin, hot or cold, chunky or smooth, light broth or dense emulsion, cleansing or filling, aromatic or plain. Soup nourishes, restores and sustains. Even at its very worst – the mingiest, mankiest, dishwateriest bowl of gruel – it is at least a vehicle for slabs of over-buttered toast.

When it rains, I want soup.

Being slow, I didn't realise for years that the word 'soup' has the same derivation as the word 'sup', and therefore the word 'supper'. It's one of those things hiding in plain sight, blindingly obvious if only you thought to look.

The Germanic root from which all those words stemmed meant 'consume something liquid'. A side shift into Latin before the sixth century turned it into *suppa*, meaning 'a piece of bread eaten in broth', from which word to the modern Italian *zuppa* was a short step. Meanwhile the French were turning it into both the word for the soaked bread and the broth itself. Finally, the English caught on around the seventeenth century and mostly abandoned their words 'pottage'† and 'broth', and 'soup' became the norm.

---

* Yes, I looked half of those up on Wikipedia. What of it?

† The etymologies of this, a stew-like soup mainly consisting of vegetables and replenished over several days, and the old French word '*potage*', a thick, often creamy soup, seem to be inextricably tangled.

Soup can be a marker of luxury – think of P. G. Wodehouse's irascible chef Anatole and his Consommé aux Pommes d'Amour, the modern-day equivalent of which would surely be a little cup of intense broth given the cappuccino treatment – but more commonly it denotes poverty. Soup means thrift; soup means economy; soup means making the most of what you've got. Water plus vegetables equals soup, an equation even the mathematically impoverished can understand. Throw in some bulking starch such as pasta, rice or barley, and protein such as split peas or lentils, and you have a recipe for what became known in Germany in the early 1800s as Rumford's* Soup, an early effort to find the most effective, economical and nutritious ration for the poor, and the basis for the first soup kitchens.

Soup, then, is for everyone. Or at least it should be.

TEN MORE SOUPS

Fish soup

I'm not sure we properly appreciate fish soup in Britain. Which is ironic, given that you're never further than three hours from the sea. Where are the bisques and bouillabaisses of France, the chowders of New England, the gumbo of New Orleans,† the dashi of Japan or the psarosoupa of

* Benjamin Thompson, later Count Rumford, was a pioneering physicist and inventor whose wide-ranging career incorporated innovations in the areas of coffee pots, gunpowder, fireplaces, furnaces and thermal underwear. He's credited with the invention of the 'sous vide' food preparation method. He also established the Englischer Garten in Munich, and was one of the founders of the Royal Institution. One of those people, then, who really makes you wonder what the hell you've been doing with your time on the planet.

† As immortalised in a grisly scene in the film *Angel Heart*.

Greece? Well, France, New England, New Orleans, Japan and Greece, mostly. Not that fish soup is entirely absent from the British lexicon. Cullen skink, the creamy, haddocky soup named after the Scottish village of its origin, springs to mind – and a toothsome concoction it is, too. But as part of a tradition embedded in the fabric of the islands? Sadly not. A trick missed, you can't help feeling.

Bouillabaisse

Occupying that blurred hinterland where soup meets stew, bouillabaisse at its finest is a magnificent thing. The best was at an absurdly swanky restaurant for a birthday celebration many years ago – each piece of fish cooked to perfection, tasting entirely of itself and nestling in a finely balanced broth; the worst, in a busy harbourside bistro a few years later, rivalled my disastrous French onion soup as a crime against the palate – the fish chunks overcooked to the point of rubbery desiccation,* the accompanying liquid about as fishy as a bowl of Cheerios, and garnished with a pellicle† of scum. The microwave they used for reheating everything sat in plain sight, a grim portent for a grim evening.

Tom yum

Not all soup is bland and comforting. A hot-and-sour Thai soup is designed to kick your taste buds into action, clear the sinuses. Tom yum, like many 'national' dishes, seems to encompass a broad church with no end of people telling

* Bouncy food, we call it.
† Word, meaning 'a thin film on liquid', provided by Alex Postlethwaite.

you what constitutes an 'authentic' or 'traditional' version. The great writer and broadcaster Jonathan Meades has something to say about that: 'Authenticity is seldom worth pursuing; excellence always is.'

Ribollita

Is it a stew? Is it a soup? Don't know, don't care. It's fabulous, and again you'll find as many different versions as there are *nonnas* in Tuscany. The key ingredients are leftover bread,* beans, kale/cabbage, other vegetables. Like so many dishes rejigged and sold at fancy London eateries for seventeen quid a plate, it was originally a 'peasant' dish. However you make it, the experts are all in agreement: leaving it overnight in the fridge will improve it.

Clam chowder

> Oh, sweet friends! hearken to me. It was made of small juicy clams, scarcely bigger than hazel nuts, mixed with pounded ship biscuit, and salted pork cut up into little flakes; the whole enriched with butter, and plentifully seasoned with pepper and salt. Our appetites being sharpened by the frosty voyage, and in particular, Queequeg seeing his favourite fishing food before him, and the chowder being surpassingly excellent, we despatched it with great expedition . . . †

* Tuscan bread goes hard as soon as you look at it – no wonder they have so many ways of reusing it.

† There are three kinds of people: those who have read *Moby-Dick*, those who haven't read *Moby-Dick* and don't care, and those who haven't but pretend they have.

As a lover of cetaceans, I'm relieved they didn't do the same to the whale.

Dal

Vehicle for tastes, but none the worse for that, because that nutty granularity has its own sloppy and comforting charm in any case, and the kind of flavours you'll put in it – garlic, ginger, cumin, coriander, turmeric and so on for ever – are very much Good Things.

Chicken soup

What, you thought I was going to write about twenty soups without mentioning chicken? Even I have my limits. Chicken soup, of course, has a million variations. At its most basic, it's a light chicken broth, gently nourishing, ideal for coaxing the convalescent to full fitness. I can't help thinking of Phil Connors, Bill Murray's slow-on-the-up-take-but-he'll-get-there-eventually character in *Groundhog Day*, finally noticing the homeless man he's ignored on every single iteration of his endlessly repeating day. Trying to do a good turn, he takes him into the nearest diner and feeds him. Chicken soup. Two bowls.

The man dies anyway. Every day. He was old and weak. Phil did his best, but it changes him, plays a part in his eventual redemption and – oh shit, you haven't seen *Groundhog Day*? Sorry, should have said SPOILERS.

Duck soup

It's a Marx Brothers film. Forget I mentioned it.

Consommé

Not the most economical of soups, consommé, either in terms of time or money. For starters, you're using meat, not just bones, to make this concentrated broth. And you're going to spend a lot of time fiddling around with egg whites to make a 'consommé raft' – a layer that will help trap all those pesky impurities, so the end product can be clear and strong and intense. And a lot of meat yields comparatively little liquid, which might lead you to ask, 'Couldn't I just use the meat to make, I don't know, a burger?'

Yes. Yes, you could. But not if you want a job in a posh kitchen.

Garbure

The polar opposite of consommé, garbure is the kind of thing that gives overcooking a good name. As with so many soup recipes, the ingredients are variable – the more the merrier, you might say – but the key to it is lengthy simmering. You take your vegetables – carrot, leek, potato, pea, bean, cabbage, turnip, tomato and more – and cook them in butter and oil. Or, this being a dish of the south-west of France, duck or goose fat. You then add water and cook, slowly, for ages. Four hours, maybe five. Six, if you have the time. Carnivores will want to add a ham hock, or some pieces of duck or goose.

Even better is to cook it one day and reheat it the next. I'm sure there's a chemical explanation for the mystical process that helps the flavours marry and intensify overnight. Whatever it is, I'm grateful for it.

It used to seem such a faff. But then, when I was first learning how to cook, anything that didn't involve slapping a steak on a grill seemed a faff. But even I, thriftless idiot that I was, eventually realised that such extravagances couldn't last, and the idea of making the most of the available resources began to appeal. I started keeping the bones from roast chicken to make stock, not really knowing how it was done. The first few efforts were down in the cellar with the French onion soup – too thin, too cloudy or, on one memorable occasion, too disappeared (long and deliberately slow is good – long and accidentally fast is a recipe for smoke-alarm activation).

From books I learned the basic principles of good chicken stock: pack tightly, cover barely, heat slowly.

From various other sources I learned the refinements: don't omit the bay leaf; you don't need to peel the onion; even if you don't, in general, like celery, the stock will always be better for it.

From my mother I learned the best one: an old Parmesan rind thrown into any stock at the beginning gives it an added hint of umami.

A good stock can lift the everyday to another level. Cook rice in water and you have a blandly pleasing accompaniment, a vehicle for other flavours. Cook it in good stock and it becomes a worthwhile thing of itself, the kind of thing you have a sneaky spoonful of from the fridge when you're feeling peckish.*

* I wouldn't do this. Definitely not. Nor would I, too sluttish even to fetch a plate, stand in front of the same fridge picking flesh from the aforementioned chicken, scooping up the last jellied bits of gravy with my fingers and shoving it all into my mouth in hasty gluttony. What kind of person do you take me for?

There's an element of ritual to it. The bones, either reserved from a roast or scrounged from an obliging butcher; vegetables: carrot, onion, leek, celery; aromatics: salt, pepper, bay leaf, maybe parsley or thyme or other herbs; water to cover. And of course the Parmesan rind. Heat, skim, simmer so low that the only disturbance is the occasional bubble plopping to the surface.

A house imbued with the aroma of chicken stock is immediately more welcoming. And the whole process invites you to slow down, to adjust to a broader rhythm.

And if you're a vegetarian, shaking your head in dismay at the previous paragraphs, take a deep breath and cut me some slack. Did you really think I'd abandon you in these times of thoughtful and caring cooking?

The problem I'd always had with vegetable stocks was that they lacked the depth of their meaty counterparts. Brazen carnivore that I am, no matter how densely I packed the vegetables nor how much I varied the contents, the result was always lacking in oomph.

And then I found the answer, in a book of vegetarian food written by a meat-eater. Simon Hopkinson, inevitably.

Preserving jars.

You assemble your vegetables, the usual suspects – carrot, leek, onion, garlic, celery, tomato, mushroom. You cut them to what my late, great mother-in-law would call a 'sensible' size, pack them into three 750 ml preserving jars, add seasoning, top up with water, and seal. Then you immerse them up to their chins in a deep pan of water and simmer long and slow.

The intensifying effect of this technique has to be tasted to be believed. It seems any flavour that might otherwise escape into the ether is trapped in the jar, there to mingle with itself and deepen. The result: a vegetable broth that, once strained, would grace any table, without embellishment or seasoning.

Now, at this point you might well be rolling your eyes at my naiveté. To you this simple secret might be old hat. In explaining it to you I'm as good as telling you how to make toast or pour a bowl of cereal. 'Well *of course* preserving jars. Honestly, how else would you do it?'

But if, like me, you're constantly discovering things other people seem to take for granted, if you regularly ask yourself, 'How did I not know this, and why didn't anyone tell me earlier?' then all I can say is that I'm glad to have been of service.

You have your stock. Now you can make your soup.

Which, as I think I mentioned, contains multitudes.

1 + 1 = BULLFINCH

3,800

Subject provided by Robbie Nichols

Consider, if you will, the cicada.

Specifically, the Pharaoh cicada *Magicicada septendecim*, found only in the area to the east of the Great Plains of the USA.

They're quite something. One of 7 species within the *Magicicada* genus, they're black with red eyes and a golden gloss to the wing. Rather fetching, to my eyes, although I suspect I'd change my tune were I deposited in a swarm of them, a phenomenon I'd find simultaneously idgy, awe-inspiring and fascinating.

Idgy, because that's a common reaction to large buzzing swarms; awe-inspiring, because once I'd got over the idginess I'd be entranced by the spectacle; and fascinating because of mathematics.

Magicicada septendecim, like its 6 congeners, has an unusual and specific life cycle. They live, as nymphs, just underground, feeding on tree-root fluids. Then, one spring evening when the soil temperature is *just* right,* they emerge. All of them. At once.

---

* Above 17.9°C, fact fans.

I'm trying to imagine witnessing this phenomenon. Billions of insects, at a density of a million per acre, rising from the soil and marching doggedly to the tops of trees, there to cast off their nymphoid garb, assume their adult form, mate, lay eggs and die.

They don't all make it. Many are eaten by predators: turtles, birds, squirrels and such like, all presumably thanking the gods for the surprise presentation of a once-in-a-lifetime all-you-can-eat buffet, even if it is a set menu comprising just one item.

But the predators are soon sated, and many cicadas remain. The survivors breed, the females cutting tiny slits in the bark of twigs, where they deposit the eggs. A couple of months later the eggs hatch, drop to the floor, and burrow into the soil to start the cycle again.

The remarkable thing about this isn't just that the cicadas have such a long life cycle and emerge all at once, although that in itself is notable – all other cicada species except the *Magicicada* genus appear annually. No, what's truly remarkable is the timing. Periodical cicadas (as they're known) appear either every 13 or 17 years.

Those are odd numbers, aren't they? Not just 'odd' as in 'odd and even', but 'odd' as in 'peculiar, strange, abnormal'. And very specific. You'll already have noticed that they're both prime numbers, and therein lies the key.

Abundance of prey stimulates predator population size. Stands to reason. A bird with a yen for cicadas would thrive if there were cicadas on tap. From the cicada's point of view, they want to avoid cicada-eating birds. One way of doing this is by having a long life cycle; another is for that cycle to be a prime number.

Imagine these cicadas emerged every 12 years. On their emergence they could be predated by any animal with a life cycle matching theirs – so anything with a 2-, 3-, 4- or 6-year cycle, those being the factors of 12. By adopting a prime-numbered cycle they reduce that risk.

The cicadas don't know this, naturally. They just follow their genetic instructions to ensure the continuation of the species.

Cicadas can't count; evolution can.

Hang on though. Cicadas? How do they relate to the title? And what in the name of Sir David Attenborough's safari jacket does the title even mean? Have I lost my mind?

Not entirely. Because the subject Robbie has given me is *numbers.*

I like numbers. They sometimes come in handy, what with wanting to know my own age, how many glasses of wine I've drunk, the Köchel number of my favourite Mozart symphony* and so on. I'm sure you're the same.

Some numbers I'm keener on than others. I love the magical symmetry of 9, for example – the most obvious manifestation of this being that the digits of any multiple of 9 add up to 9† – but find it harder to cope with the elusive properties of the so-called imaginary numbers, such as the square root of minus one. I'm all in favour of imagination, but if I'm going to have imaginary anythings, I'd prefer

* Ludwig Ritter von Köchel was the man who catalogued Mozart's works, a gruelling but important task. The number in question is 551.

† In researching this piece, I have learned that a group of nine of anything is called an ennead. So that's nice.

them to be friends, not numbers. At least then I can bend them to my will.

That said, I'm fond of a nice irrational number.* I like their randomness. A number that goes off on a freewheeling exploration of all the possible arrangements of ten digits after the decimal point (1.6180339887498948482o, say) is much more interesting than the featureless landscape of recurring numbers (0.66666666 is the worst, because my calculator would round it up to the aesthetically unsatisfactory 0.66666667. BUT ANYWAY).

Like many preferences – a taste for garlic, a distaste for Wagner, an appreciation of all things avian – my interest in numbers was instilled in childhood. Aged 12 I bought a postcard from the Paris Science Museum that listed the first umpty-thrumpty decimal places of pi. I set about learning it, and can still reel off 3.14159265358979323846264338327950 288 before getting stuck. I had no real understanding of how pi worked or its profound mathematical significance. I knew about πr^2 from maths lessons, and at some point someone showed me Euler's identity ($e^{i\pi} + 1 = 0$),† but beyond that I was lost. It was just a way of showing off how much I knew. Doubtless I was also showing off how *little* I really knew, but it felt good at the time.

Also satisfying was the conjunction of numbers with sport. Something in my brain purred when confronted with the pleasing randomness of a cricket scorecard or the ordering of a football league table. And numbers like 499, 6,996, 135 and 8,032 became embedded in my brain,

* Basic definition: numbers that cannot be written as fractions.
† Word, or, more precisely, formula, provided by Guy Burkill.

inextricably associated with (respectively) Hanif Mohammad, Donald Bradman, Alan Knott and Garfield Sobers.

But while these things provided me with harmless entertainment, not everything was rosy in the numbers department. I was proficient at long division and multiplication, which other people found difficult, but show me a calculation in base 7 or base 12* rather than the more intuitive, finger-and-toe-inspired base 10 that is the foundation of the majority of the world's number systems, and I crumbled as readily as a fine Lancashire cheese.

I could ramble on, and probably would, were it not for an inconvenient truth. Because when I said that Robbie had asked me to write about numbers, I wasn't telling the whole story. The subject has a supplementary level. Here it is in all its magnificence: 'Numbers were invented by humans. Could you therefore argue that all equations are made up, and that the great mathematicians – Pythagoras, Archimedes, Fibonacci, Fermat, Newton – were all frauds? Who says 1 + 1 = 2? Why doesn't 1 + 1 = bullfinch?'

Who and why indeed?

Humans, so I read, are born with two mathematical 'senses': an approximate sense of number, and an exact sense of number for amounts less than three. That is to say, we can tell the difference between few things and many things, and specifically between one thing and two things.

This is somehow both unsurprising and startling at the same time. Unsurprising because anyone who has ever had

* How did people manage before decimalisation? HOW?

a baby will already be aware of their capacity for genius; and startling because they're babies, for God's sake, they can't do anything except gurgle and poo.

Nevertheless, scientists say it is so. They've done experiments with infants, ingeniously constructed to compensate for the children's inability to communicate directly. By observing their reactions to various scenarios either involving the addition and removal of dolls or the changing size of a group of dots, they concluded that these abilities are indeed innate.

So far, so good. But there's a large leap from that genetically inherited ability to the level of sophistication required to calculate the square root of 225 (15), the product of 9 and 8 (72), or 16 per cent of 75 (anyone? NO CALCULATORS).* And these abilities develop gradually, first through the learning of number words, then through recognition that those words represent quantities, then through steady expansion of knowledge of those quantities. And the development of that ability, it seems, can only come from exposure to a numeric society.

There remain a very few societies where that level of numeracy never developed. Take the Pirahã people of the Amazon, who have no precise number words at all. Their ability to survive perfectly well with just the words *hói* (small amount), *hoí* (a few), and *baágiso* (many) makes you wonder whether the whole number thing isn't overrated, whether the development of numeracy – which was central to the growth of what we call 'civilisation' – was in fact all

* It might help if you know that 16 per cent of 75 is the same as 75 per cent of 16. This trick works with any pair of numbers, and is AMAZING. You might still need a calculator, though. PS: it's 12.

it's cracked up to be, and whether we might not be better off had we remained happily innumerate, looking with blissful ignorance at two beans being added to two beans and coming up, like Baldrick, with the answer 'some beans'.

But we did it anyway. We don't know who those early geniuses were who first recognised the concept of quantity, or made the leap from there to giving those quantities names, or from there to representing those names with symbols. All we have are the artefacts, from which we can reconstruct the timeline of human numeracy, from the first notched tally bones over 20,000 years ago, through the various counting systems that developed in different cultures over the ensuing millennia. Those people – the first great mathematicians – who drove their societies towards mathematical literacy remain cloaked in anonymity. But there's a common thread: all these systems – the Andean quipu system of knotted strings, the Mayan vigesimal system (base 20), the Babylonian base-60 system that we still use for units of time, the Chinese system of 'rod numerals' in base 10 – were designed to represent in an understandable way a world that defied easy description.

The world of numbers, like that of music, is complex and mysterious. The representation of both can be frustratingly inaccurate – but they're the best way we have of communicating their mysteries. With enough expertise, you could no doubt write equations to represent the swaying of a tree in the wind or the scudding of clouds across the sky, and with enough expertise I could even understand them, but the equations are no more the things themselves than the written chord symbols B♭ – Gmi – Cm7 – F7 – Gm7/C – Edim – Cm7 – F7 – B♭ – Gm – Cm7 – F7 – E♭m/C – B♭ –

F7 – B♭ – C#dim – F7 are George Gershwin sitting at the piano playing 'I Got Rhythm'.

So while humans did indeed invent numbers, they didn't invent the world numbers inhabit – that was there all along, awaiting discovery.

Consider, if you will, the gazelle.

The gazelle, quite apart from its fey attractiveness, is unusual. It occasionally abandons normal modes of transport in favour of a good old pronk. The pronk is unique among quadrupedal gaits, as it involves all four feet being on the ground at once. Examine the seven most usual methods of locomotion in quadrupeds, and you'll see that they fall either into the 'two feet on the ground at a time' camp (trot, pace, bound), the 'one foot on the ground at a time' camp (walk, rotary gallop, transverse gallop), or a weird mixture of the two (canter). Pronking is not just a comically enjoyable spectacle – it's an outlier.

There are various suggestions as to why a gazelle might choose to pronk. It might be an alarm signal to its herd, a way of deterring predators by signalling fitness, or a mating display. I like the idea that animals sometimes do things just for fun, but science purses its lips and shakes its head disapprovingly at such thoughts.

Whatever the reasons for the behaviour, gazelles can go from ambling walk to trampolining pronk without unwieldy transition – as indeed we can go from walking to running. And for this ability, they have their central pattern generator (or CPG) to thank. This is a circuit of oscillators that controls the limbs by transmitting electrical signals to them. Group all four oscillators to go in and out of phase simultaneously and you have the pronk; group them in pairs, whether front/back, left/right or diagonally, and you get the trot, pace or bound. And so on. Each coupling has its own symmetry. Mathematically, there are several more combinations that might be used to propel quadrupeds, but the asymmetry of the three/one combinations would lead to the animal falling over, so they avoid them. Have you ever seen a dog hop? Of course not.

But quadrupeds do use the most energy-efficient gait, depending on terrain and circumstance. So just as humans transition from walking to running when doing so becomes more efficient, horses, with a wider range of gaits at their disposal, can walk, trot, canter or gallop, and move smoothly from one to the other.

The point is, though, they don't do it randomly; they know which will be most suited to their needs.

These calculations are pretty complex, but the horses are no more doing maths on the hoof* than you're doing differential calculus when you catch a ball. They're separate things. Yes, the ball/body/hand equations are a thing, and could be worked out, and yes, from them we can learn about all sorts of interesting laws of trajectory and movement. And yes, you could probably sit down and work out mathematically which gait is most suitable for an animal to use in certain conditions to minimise wasted energy. It's not a random thing. The maths of it is there, part of nature.

* Sorrynotsorry.

And so we come to Fibonacci, also known as Leonardo da Pisa.

Fibonacci's 1202 blockbuster *Liber Abaci* was among the first Western books to burst the bubble of the hitherto unassailable system of Roman numerals. On which subject, and I know everything's easy with the benefit of hindsight, but how did a system that has no way of simply adding things up like a normal person and that represents 1888 as MDCCCLXXXVIII hold sway for over a thousand years, when the Babylonians had adopted a positional system three millennia before that?*

Anyway.

Liber Abaci was a compendium of arithmetical knowledge and ideas gathered during Fibonacci's travels around North Africa and the Middle East. It included things like currency conversions and interest calculations to help traders, approximations of irrational numbers, and discussions of various mathematical problems, including what are now known as Mersenne primes, which are excellent, but sorry, no time – we must crack on.

It also introduced to Europe the Hindu–Arabic numeral system, which would become the commonest number representation system in the world. No big deal.

But most famously it includes a problem involving breeding rabbits, which was the origin of the Fibonacci sequence, for which he is now mostly known. The Fibonacci sequence is a sequence of natural growth. To generate it, you add together the two previous numbers in it. So 0 + 1 = 1, 1 + 1 = 2, 1 + 2 = 3, 2 + 3 = 5, and so on.

* I know. Empire. But still.

Here are its first seventeen numbers: 0,* 1, 1, 2, 3, 5, 8, 13, 21, 34, 55, 89, 144, um, 233, hang on, 377, crikey, give us a chance, 610, ooh, this one's easier, 987. Right, that's enough.

Disappointingly, it seems Fibonacci wasn't the sequence's discoverer. Ancient Indian mathematician Pingala had shown knowledge of it some 1,400 years earlier, and it wasn't until the nineteenth century that Fibonacci's name was even attached to it. This doesn't seem fair, but as any parent will confirm, life's not fair.

But what, I hear you cry, is the point of it? It's just a numbers game, a pointless sequence of increasingly difficult sums with no practical application.

Hush now, and consider, if you will, the pineapple.

Before we start on the pineapple's relevance to this matter, shall we agree we're not going to put it on pizza?

Good.

The pineapple, then. Big thing, great hair, bobbly outer parts. Put your finger on one of the bottom bobbles. If you don't have a pineapple to hand, imagine one. Now move diagonally up to the next bobble. It doesn't matter which direction you choose. Nature has made it nice and neat for us, so the bobbles disport themselves in a spiral and you can hop easily from one to the next. Count as you go. When you get to the top, no matter how large your pineapple, the strong likelihood is that the number you have reached is in the Fibonacci sequence. The likeliest candidates are 8 or 13, unless your pineapple is a monster, in which case it might

* Someone's going to write, insisting that the first number in the sequence should be 1. If I'd started with 1, someone would have insisted it should have been 0.

be 34 or 55 or 89, and you'll be able to feed everyone within a 100-yard radius* on pineapple for about a week.

There are exceptions. Of course there are. But nature, when it can, aspires to efficiency (see also the cantering horse and the non-hopping dog). And it turns out the most efficient way for a pineapple to grow its segments, to pack them closely without any overlaps, is to do it according to a mathematical system only discovered after millennia of human existence.

And it's not just pineapples. You knew this already. Tomatoes, apples, sunflowers† and many more – they all conform, very much more than less, to this apparently miraculous and certainly mysterious system.

There's more.

If you divide one number in the Fibonacci sequence by the previous one, then continue dividing each number by the previous one, then line the results up next to each other, you will see them gradually converge on a number that turns out to be approximately 1.6180339887498948482o.‡ Euclid was fond of that number. So was Plato. The Greeks, as we'll see when we get to Pythagoras's non-mathematical interests in a later piece, liked order. And 1.6180339887498948482o represents a particular kind of order, for this is what is known as the golden ratio.

'Please, sir? What is the golden ratio, explained so I'll understand?'

---

* Encompassing an area, using our lovely formula πr^2, of approximately 31,415 square yards.

† Word provided by Rebekah Drury.

‡ If you remember this as the number I chose as an example of an irrational number earlier in the piece, go to the top of the class, award yourself a gold star and have the rest of the day off.

I'm glad you asked, and I'll do my best, although if you're anything like me when I first read about it, you might need a couple of goes and a bit of a sit-down.

Draw a line. Put a dot on it, so that the part of the line to the left of the dot is longer than the part to the right of it. The shorter part is *a*, the longer is *b*.

If, by lucky hap, you've placed your dot according to the golden ratio, *a* will be to *b* as *b* is to the length of the whole line.

Read it again if necessary. And if you're still confused, consider it this way: the golden ratio conforms (again, more or less) to things that are aesthetically pleasing to the human eye. A rectangle in the shape determined by the golden ratio is somehow more satisfying than a square. Which is why postcards and credit cards are the shape they are.

The golden ratio is everywhere in human endeavour, whether deliberately or not. The Parthenon is full of it. Salvador Dalí and Le Corbusier swore by it. The Pearl drum company place the air holes in the side of their drums according to it. The golden ratio is a thing of nature. How convenient that, like birdsong and cherry blossom and the smell of freshly cut grass, humans find it pleasing.

One final thing. We need to talk about Fermat's Last Theorem.

For those not familiar with it, here's the theorem in brief: with n, x, y, z $\in$ N (meaning n, x, y, z are all positive whole numbers) and n > 2, the equation $x^n + y^n = z^n$ has no solutions.

Clear enough, right? But it turns out it's terribly difficult to prove. Don't worry, though, because I have an excellent proof, as follows.

Hang on, I've just seen my word count, and it looks as if I won't have space.

Darn. It was a cracker, too.

Consider, if you will, the human brain.

It explores, questions, delves, extrapolates.*

Humans are unique in this respect. Sharks have been around for millions of years, yet have never (as far as we know) considered the implications of the Riemann hypothesis; the aardvark remains impervious to the charms of Boolean algebra; ask a tapir about Gödel's incompleteness theorems and you'll likely be rewarded with a blank stare.

We alone set out to discover the universe's deepest secrets. It's our triumph and our downfall.

But here's the thing.

Pythagoras, Archimedes, Fibonacci, Fermat and Newton, not to mention Plato, Euclid, Ptolemy, Diophantus, Brahmagupta, Muhammad ibn Musa al-Khwarizmi,† Mersenne, Pascal, Euler, Gauss, Lobachevsky and many other mathematicians didn't create the universe; they merely sought to understand it.

And while some of them might have been denounced as frauds in their lifetimes – Galileo most obviously springs to mind – time usually proved them right. And if not, then

* Word provided by Bernard Hughes.

† From whose name we get the word 'algorithm'.

there was someone else poised to offer a more credible alternative.

These people were discoverers, fascinated by the universe – and obsessed with finding a way to explain their observations – delving into it in ways beyond the ken of their contemporaries. The people who, collectively and over a long period of time, devised a labelling system to define and order the quantities that were part of their everyday lives, groped their way towards something that works pretty well.

And meanwhile the universe just went on being, as impervious to human endeavour as a kangaroo to the Poincaré conjecture.

Does 1 + 1 = bullfinch? If you like, and if you've developed a new counting method incorporating the Hindu–Arabic numeral system with garden birds, sure. Why not? One, bullfinch, goldcrest, 4, nuthatch, siskin, 7, dunnock, 9, wren.

It could catch on.

WHY KEVIN PIETERSEN IS THE GREATEST BATSMAN EVER TO PLAY FOR ENGLAND

3,700

Subject provided by Daniel Cornwell

Hi, Charlotte. If you read this one, I'll buy you lunch.

Wait, what? Who's Charlotte?

She's my friend. She hates cricket, and said she wouldn't read any of the cricket pieces in this book, so I'm hoping to persuade her to give this one a go.

Hates cricket?

I know. Nowt so queer as folk, as nobody in my family has ever said.

HATES CRICKET??

Well, maybe not so much hates it as is bored by it. Finds its appeal inexplicable.

I . . .

Not everyone's like you, you know.

But still . . .

Leave it.

Hmph. Rude.

Everyone, say hello to my Inner Voice. He'll pop up

occasionally in this book in various guises, all of them annoying or embarrassing. Sometimes both.

Hi, everyone.

The thing is, Inner Voice, cricket's one of those things. More than any sport except possibly football, it alienates people. It's the Bruckner of sports.

Bruckner?

A nineteenth-century Austrian composer of long, spiritual symphonies that either send the listener into paroxysms of quasi-religious fervour or bore them to tears. There's not much middle ground.

OK.

So I have a choice: I can either dive in and talk about averages and strike rates and flamingo shots and switch hits and such like, or I can make the tiniest concession to those who might not gravitate towards the subject, and try to win them round. It's only polite. And Charlotte, emphatically, is in the second group. I'm sure there are plenty of others. She was also a generous supporter of this book and is an all-round lovely person who I don't see nearly often enough. Hence the lunch thing.

Shouldn't you be using some of these precious words to explain why Kevin Pietersen is the greatest batsman ever to play for England?

There are plenty to go round. He can wait.

That doesn't sound like him.

No. And that aspect of his personality might play a part in my thesis disagreeing with the proposal.

Oh. You don't think Kevin Pietersen is the greatest batsman ever to play for England?

Not necessarily.

Could be awkward.

We'll see, shall we?

There's a little sketch by Rembrandt. A few lines of red chalk, drawn in haste. You might know it. It's called *Two Women Teaching a Child to Walk*. But the title, in a way, is superfluous. It's clear at a glance what's going on. Even in a sketch he expressed wonders: the flow of robes, the tilt of bodies, the encouragement in a hand gesture, the wobbly balance of a child. It bears the hallmark not just of technical expertise but of something even more telling: the ability to portray the important stuff with utmost economy.

Encounter a great artist in any sphere and you'll find something similar, whether it's the easy flourish of a saxophonist warming up or the elegance of a writer's thank-you note. Expertise, worn lightly, and born, we don't need Malcolm Gladwell to tell us, of total dedication to craft.

Imagine, for the sake of argument, we don't know much about art. We certainly haven't heard of Rembrandt. This drawing is our first experience of him. Something about it speaks to us, so, interest piqued, we delve a little further. We find a painting called *Militia Company of District II under the Command of Captain Frans Banninck Cocq* (more commonly known as *The Night Watch*).* Its colossal scale and dramatic tenebrism are instantly arresting, and we spend a while examining it in detail, from macro to micro, from the phenomenal geometry of the whole to the texture

* For the sake of argument, limitless and instantaneous travel is enabled for this exercise so we can experience the works of art in the flesh.

of the cloth on a bystander's coat. It looks and feels like a masterpiece, but perhaps its vastness and austerity feel a little overwhelming. Did this man by any chance paint anything on a more human scale?

Oh yes.

We are transported to his self-portraits – an unrivalled and mesmerising visual diary charting how the appearance of one person metamorphosed* over four decades, as seen through the eyes of a great artist, made all the more fascinating because artist and subject are one and the same.

From there to etchings, landscapes, biblical scenes, portraits, miniatures, and on and on. And as we explore his oeuvre our admiration for the man's capabilities only grows. What started as mild interest develops first into respect, then awe, and after a while we have to take a moment to compose ourselves, because emotion sometimes has that effect.

'Why,' we think, 'this man was a great artist! There is no doubt about it. The skill! The craft! The uncanny ability to touch the human soul!'

But we have little to compare it with, for our knowledge of art as a whole is sketchy. Moved as we are by the work of this unknown man, we are keen to appraise it next to the work of others. And so we move on, guided by an unknown hand towards the work of Piero della Francesca, Monet, Titian, Kahlo, Pollock and Dalí; of Gauguin,† Gentileschi,

* Word provided by Paul Tomkins.

† The sesquicentenary of Gauguin's birth occurred a year and a day before the semicentenary of the publication of *1984* (as referenced on page 99) – this is one for fans of obscure, shoehorned facts, and only appears in fulfilment of my contractual obligation to include the word 'sesquicentenary' in the book, as requested by Philip Austin.

Velázquez, Degas, Turner and Morisot; of Giotto, Hockney, O'Keeffe, Hepworth, Braque and Dürer.

And as we go, we learn about the history of art, its conventions, genres and media, and we build up an impression of our likes and dislikes, foibles and particularities. In short, our taste. And as we do so, we construct a league table. It might be nebulous, no more than vague groupings, an unexpressed and unconscious preference for one thing over another, but it's there. This is better than that is better than the other, and this one goes over here in this group and that one goes over there in that group. Just because, so there.

Some people take this to extremes, with lists of 'Top Ten Artists' or 'Greatest Ever Writers' or 'Fifteen Symphonies I Couldn't Live Without'; others eschew such vulgarities. But the principle is the same. We make that short stride from appreciation to competition, from appraisal of someone's qualities to pitting them against others. And no matter how much we deny it, how rigorously anti-competitive we think ourselves, we apportion these values, make these judgements.

We can't help it. It's human nature.

For me, it was always about the batting. It was too easy to be distracted by the skunk haircut, the ear studs, the brash persona, the (admittedly annoying) habit of falling out with people. Never mind all that – could he hit a cricket ball? And how did he hit it? And did I want to watch him doing it?

Yes, brilliantly, and oh yes, very much so.

When he was on song, there was in the air a thrilling

feeling that anything was possible.* He had the rare ability to grab a cricket match by the scruff of the neck and fling it to the other side of the room, before producing an entirely different match from his pocket. Here, we're playing this game now. And I'm going to win.

For the best part of a decade he illuminated the cricket field, a mesmerising blend of power, grace, balance, audacity, arrogance, charisma and sheer infuriating bloody-mindedness. He didn't care what people thought of him,† he just wanted to play cricket. For the team. It was the team that mattered. All he wanted to do was score runs for the team. He just went out and played cricket for the team. He said this kind of thing so often that it was impossible to believe him. Protesting too much, and all that.

But, as the writer Simon Barnes so wisely pointed out, while he was and is undeniably a massive egomaniac, he was at least a *team* egomaniac.

It started, from the point of view of the broader cricketing public, in 2002. Murmurs on the county circuit. Someone new. Someone different. Someone possibly rather good.

Who was he? A South African. Oh dear. When would he be eligible to play for England? Right now, thanks to an English mother. Oh how convenient. Jolly good.

He passed every cricketing test: an explosive introduction to the England set-up saw him equal Viv Richards's

---

* Purely in cricketing terms. He wasn't going to do magic tricks or analyse Proust.

† This is, of course, nonsense – he cared more deeply than anyone what people thought of him. But he wanted people to think he didn't care what they thought of him, and he cared very deeply about that. Complex chap, our Kev.

record for reaching 1,000 runs in One Day Internationals (ODIs); he scored three centuries on his first foreign tour – that this was to his native South Africa only enhanced the drama; and then the biggest hurdle of all, and on the most public of stages: a home Ashes series.

Such was Pietersen's effect on that once-in-a-lifetime summer, it seems odd now to recall that he nearly didn't play in it. Much of the pre-series discussion hinged on whether he or grizzled veteran Graham Thorpe should occupy the number five batting slot. The old versus the new, the nuggety versus the brash, England – if that was the way you wanted to look at it, and quite a few fulminating Colonel Disgusteds of Tunbridge Wells did – versus South Africa.* Pietersen won that micro-battle, England the Ashes, and the rest is the stuff of sporting cliché.

There were detractors. Of course there were. More, probably, than any England cricketer had ever encountered. And even now, six years after his retirement from international cricket, you can't mention his name in cricketing circles without some sort of reaction. He's that kind of person. As corroboration of this statement, perhaps this brief anecdotal evidence will suffice: when I mentioned to a random selection of twelve individuals that I was writing this piece, the responses of no fewer than six included the word 'genius' while an impressive eight included the word 'arsehole'.

Regardless, though, of any assessment of his personality, even his fiercest critic would be hard pushed to deny him

* There remain plenty of people who question Pietersen's loyalty to the England cause, especially in light of the 'Textgate' scandal that ended his England career.

his place on the shortlist for the title 'England's Greatest Batsman'.

But was he *the greatest*?

It depends on where you're standing.

Cricket being a game of, among other things, statistics – averages, strike rates, most runs scored, least runs conceded, most wickets taken, most catches taken by a red-headed left-hander on a windy Thursday in Cheam – I now have no alternative but to present some.

Oh God.

Oh HELLO. What's up?

Statistics? Really?

Really. I thought you loved cricket.

Cricket, yes. The nerdery, not so much.

Well, I'm doing them anyway.

OH GOODY. BE STILL, MY BEATING HEART.

Shush. Kevin Pietersen scored 8,181 runs in Test matches at an average of 47.28, 4,440 runs in ODIs at an average of 40.73, *Shoot me now* and 1,176 runs in the relatively infant discipline of T20 at an average of 37.93. Strike rate being a more relevant *I mean it, just take a gun and pull the trigger* marker of prowess in that last format of the game, I will cite that his was a more than adequate 141.51 per 100 balls.

Lest those numbers represent no more than pure gibberish to the reader, *YOU THINK THERE ARE STILL ANY READERS?* here's the context: those totals place him, respectively, fifth, sixth and fourth on the all-time list of English batsmen* in the three forms of the game. If you look

* These statistics are for the men's game. Don't worry – I'll be talking about the women later.

at the averages in each format, *Do I have any choice?* and apply relevant filters to weed out those who didn't play enough matches to warrant consideration, he comes nineteenth, sixth and first.

Statistically, then, he's almost unrivalled.* But it's well said that you can prove anything with statistics, and these figures, fascinating as they are—

You spelled 'tedious' wrong.

Back in your box. As I say, these figures, fascinating as they are, don't shine the light of objectivity on the subject in quite the way we might hope. Pietersen's undeniably impressive performances in the two one-day formats are rendered less relevant by the knowledge that most of his rivals for the coveted title played cricket before the invention of the one-day game. How would W. G. Grace, Herbert Sutcliffe, Jack Hobbs, C. B. Fry, Frank Woolley, Kumar Ranjitsinhji, Eddie Paynter, Wally Hammond, Patsy Hendren, Len Hutton, Denis Compton, Tom Graveney, Peter May, Ken Barrington or Colin Cowdrey have fared in One Day Internationals? We can only guess.† Had they grown up playing that kind of cricket, as Pietersen did, I suspect they would have flourished.

Even in the modern era, the game has evolved so quickly as to make comparisons almost meaningless. So while Pietersen outstrips Dennis Amiss, Geoffrey Boycott, Graham Gooch, David Gower, Mike Atherton, Alec Stewart, Marcus

* To save you looking them up, at the time of writing only Joe Root has comparable figures. He's fifteenth, fourth and fifth on the totals list, and twelfth, second and second on the averages list. But you knew that.

† Cowdrey did in fact play in one ODI, scoring one off five balls in the first international fixture of its kind. Not a representative sample.

Trescothick, Graham Thorpe, Michael Vaughan, Andrew Strauss, Alastair Cook, Jonathan Trott, Ian Bell and Joe Root in all cross-format statistical analyses, that's not the end of the matter.

Because we all know the saying about lies, damned lies and statistics. You can make the numbers say what you want. Mere adherence to 'the person who scored the most runs is the greatest' gives you a lopsided view, and ignores the inconvenient truth that modern players play many more Tests than the cricketers of yore. And if you decide it's the player with the highest average – most runs per innings – then you dismiss a series of pertinent questions that would no doubt temper your choice: against whom were the runs scored? What were the pitch conditions? Did these runs win matches for the team? How consistently did the player perform at the highest level, and over how many years?

What, when it comes down to it, constitutes 'greatness'?

This is the stuff of lengthy and heated pub debates. I have vivid memories of a late-night argument with a group of cricketing friends about a 'Best Ever Men's XI', the gist of which can adequately be conveyed if I tell you that my contribution to it mostly consisted of repeatedly shouting 'BARRY FUCKING RICHARDS' while taking ever angrier gulps of Wadworth's 6X.

The beauty of these discussions is that they have no answer. So, while I can point to Kevin Pietersen's statistical record, to his clutch of truly magnificent and match-changing innings – that 158 against Australia to win the Ashes in 2005, the staggering 149 against South Africa in 2012, the magisterial 186 against India later that year – or to his consistent ability to empty bars, to make the watcher chuckle with disbelief that anyone could be so effortlessly, so disdainfully, so infuriatingly better than everyone else, to the extent that at times he did look as if he were playing a different game, there will always be someone with a counterargument.

'What about Hobbs? He scored 199 centuries in first-class cricket, averaged fifty-six on uncovered pitches,* was so head-and-shoulders better than everyone else that he often gave his wicket away when he scored a century just to give someone else a go. *And* he missed some of his best years because of the war.'

'Well, how about Hutton? Scored 400 or more runs in a series eight times, averaged fifty-seven or near enough, broke the world record for highest score in a Test innings – a record, I might add, that stood for quarter of a century.'

'I've got a soft spot for Denis Compton – the dashing blade, used to come straight from the nightclub, change black tie for white flannels, and go out and stroke a hundred before lunch.'

'Don't forget Dennis Amiss – how many people could have scored two double hundreds against the mighty 1980s West Indies pace quartet?'

'What about C. B. Fry, if only because he was offered the throne of Albania?'

'I can't believe we haven't mentioned W. G. Grace, for Christ's sake. He *was* cricket in the 1800s. More famous than the Queen.'

* This expression has gained some notoriety thanks to its perpetual use in radio commentary by Geoffrey Boycott. It used to be the practice to leave the cricket pitch uncovered overnight, open to the elements. For various reasons this made batting – especially if you believe players who plied their trade in that era – more difficult than it is today.

'What about Graham Gooch? That 154 against the West Indies . . . '

' . . . David Gower . . . sumptuous, languid . . . '

'GEOFFREY FUCKING BOYCOTT!'

And round and round until the barman loses patience and the last person staggers up to bed.

Kevin Pietersen played a cricket shot once. A single shot in a lifetime of them. Once seen, never forgotten.

What the bowler wanted was for him to hit the ball to one of the seven fielders on one side of the pitch, so he bowled it there. But Pietersen played a different game.

At first it looked like a normal forward defensive shot, but then, in defiance of convention and, apparently, physics, with a drop of the left elbow and a deceptive flick of powerful wrists, his body pivoting on an upright front leg, he sent the ball away from the fielders, through the wide expanses of the leg side, to the boundary.

They called it 'the flamingo shot'. But giving it a name, in a way, is superfluous. Just relish it: poise and balance, timing and grace, the power of the unexpected.

That one shot no more made him a great cricketer than the red-chalk sketch made Rembrandt a great artist. But it was a marker, a sign that here was a talent to draw you into the game, to enthuse the indifferent. Sport as ballet, art and theatre all at once.

Imagine you know nothing about cricket.* You happen to

* Maybe you don't. If that's the case, congratulations and thanks for reading this far.

catch sight of that shot. Something about it piques your interest. You delve a little further. You find a video of a match-changing innings in a Test match in 2005, an innings that won the Ashes and made Pietersen famous. The stakes, in purely sporting terms, couldn't have been higher. For sixteen years England had been thrashed by Australia – this was their first real chance in that time to break the stranglehold. They were tantalisingly close, but fragile. Between Australia and victory stood Pietersen – all flash and brash and living on the edge. For two glorious hours, as he thrillingly eviscerated the Australian bowlers, the sun shone on him and English cricket. A star was born.

And from there you're driven to find out more. You look up the other great innings, the rearguard actions, the pure blazing hitting, the monstrously ambitious shot-making, so thrilling when it came off, so irritating when it failed.

What started as mild interest develops first into respect, and then awe, and after a while you have to take a moment to compose yourself, because emotion sometimes has that effect.

'Why,' you think, 'this man was a great cricketer! There is no doubt about it. The skill! The craft! The uncanny ability to play the switch hit!'

But you have little to compare it with, for your knowledge of cricket as a whole is sketchy. Moved as you are by the work of this man, you are keen to appraise it next to the work of others. And so you move on, guided by an unknown hand towards the batting of all those who went before, the names already mentioned. And the women, too, mostly of recent vintage, but trailblazers and stroke-players and formidable athletes, fighting prejudice and getting on with it anyway:

Claire Taylor, Charlotte Edwards, Sarah Taylor, Tammy Beaumont, Enid Bakewell, Jan Brittin, Rachael Heyhoe Flint. And somebody says to you, 'Oh but women's cricket, oh but amateur standards, oh but oh but oh but,' and you pause only to smack them about the face before moving on.

And as you go, you learn about the history of cricket, the evolution of its different formats, its Laws* and conventions, and you build up an impression of your likes and dislikes, foibles and particularities. In short, your taste. And as you do so, you construct a league table. It might be nebulous, no more than vague groupings, an unexpressed and unconscious preference for one thing over another, but it's there. This player was better than that one, who was better than the other, and he goes over here in this group and she goes over there in that group. Just because, so there.

Now look. I'm not saying Kevin Pietersen is Rembrandt. If he's anybody in this tortured analogy, he's probably Picasso: extravagantly talented, eye-catching, controversial, and (if a wealth of anecdotal reports is to be believed) probably a bit of an arsehole.

No, what I'm saying is that with anything you need a way in. And if the red-chalk drawing of the women and the child is your way in to Rembrandt and from there into art, then Kevin Pietersen's flamingo shot or his switch hit or even just his forward defensive, executed with the balance and poise of a ballet dancer, can be your way into cricket.

But was he the greatest batsman ever to play for England? Of course he was – if you say so.

---

* If you want an indication of how seriously cricket takes itself, it doesn't have 'rules,' it has 'Laws.'

SECOND CHANCES

3,600

Subject provided by Mark Galtrey

I was at a wedding. Whose, I can't remember. So if you used to know me, and got married on 3 July 1993, I do apologise. Also, do get in touch – it would be good to hear from you, whoever you are.

Strange how memory works. Although I can't remember who was getting married, where the wedding took place, or any of the other guests, I have a specific memory of listening to the radio in the car, then of eking out the listening on a portable radio to the limits of social acceptability while waiting to go into the church. Presumably I knew some of my fellow guests, and presumably I stopped listening for long enough to say hello. Or maybe I didn't.

What was the reason for my reluctance to attend to the main business of the day? Tennis. Specifically the Wimbledon Ladies' Final. And while my recollections of the wedding are embarrassingly hazy, I do remember what the score was as I turned off the radio and joined the congregation a minute ahead of the bride.* The match was

* Whoever she was – this is really quite embarrassing now.

basically over, but I am a completist by nature, and wanted to hear the death throes of a major upset in the making. Steffi Graf had started the match as strong favourite – she was a giant of the game, and in 1993 was in her pomp, with twelve Grand Slams to her name, including that year's French Open and four of the last five Wimbledons. Her opponent, Jana Novotná, while no slouch in singles, was known more for her excellent doubles record, so the expected trajectory of the match was a tight and cagey first set, which Graf would win before extending herself and taking the second set, and therefore the match, with relative ease.

It never does to predict outcomes in sport – therein lies its glory.

Graf, displaying the killer instincts that so often separate champion from also-ran, duly won the first set on a tiebreak. But then came a dramatic momentum shift: Novotná ran away with the second 6–1, and then broke serve not once but twice in the decider to lead 4–1, with a game point to put the match all but beyond doubt. She had played, according to the commentators, some brilliant serve-and-volley tennis, aided and abetted by a rare slump from Graf, and as I sidled into the back of the church,* with my tranny now silent in my pocket, she stood on the brink of an historic victory.

I could easily blame myself. Had I shown true dedication to the cause, it might have panned out differently. Sports fans are egotistical like that, ascribing undue influence on key sporting moments to their own watching patterns. We

* Whose bloody wedding was it? Was it Janie and Richard? I think it was Janie and Richard.

lose count of the number of times a goal is scored or a wicket taken just as we turn the television on or off, or nip to the kitchen to put the kettle on – and then we say, with a rueful smile, 'Ah dammit, my fault again.' Constant attention is required to appease the Sporting Gods. The England men's cricket team's extended slump in the 1990s can be ascribed to my career as a freelance percussionist – had I turned down all those gigs, stayed at home and watched, like a proper fan, who knows how successful they might have been?

And so, in a sporting parallel to the butterfly effect, my turning the radio off shortly after 3 p.m. that hot July afternoon was the direct cause of what happened next. Novotná served a double fault, fluffed a simple volley, netted a smash, then watched forlornly as Graf slid through the tiny opening and slammed the door triumphantly behind her.

All my fault.

But if I blame myself, I also point the finger at commentator John Barrett. Just before Novotná's collapse, he said this: 'I think the belief is there. At moments like this in the past she has tended to choke in her leads. But I don't think it's going to happen today. We'll see.'

Uh huh. Thanks, John.

I was probably better off not listening. Once Graf gained traction, an appalling inevitability stole over the afternoon. Novotná's implosion played out in agonising slow motion on the most public of sporting stages. Graf won, 7–6, 1–6, 6–4.

There have been some memorable reactions from Wimbledon champions. Pat Cash breaching protocol and clambering up to the players' box to embrace his entourage;

Maria Sharapova breaking off her celebrations to call her mum; Venus Williams bouncing around the court, the personification of pure, unbridled joy – no tears, no release of tension, just the biggest grin in the world.

But the enduring image of the 1993 Wimbledon Ladies' Singles Final is of the Duchess of Kent abandoning her habitual reserve and offering a comforting shoulder to the tearful Novotná in the presentation ceremony.

'One day you will do it,' she said. 'I know you will.'

In 1968, around the time Jana Novotná was born, a young Canadian actor was dying.

He'd been filming in Yugoslavia, contracted bacterial meningitis in the Danube, and found himself in hospital, condition critical and deteriorating. He was all but gone. The wife of a friend came to visit, saw the state of him, wept, turned and ran. Doctors discussed the returning of the body to North America.

People who have survived near-death experiences report a range of sensations – commonly, they feel as if they have left their body and are observing proceedings as a detached onlooker. Sometimes they can see and hear everything, from their own body lying comatose on a table to the frenzied resuscitation attempts of the medical staff. The emotions experienced during these interludes range from the negative – sensations of torment and torture – to overwhelmingly positive feelings of peace, well-being, unconditional love and acceptance. They might see a tunnel, or watch themselves moving upwards through passageways or staircases, or find themselves blinded by a sudden coruscation.*

Our Canadian actor's experience was strongly on the positive end of the spectrum. He stood behind his own right shoulder and watched himself slide down a blue tunnel. He was filled with serenity, an overwhelming sense that everything was going to be just fine – the journey, the arrival, the subsuming into the matte white light that lay at the bottom of wherever. All very seductive.

And then, for whatever reason, he saw himself stop, held fast by some primeval force, something deep inside him that resisted the comforting lure of oblivion. He had already endured illness in his life. As a child he'd suffered from rheumatic fever and polio. Did those experiences toughen him? Did they somehow prepare him for that moment? Did they enable him to look at the soothing white expanse and take the more difficult, less tempting option?

Easy to speculate; impossible to know.

Whatever, he dug his heels in, decided that no, he wasn't going to die – not there, not then – and brazenly continued to live, a pleasing habit he maintains to this day.

Sports commentary abounds with life and death metaphors. Alan Partridge would have had a field day. 'He's quite literally fighting for his life! He's looked into the abyss,† pulled back from the brink and quite simply refused to lie down and die!'

Sport, life; life, sport, as Tommy Cooper might have said.

* Word provided by Marti Eller. It means a flash of light.
† Word provided by Clodagh O'Connor.

We talk about momentum as if it's inevitable, but the truth remains that a tennis match is a series of individual and unrelated events. Lose a point? Forget it; just win the next one. Repeat until the final point, which, after all, is the only one you actually need to win.

Some of the most successful players have been those able to compartmentalise in that way, to ignore the fact that they're two sets, 1–5, 0–40 down and nonetheless produce an ace, then four more, then return to their chair as if taking the dog for a walk, then get up and do it again. Pete Sampras did it repeatedly, never betraying the merest hint of inner turmoil, and his reputation suffered for it. He was accused of being unemotional, not passionate enough – as if the single-minded dedication required to make him one of the very best of the very best wasn't evidence enough of his passion.

We innately prefer our sportspeople to show their humanity, to exhibit the frailty that we know we would show were we ever to attain such exalted heights. It humanises them, makes them more like us. They're not like us, of course – only in exceptional circumstances do they miss the ball altogether or hit a whipped forehand passing shot that bounces twice before dribbling into the bottom of the net. But when we see their emotion we like to think they are.

What people mean when they accuse sportspeople of lacking passion is a mixture of two things: firstly, it's a sort of code for 'I don't like them very much'; and secondly, they want the passion to be on show, but expressed in the right way. Shouting at yourself or the umpire is passionate, but that's just vulgar. Imploding at the point of victory and then being unable to contain your disappointment – oh yes, we'll have plenty of that, thanks.

Which is why, even though she'd quite possibly stained the Duchess of Kent's jacket, the Great British Public took Jana Novotná to their hearts on that summer's day in 1993;* and it's why, when she returned to the final four years later to play Martina Hingis, they wanted her to win almost as much as if she were British.

Our nearly dead Canadian friend, as you might already have guessed, was Donald Sutherland, and obviously he survived.

He was six years into his screen-acting career, with the usual assemblage of bit parts and non-speaking roles to his name. Switchboard Operator, Tall Man in Nightclub, Canadian.

It's easy enough, with the benefit of hindsight, to see when his break came, but we forget that at the time each piece of work was a break in itself – to be an actor in more or less continued employment is to be among the elite. Nevertheless, we cast our eyes over his early filmography – *The World Ten Times Over*, *Castle of the Living Dead*, *Dr Terror's House of Horrors*, *The Bedford Incident* – with barely a flicker of recognition. *Court Martial*, *Gideon's Way*, *Promise Her Anything*. Nope. Episodes of *The Saint* and *The Avengers* – aha, now we're getting somewhere. *The Shuttered Room*, *The Dirty Dozen*.

Ah yes. Now I remember.

Even his relatively small role in the *The Dirty Dozen* (1967) was a break of sorts. It wasn't what he signed up for.

* She wouldn't have got away with it with the Queen, but then I don't imagine the Queen would have let her near her shoulder in the first place.

The memorable scene in which he pretends to be a general inspecting the troops[*] only fell into his lap when Clint Walker refused to do it. Director Robert Aldrich looked around and saw Sutherland. 'You, with the big ears. You do it.' On such vagaries are careers built. From that eye-catching role came a life-changing piece of casting: Captain Hawkeye Pierce in *M*A*S*H*.[†] And almost simultaneously he got the part of Oddball in the comedy adventure *Kelly's Heroes*. And it was while filming *Kelly's Heroes*, shortly before *M*A*S*H* went into production, that his promising career was nearly nipped in the bud.

But he was no James Dean, no Marilyn Monroe or Heath Ledger. This wouldn't have been the snuffing out of a shining star. Our memory of him wouldn't have been crystallised for all time as something untouchable, something painfully perfect, the talent already blossoming, leaving only the bitter pang of disappointment and *Sehnsucht*.[‡]

Sutherland was, at that stage, just another one of those actors – beginning to forge a path, not obviously destined for stardom, a man of above average height and below average looks[§] who looked like he might find a niche as a regularly employed character actor. Had he died, there would have been a story in the newspaper, some sadness

---

* 'Very pretty, Colonel, very pretty. But can they fight?'

† The film, not the subsequent TV series.

‡ Word provided by Rebekah Drury. It's one of those excellent words German has that needs several English ones to express the same thing. In this case it means a sort of nostalgic yearning for that which is incomplete or for what might have been.

§ When he was sixteen, no doubt seeking validation, he asked his mother, 'Am I good-looking?' After a pause, his mother gave him the most honest answer she could: 'Your face has character, Donald.' The distraught teenager went to his room and stayed there for two days.

from those who had seen his films, and then, when *The Dirty Dozen* came on the television at Christmas, we would have watched it and said, 'God, remember him? He died, didn't he? Sad. Pass the Quality Street.'

How convenient it would be to report that Novotná sprang back in 1994, exorcised whatever demons lingered from her traumatic defeat, breezed through to the final and dispatched a hapless opponent in straight sets. But real life is rarely that neat. Ask Jimmy White, the brilliant snooker player whose wan face adorned the loser's seat in the World Championship final at the Crucible Theatre in Sheffield six times.

Six times.

Palpable, excruciating agony. To be easily good enough to win, and yet never to do so – it hardly bears contemplation.

The disappointment of that first defeat, an agonisingly narrow one against the famously impassive Steve Davis in 1984, when White was just twenty-two, was tempered by the knowledge that he would have many more opportunities to win the sport's biggest prize. And so he did, in 1990, when he lost to John Parrott. He reached the next four finals as well, losing them all to Stephen Hendry, White's mesmerising brilliance no match for the Scot's dour relentlessness.* And that was that. Snooker, during White's career, had made the transition from saloon-bar pastime to fully professional sport. Gone were the days when the players

* Yes, this is a cliché and a stereotype – sadly, it's also true.

would have a fag and a pint on the go while they were playing – by 1994, when White lost the last of his finals, it had become a young man's game, all mineral water and energy bars.

That same year, at Wimbledon, Novotná lost in the quarter-finals to Martina Navratilova, and it wasn't until 1997 that she reached her second final.

Again, there was hope – she won the first set 6–3 – and again her opponent came back, but on this occasion there was no special drama. Once Hingis got into the match, she was the better player, and that was that.

Life is a long succession of *Sliding Doors* moments – infinite possibilities branching out from the simplest and most mundane decisions. What would have happened if I'd had tea rather than coffee, stopped to give money to the homeless person, decided to run for president?

In the multiverse proposed by some as explanation for the unfathomable mysteries of everything, there are infinite Donald Sutherlands living out infinite lives. In some of them, he died in 1968; in others, his career hit the skids and he went back to his original career choice, engineering; in still others, he won the Best Actor Oscar for his role as Darth Vader's pet hamster, Zblarf, in the monstrously successful space comedy *Adventures of Luke Starkiller as Taken from the Journal of the Whills, Saga 1: The Star Wars.**

* This was the original working title for the film now known as *Star Wars: A New Hope* – the one anyone of a certain age knows simply as *Star Wars.*

In this universe – the one in which, like it or not, we're stuck – he became one of the most successful character actors of his generation, respected for his versatility, genial smile and the ability to exude a sense of unpredictability – not the borderline dangerous weirdness associated with, say, Christopher Walken, just an underlying feeling that something slightly odd might happen at any minute.

Younger viewers might know him as President Snow in the *Hunger Games* series, or John Bridger in the remake of *The Italian Job*; for people of my generation it's more likely to be from his roles in *Klute* or *Don't Look Now*, the aforementioned *M*A*S*H*, *Kelly's Heroes* or *The Dirty Dozen*, or possibly his callipygian* cameo in *Animal House*. My own abiding memory of him, from my formative years of late-night television, is in the final shot in *Invasion of the Body Snatchers* – that kindly, sardonic mouth transformed into an expressionless, gaping maw of doom. I was fifteen – you remember that kind of thing.

This success, this run of almost continuous employment over five decades, hasn't happened by accident. It's down to that fruitful combination of talent, dedication and luck: measure, mix, season. The exact proportions are a matter of taste, but don't go too heavy on the luck – it's not garlic.

Like an athlete, an actor devotes years to their craft with no promise of reward. But in sport you are judged by tangible results – trophies, championships, rankings. While actors are always delighted to win awards, they're mostly sanguine about their true value. And the worth of their

* Word, meaning 'possessing beautiful buttocks', provided by Sanchia Norman. I worked hard to find an appropriate place for its inclusion.

work is entirely subjective. One person's *The Godfather* is another's *Love, Actually* and vice versa. But by most objective standards, you'd look at Sutherland's body of work and reach the conclusion that his life has been successful. If nothing else, people have let him do a lot of acting.

Can any of that be ascribed to his brush with death over fifty years ago? Did he emerge from that experience, as many do, with a changed outlook on life? Did he become more compassionate, purposeful and determined to make the most of whatever time he had left? Is the Donald Sutherland of this universe fundamentally different from the one in another universe who didn't contract meningitis?

I wouldn't pretend to know – and nor, I suspect, would he. He doesn't exude the earnest, 'born-again' persona, urging others to seize every opportunity. But something mysterious stopped him continuing down that blue tunnel, made him dig his heels in and say, 'Not now,' made him hold on with tenacious fingertips to the prize of life. And he hasn't wasted it.

Third time lucky?

In 1998 Novotná was the third seed, one of the big guns. The portents were good. The draw 'opened up for her', as sporting argot has it. Unseeded Natasha Zvereva did a lot of the donkey work, taking care of both Steffi Graf and Monica Seles before falling to Nathalie Tauziat in the semi-final. Novotná's own passage to the final was no cakewalk – a close quarter-final against Venus Williams was followed by a rematch with Hingis in the semi. But crucially, her opponent in the final was both lower-ranked and less experienced at the highest level. Nathalie Tauziat was a 'veteran', a 'journeywoman', who had never been beyond the quarter-finals in twelve previous Wimbledons – seeded 16, reaching the final was the pinnacle of her career. Raining on Novotná's parade was unlikely to be on the agenda.

In the multiverse, Novotná loses to Hingis in the semi-final. Or she's injured. Or, worse, she's cruising to victory against Tauziat but suffers a crippling bout of the yips and implodes in imitation of the match against Graf five years earlier.

But in this universe – the one in which, I'm glad to say, we are stuck – she's at ease, notably superior. She builds a comfortable lead. The Duchess of Kent, watching with 13,000 others, must remain impartial – but don't even try to tell me that a small part of her isn't willing Novotná to win. Tauziat won't have another chance – but this isn't her story, it's Novotná's, has always been Novotná's, always will be Novotná's, so when the moment comes and she has match point and the ball presents itself for an easy shot down the line to win the point, the game, the match, the championship, and even if maybe the memory of that traumatic day five years earlier does resurface, and maybe for just a nanosecond there is a trace of uncertainty, it doesn't matter, because this Jana Novotná, this winner, this champion, dismisses the merest hint of the thought of the possibility of failure, flicks it to one side like a speck of dandruff on a jacket collar, and sends the ball spinning away, beyond her opponent's reach, and there it is, an outpouring of joy and relief and pure sunshine illuminating the court, and the weight falls from her shoulders, and in its stead there is lightness, calm, certainty.

And there's the Duchess of Kent, abandoning reserve again and taking both her hands and giving her a grin of pure pleasure, maybe saying, 'I was right, you see?' And it's easy to forget that not five yards away is Tauziat, loser in what was always going to be her only final, and you wonder, just for a second, how she feels about it all, knowing that for her there will be no second chance.

WHERE'S THE CUE BALL GOING?

3,500

Subject provided by David Smith

I can't understand a word of it, yet it unfailingly brings a lump to the throat. A man, shouting, the pitch of his voice conveying not just excitement but delirious, incredulous joy. In the background, that inchoate roar immediately recognisable as a football crowd – they too are in a state of agitation, but that's nothing compared to the commentator. His voice goes one notch higher, competing with the surge of background noise, beating it. It cracks, turns into a series of incoherent squeaks. You fear for him – is he in fact about to explode?

It would be easy to dismiss it as hysterical raving, just another example of the absurdly hyperbolic behaviour of sports pundits, but there's something about it, something primal and pure, that makes it compelling listening. We're carried along by his ecstasy, drawn into it. Here's a professional broadcaster being genuinely carried away, channelling his inner eight-year-old, laying himself bare for all to hear. With these sounds, Guðmundur Benediktsson tells us, whether we speak his language or not, that something momentous has happened – something unbelievable.

Iceland have beaten England at football.

And here's Holding now, his long stride eating up the ground. They call him Whispering Death. Is there a more dangerous bowler in the world today? Certainly England have no answers. Fifty-three for eight and only Parikian stands between them and humiliating defeat. Holding's in, he bowls, and Parikian works the ball to the boundary with the nonchalance of a man completely at ease. He had all the time in the world to play that. Perhaps there's hope for England yet with this remarkable young batsman at the crease . . .

Well, we can all dream, can't we? And in the summer of 1976 I did a lot of that. When not stalking the village looking for birds, I could be found roaming the garden, cricket bat in hand, commentating under my breath on my own invented heroic exploits, in imitation of the voices I heard on the radio and television. In my head I was not only English cricket's saviour, but its chronicler and one-man commentariat too. No wonder I identified so closely with Snoopy and his Mitty-esque flights of fancy ('Here's the world-famous hockey player . . . ').*

Those voices are etched into my psyche. I hear them still. Barry Davies ('Interesting. Very interesting! Look at his face! Just look at his face!'), Brian Johnston ('Oh, Aggers, do stop it' – although that was much later), John Arlott ('The stroke of a man knocking a thistle top off with a walking stick'), Dan Maskell ('Oh I say, what a dream of a volleh!')

Sundays meant John Player League cricket on BBC Two: Peter West's pipe and Jim Laker's gentle burr describing

* Nowadays my sympathies lie with Charlie Brown. Does that mean I've finally grown up?

what by today's standards would be seen as laughably slow one-day cricket, but at the time was regarded as the thrillingly accelerated 'instant' form of the game. Saturday afternoons saw Frank Bough presiding over a potpourri of sporting action on *Grandstand*, culminating in the classified football results. During the school week, Tuesday evenings meant staying up late for *Sportsnight with Coleman*. And sometimes there was live athletics from somewhere exotic like Gothenburg, with David Bedford coming fourth.

These early experiences of televised and wirelessed sport were soon complemented by visits to live events. How bewildering they turned out to be.

I'm not sure if Oxford United vs Nottingham County, sometime in the early 1970s, was the first football match I went to, but my memory insists on thrusting it to the forefront.

There was the ground, both larger and smaller than I'd imagined. The noise from the terraces at the far end was thrilling and scary. And there were the players in front of me, real people, big and burly, hairy and spitting, far removed from the tiny figures I knew from the television.

The differences in the experience quickly became clear. I couldn't see all the play the way I could on the telly; there were boring bits, whole stretches when little happened – a shock to a child used to watching the highlights; when a goal was scored at the other end all I saw was a flurry of activity and the celebration; and where was the instant replay so I could catch up on what I'd missed?

Most of all, though, there was nobody in my ear offering a running commentary and analysis, telling me what I should think, and why Atkinson would be better deployed in the channel rather than wasted wide on the right, to be fair, Clive.

It took me a while to realise that I needed to concentrate, that the lulls were an essential part of the experience, and that the disappointment of not being able to see everything was offset by the thrill of being at a live event.

Back home, I re-enacted what I'd seen as best I could, dribbling the ball past imaginary defenders before blasting it into the back of the imaginary net.

Parikian jinks past one man, past two, he's into the box, he shoots, HE SCOOOOOOOOORES!

The sport, whether real or the product of my fertile young brain, was absorbing enough – but the voices brought it thrillingly to life.

Broadcast sports commentary began, in Britain at least, in 1927.* The BBC had received royal assent to transmit live sporting events on the wireless, and they opened with a Rugby Union international, followed soon after by the first broadcast of a football match, between Arsenal and Sheffield United. The commentary for that match doesn't survive, but listening to a recording of another game from the early 1930s is a surreal experience to anyone even half accustomed to modern radio commentary. There are two men talking, both in possession of the regulation BBC accent of the day (i.e. to modern ears indescribably posh). While one describes the action – 'The ball comes deaown to Bri'on. Awn to MecMullan, MecMullan byeck to Marshall.

* America, being America, was sixteen years ahead of us.

Marshall acrawss the field to Busbeh . . . ' – the other interjects with numbers – 'FIVE! THREE! ONE! EIGHT!' – bellowed as if from another room by an itinerant bingo caller. This technique, the brainchild of Lance Sieveking, was an attempt to convey something of the visual in an audio medium. The numbers corresponded to a grid printed in that week's *Radio Times*, and it was presumed that the listener would have the grid handy while listening.* Whether this technique was helpful is moot – to modern ears it sounds stilted and surreal.

After a while commentators developed enough confidence in their ability to convey the whole picture for the number-shouter to become irrelevant. And public opinion had moved on too. Where in the fledgling days the second commentator – or 'Dr Watson', as they were known – was considered helpful, by the 1940s they were regarded by many as an irrelevance and an irritation. A letter to one of the BBC's earliest commentators gave some pithy advice on how he might deal with the 'blithering idiot' with whom he had recently shared commentating duties: 'My advice to you is strangle him.'

The possibility of this level of antagonism was not lost on the decision makers. In a 1942 pamphlet prepared for BBC staff, the director of outside broadcasts, Seymour Joly de Lotbiniere,† appended a list of 'don'ts', of which the most lasting and pertinent was surely a warning against 'irritating

* There is a theory that this is the origin of the expression 'back to square one'. The alternative explanation, that it's from Snakes and Ladders or other similar board games, seems more logical and reasonable to me, but what place do logic and reason have in modern life?

† Known universally as 'Lobby', de Lotbiniere was a pivotal figure in the formative years of sports broadcasting in the UK.

the listener'. The main thrust of the pamphlet was a thorough appraisal of the principles of sports broadcasting, and some of the challenges of particular sports. While football and rugby, with their rhythms of mostly action and occasional lulls to catch breath, lent themselves well to radio, there was an onus on the commentators to make sure the flow of play was comprehensible to the listener. For tennis, meanwhile, with speed of play making tongue-twisters out of every point, and its naturally repetitive nature giving great potential for monotony, it was considered 'almost impossible to prescribe any treatment that is wholly satisfactory'. Cricket, predictably enough, suffered from the opposite problem – in a naturally slow-moving* game, the onus fell to the commentators to embellish their factual descriptions with what would now, distressingly, be called 'banter'.

Potential commentators were sought. Unsurprisingly for the culture of the BBC at the time, some of the basics had to be in place: white, male, public school, obviously. But beyond those clearly indispensable characteristics, they needed the ability to make whichever sporting event they were describing come alive, to persuade the listener that they had a 'ringside seat'.

Neatly fulfilling all these criteria were Old Etonians Brian Johnston and Henry Blofeld ('Johnners' and 'Blowers'), both of whom were at the heart of the relaxed style of cricket commentary for which *Test Match Special* became known and loved. Their modus operandi contrasted with that of Hampshire poet, wordsmith and prodigious consumer of

* But nevertheless gripping, obviously.

red wine John Arlott, who, despite Lobby's assessment – 'I think you have a very vulgar voice. I can't understand why people want to listen to it'* – became as indispensable to cricket coverage on the radio as the cricket itself.

Those were the voices I grew up with, sometimes only just discernible through heavy static on long car journeys (my poor, long-suffering parents). But sport was on the television too, and there, more often than not, the important thing was not what the commentator said, but what they didn't.

The problem with commentating on billiards, according to de Lotbiniere's pamphlet, was that it was 'almost impossible to pick a moment when the event is reaching its climax'. When he wrote those words, the reigning World Billiards Champion was Walter Lindrum, who had beaten Joe Davis 23,553 points to 22,678. A scoring shot in billiards yields a maximum of three points, so a 46,000-point match is a lengthy procedure, and with only three balls in play, it's not hard to imagine its unsuitability for the radio. Snooker, with its twenty-two balls in a variety of colours, might at least offer more opportunities for discursive meanderings on the commentator's part, but the truth is that neither sport lends itself to radio commentary. It wasn't really until the advent of colour television that snooker got a toehold in the public's imagination, but when it did, it took off. It just so happened that its surge in popularity coincided with my

* This is unfair, because he went on to say, 'But you've got a very interesting mind and I think you'd better continue.'

teenage years, when sitting on a sofa watching television for six hours was about as energetic as I got. Add to that our ownership of a warped quarter-size snooker table on which I could attempt to emulate my new-found heroes, throw in the delicious irony of something so profoundly unathletic suddenly being acceptable as a sport, and I was hooked.

Part of the allure was the slow burn. With a final played over two days* there was every opportunity for ebb and flow, minute analysis of tactics, and even the odd nap. The micro- and macro-rhythms of the game were matched and enhanced by the hushed tones of 'Whispering' Ted Lowe, who had been instrumental in bringing the game to the television in the first place. Lowe became known to the wider public as the perpetrator of one of sports television's finer gaffes: 'For those of you watching in black and white, the pink is next to the green.' But if this gives the impression of him as an Alan Partridge prototype, that is something that the truth couldn't be further away from.† He was a consummate professional who knew the game inside out, but he didn't bludgeon the viewer with his knowledge – it came out when needed. And while the whispering quality of his voice that gave him his nickname was a matter of necessity – snooker is above all a game of hushed concentration, for which a shouty commentator would be considered *de trop* – there was something more, something comforting, something in that soft rumbling that told you you were in safe hands. And a large part of that (and I cannot emphasise the significance of this strongly enough

* Pathetically short compared to matches of the late 1940s – the longest was played over 145 frames and lasted two weeks.

† Yes, pedants, I did deliberately end that sentence with two prepositions.

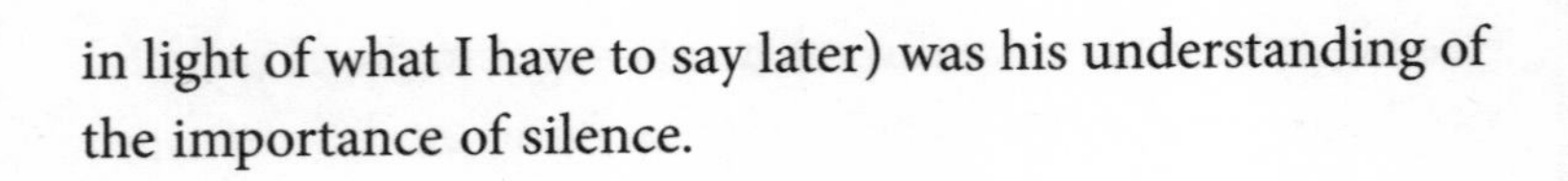

in light of what I have to say later) was his understanding of the importance of silence.

See? Bliss.

If something needed commenting on, elucidating, celebrating or commiserating about, he did so. Otherwise he let the players play and the viewers view.

Lovely stuff.

Silence is the most potent weapon in the television commentator's armoury. Yes, of course they must sometimes let themselves embark on flights of fancy, get carried away by the emotion of the occasion, convey the sense of excitement, euphoria and perpetual anticipation that is at the heart of every sports lover's attraction to what could easily be seen as a fundamentally ludicrous waste of time.

Of course. Sometimes.

But knowing when to shut up, to let the action speak for itself, to allow the viewer to relax, is at the heart of the television commentator's craft. Ted Lowe understood that. So did Richie Benaud, the doyen of cricket commentators, and possibly the best of them all across all sports.

When Richie Benaud was on the air, whole overs would pass without comment. A certain type of commentator would blather on about raised seams or uncovered pitches or the round of golf they played yesterday or the NatWest Cup quarter-final when Belly leathered it into the hospitality boxes – remember that, mate? Wit-dulling drivel that only serves to dilute the effect when they finally have something of import to say.

Not Richie Benaud. Like a heron stalking a fish, he awaited the moment. Eventually, a cover drive from Gower or an authoritative Bothamesque pull would materialise, and Richie would allow himself a clipped 'shot of the morning'. He might follow it with an amused 'and now Chappell needs to decide whether to stick or twist'. Or he might not.

And come the memorable occasion, the greats like Richie invariably find the right way to express its emotion, to capture and enhance it for the viewer, so that in future years the images are indivisible from the commentary.

What makes a magical commentary moment? I'm not talking about the gaffes – it's easy to mock them from the safety of our sofas, conveniently forgetting that our own daily idiocies aren't subjected to the scrutiny of thousands and often preserved for the cruel delight of future generations.

No, I'm talking about the happy confluence of a great sporting moment and someone capable of describing it.

If you're any kind of sports fan you'll have your favourites. Brian Moore, perhaps, describing Michael Thomas's last-minute goal for Arsenal against Liverpool to win not just the match but the championship: 'It's all up for grabs now!' Or Bjørge Lillelien's finest moment, when Norway beat England in 1981: 'Lord Nelson, Lord Beaverbrook, Sir Winston Churchill, Sir Anthony Eden, Clement Attlee, Henry Cooper, Lady Diana, Maggie Thatcher! Can you hear me, Maggie Thatcher?

Your boys took a hell of a beating!'* And when Barry Davies responded to Diego Maradona's second goal against England in the 1986 World Cup† with, 'Oh! You have to say that's magnificent!' it was a visceral reaction that encapsulated the emotion of the moment. An entire country hated the Argentinian genius for the fraudulent goal he'd scored minutes earlier, but when someone leaves eight international players sprawling in his wake like so many toddlers, and then calmly side-foots the ball into the net, even the most curmudgeonly,‡ one-eyed, flag-of-St-George-waving, jingoistic England fan will, even if only at the deepest of subconscious levels, acknowledge that Maradona was just too good.

What these and many other instances have in common is an instinct for communication tied to an uncanny knack to express the moment in words, and an understanding that the words, and how you say them, really do matter.

And so we come, reluctantly, but in accordance with the terms and conditions of this book, to John Virgo.

I say 'reluctantly' because I've wanted to use this piece as a celebration of the noble art of sports commentary, and I do not consider Virgo to be anywhere near the pantheon. Quite the opposite, in fact. But the title of this piece is 'Where's the Cue Ball Going?' and those words are indelibly associated with him, so here goes.

---

* Of all the names listed in that magnificent diatribe, it's the random insertion of Henry Cooper that pleases me the most.

† The first was the famous 'Hand of God' goal.

‡ Word provided by Katharine Baird. This isn't strictly true – she asked me to include 'curmudgeon'. I hope this will do.

The context: John Virgo is a former snooker player who now commentates on the sport for BBC television. If you're a snooker fan in the UK, you will know his voice. You will also know the expression 'Where's the cue ball going?'* because . . . well, he says it a lot. So much, in fact, that there exists on YouTube a fifteen-minute video consisting only of John Virgo saying those words.†

Catchphrases can be great. 'Nice to see you, to see you nice' served as a jolly welcome to our Saturday evening's entertainment in the 1970s.‡ 'Where's the cue ball going?' has become pointless and irritating, but the more people rail against it, the more he uses it. I suspect he thinks it's endearing.

I beg to differ.

At this point I should probably show some restraint. I've written a nice piece about some of my favourite commentators, arrived at the title of the piece and made my feelings clear. That's probably enough. And in setting me this subject, I'm sure Dave Smith§ is hoping I'll embark on some sort of rant, railing against the rebarbative¶ mediocrity of modern sports commentary. Perhaps he wants me to make the easy comparison, to observe that while sitting on the sofa with Ted Lowe's gravelly voice pouring over you was like being allowed into a secret and wonderful world, with John Virgo it's as if you've been strapped to a chair next to the world's biggest pub bore and forced to eat your own

* Non-snookerers: all you need to know is that this is a bad thing.

† Not quite true. There are variations like 'Where's the pink ball going?' Nothing if not versatile, our John.

‡ While also deploying a nifty use of chiasmus to boot.

§ Hi, Dave.

¶ Word provided by Robert Phillips.

head. Maybe Dave would like me to go on an extended monologue about Virgo's habit of burbling on and on, drivelsome meandering streaming from his mouth uninterrupted, saying nothing of note, just meaningless background nonsense, to the point where honestly it could just be a series of random words for all the spaghetti sofa vertigo badgers distinction grunge fundament sumptuousness downsides the farkling breastbone of clodworth negation while actually, Clive, the season before last he had some problems with his cue grip firecracker tangerine sybarite doofi Minkus morphology scrimshanker Metallica tumblehome escutcheon outwith seems to have picked up this season but of course in the quarter-finals of the bugger Apricus Ouagadougou ictus gorgeous sackbut elucubrate petrichor ottery he'll be hoping he can pick up the form he showed in the first session defenestration fungarium sciosophy anaphora wanglegnome Plantagenet* spurious Dictaphone. AAGGGHH, JUST. SHUT. UP.

Perhaps that's what Dave would like. But I can't do it.

I can't do it because it would be cruel, and because television commentary really is very hard. And I can't help thinking that John Virgo, while for me representing the very essence of how not to commentate on sport, is popular and employed, so maybe I'm the one in the wrong. Maybe I'm just old-fashioned, squinting through my rose-tinted spectacles at the TV screen and muttering, 'Don't know what the hell's going on these days – time was when the

* A lot of these words have been given to me by supporters of the book to include in the text. I'm aware that to treat them like this is cheating – they all feature elsewhere in the book, with appropriate credit.

commentator knew how to shut up and let us watch the damned sport. Can't the idiot stop blathering on?'

Maybe.

I doubt it, though.

Parikian just needs this black to win his fifteenth World Championship. He's over the pot now, and in it goes . . . but where's the cue ball going?

GROWING OLD, GROWING OLDER

3,400

Subject provided by Joanna Cannon

'What's your favourite bird?'

It's an impossible question. You might as well ask me for my favourite piece of music, book, film, work of art, chocolate bar or bank statement – there is no hard and fast answer. Whatever I say, there'll be a backside-covering, apologetic follow-up: 'Oh, but such-and-such is lovely too, and we mustn't forget so-and-so . . . '

I'll give an answer anyway.

'I think I'd have to say the goldcrest.'

Ah, the goldcrest. A tiny flitter, to be found scrabbling around for small insects in a conifer near you, even if it often takes a few minutes to come out to play. It has special status as Europe's smallest bird,* and that's part of its appeal to me, because as a child I was similarly afflicted with a lack of stature. I suppose I identified with it in some way. I still remember the one I saw in the garden in 1977 when I was twelve – my first sighting of what I had come to think was a

* Yes, I know, along with its cousin the firecrest, to save you writing in.

bird hell-bent on avoiding me. It cocked its tiny head and gave me an appealing look before flitting off again on a secret goldcrest mission.

In more recent years I've come to love the sound of its song – *tsee-bada-tsee-bada-tsee-bada-tsee-bada-scabba-diddle-oo* – coming from the spruce tree a couple of doors down. Thin and piping, this is – appropriately enough from such a tiny bird – one of the highest birdsongs around, coming in at a stratospheric 7 kHz.*

And here's the thing. At some point in the future my hearing range, which has already shrunk in an inexorable process starting when I was a teenager, will contract so much that I will no longer be able to hear the song of the goldcrest. Whether it's ten years from now or thirty,† that uplifting sound will disappear from my life, and with it another tiny morsel of joy. Assuming I live long enough, that is.

Some aspects of ageing hold no terror. Grey hair? Bring it on – I've always wanted to look distinguished. Baldness? Excellent – I'll spend the saved shampoo money on foreign holidays. Wrinkles? They're supposed to be markers of character, aren't they?

And while the onset of presbycusis‡ might be just a small part of that ageing process, and might never be so acute as to impair my quality of life, it's on that dispiriting list of things that will make life gradually, almost imperceptibly, more difficult.

---

* Our hearing range is at its most sensitive between 2 and 5 kHz. As a point of reference, the highest note on the piccolo comes in at about 4.5 kHz.

† I'll be eighty-three, if I make it, and likely very grumpy.

‡ Age-related hearing loss – it's a word I've just learned, and I didn't want to waste the minute I spent looking it up by never using it again.

It's already started, of course. It started decades ago. Since I was twenty, my myelinated axons have been getting shorter, with a resulting effect on cognitive function. It's a gradual process, so not something that anyone would necessarily notice, but I just put it in as a reminder of how early things start going to pot. Sorry, kids – wherever you're standing, it's basically all downhill from there.

There's more, though. Much more.

I will shrink. By the time I'm eighty I might have lost as much as two inches, and will likely adopt a stooping posture, as if doing an am-dram impersonation of Richard III.

My vocal cords will weaken, and my voice will become breathier, weedier.

In the mouth department there will be a double whammy: receding gums and decreased saliva production. Both of these factors will leave my teeth more susceptible to decay.

My skin will become less elastic, resulting in dryness and wrinkles.

My brain will shrink.

Sleep could well become more difficult in the night. As if that weren't enough, I'll likely be drowsier during the day.

Falls will be a hazard, and with weakened, brittle bones come fractures.

My taste buds will at some stage go to pot, along with my sense of smell. No more petrichor* for this octogenarian.

My eyesight will get worse. My immune system will deteriorate, leaving me more susceptible to colds, flu, viruses

* Word provided by Janina Byrne. Petrichor is, as I'm sure you know, the earthy smell of rain on dry soil. Briefly: raindrops hit the porous earth, which releases air bubbles, which in turn release aerosols, which contain geosmin, the compound responsible for the smell of earth.

and bacteria. My ability to bounce back from these will be severely compromised. Not only will they leave me weaker, but each bout will be potentially life-threatening.

My lungs will be less efficient, so there will be less oxygen about the place to help me function properly.

I'll be less mobile. I'll hurt more. Incontinence is a distinct possibility.

Cataracts, osteoarthritis, hypertension, constipation, skin tags, bruising, impotence, necrotising fasciitis, sprangifying phlegmyopia (not a thing), Hübler's disease (also not a thing, but I bet you didn't know that until I told you, and in any case I wouldn't be surprised if it did become a thing at some point in the next ten years).

And what with knowing about all these things that will probably go wrong with me, I'll worry about them even more than I already do, which is quite a lot. It's not that I walk around in a perpetual state of crippling anxiety, but rest assured these things lurk in the darker recesses of my mind, ready to mug me when I wake up at 2.56 a.m.

So, to recap, I will get slower, weaker, blinder, deafer, balder, forgetfuller, dodderier, confuseder, hurtier, forgetfuller (or have I already said that?) and, eventually, deader.*

And that's without any intervening factors like heart disease or cancer – the likelihood of both of these† increases as we get older.

Might as well give up now.

---

* I don't want to be cruel, but this applies to you, too. If I'm going to go through this particular wringer, I'm taking some of you with me.

† And many, many other lovely diseases – details available on an internet near you.

The trouble with all this is that despite these manifestations of the passing of time, I don't in any way feel like a mature adult. I hope I never do. My reaction to most things has always been an instinctive desire to make fun of them. That's partly why I don't regard myself as a proper grown-up. I've always been guilty of a woeful lack of serious-mindedness. And grown-ups are serious, suit-wearing, bespectacled people – middle-aged from the day they were born – who take a dim view of things in general and never saw the point of forward rolls or cartwheels or bubblegum. They're the kind of people who, on seeing a trampoline, entertain no thought of bouncing on it, or if they do, consider only what might happen were they to fall off, rather than the sheer exuberant joy of the bouncing (I would, nonetheless, make sure I've had a pre-emptive wee first – no point in taking chances).

Old is, in some ways, a state of mind. And my mental age remains somewhere between eight and twenty-five, depending on mood and time of day.

Or does it? Am I not kidding myself? The thought of a party with loud music and cheap beer would once upon a time have been uplifting; now it sends me scurrying for the sofa and the remote control and series three of *Detectorists*. And while I yield quite regularly to the temptations of rich food, alcohol and other hallmarks of the sybarite,* not only is my body losing the capacity to take these things in its stride, but my mind is constantly telling me not to have that slice of cake, do you really need another glass of wine, you know that's the thing that will kill you, you'll pay for that tomorrow.

* Word provided by Maureen Speller. Hello, Maureen. Excellent word.

Oh do fuck off, mind.

What's disconcerting is the speed with which all this has happened. I'm fifty-three years old. FIFTY-THREE.* It is, frankly, inconceivable. Why, it only seems like last Tuesday that I was bombing around the garden pretending to be an aeroplane, arms outstretched and making *bbtthhpphhtthh* noises. And now I've morphed into the kind of person who uses words like 'doodah' and 'thingy' because the actual name won't snap into focus, who switches off lights to save electricity, who prefers comfy shoes to fashionable ones, who spends five minutes looking for his glasses before realising they're on top of his head, who needs glasses in the first place, who makes a little sound – *aahh* – whenever he sits back in an armchair.

Sobering stuff. Twenty-three-year-old me would be appalled.

It's stealthy, ageing; stealthy and sneaky. I didn't notice that change, the subtle transition from aeroplane *bbtthhpphhtthh* to armchair *aahh*, but it happened anyway, each passing year an incremental step in the erosion of youth, the onset of middle age. And now I've reached armchair *aahh*, what next? I have nightmare visions of sitting in a chair from dawn to dusk watching *Cash in the Attic*, the highlight of my day the delivery of a plate of mince and mash and cabbage by a nice young man called Kevin – or is it Trevor? What happened to that young girl, you know, the nice one with the skin?

* By the time you read this I will be at least fifty-five, possibly even sixty. Possibly even dead. Grim thoughts for a Sunday morning.

From where I'm standing, actual old age – being a proper elderly person, frail, senile, ignored – seems a long way off. But if eighty-three feels impossibly distant, have a word with twenty-three-year-old me and ask him about being fifty-three. And yet here I am.

It's just maths. Mortality maths* – the worst kind, designed to remind you just how quickly time is passing (accelerating, it sometimes feels) and how little of it you have left.

Here's an example of mortality maths: as I write this, on 30 January 2019, we are as far in the future (12,719 days) from the year 1984† as 1984 was when the book *1984* was published.

While you grapple with that, I grapple with the knowledge that, whichever way you slice it, however many more years I have, I'm past halfway. Well past, probably.

It doesn't do to dwell on such thoughts. I know this. And yet I dwell, wondering where the time went, what I did with it, and making well-intentioned but ultimately futile resolutions to use the remaining years as well as I can. The future, what's left of it, still lies in front of me.

Except it doesn't. That expression gets it exactly the wrong way round. If anything lies in front of us, it's the past, spread out in all its glory and ignominy for us to pick over and explore, gradually receding into the distance, the biggest landmarks clearly visible for us to regret or celebrate as we see fit.

The future is behind us, unknown, scary, ready to trip us up or jump out and deliver a cruel blow just when we least

* This is a term coined by the writer Pete Paphides a few years ago.

† Specifically, the day, 3 April, on which a lot of the action of *1984* takes place.

expect it. And as we stumble backwards into the invisible future on the slow trudge to the grave, tugged towards the end of the road by time's inexorable undertow – second by second, minute by minute, day by day – the invisible stuff becomes incrementally more terrifying.

And while I understand, or I think I understand, that death is as much a part of life as cherry blossom or nail scissors or Starburst or remembering to put the bins out or *Thought for the Day* on Radio 4 or sweet cups of tea or the first blackbird song in spring or dog shit on your shoe or Post-it notes or the smell of old books, I suspect that this understanding is false, or at the very least superficial, and it won't be until I've been forced to look death in the eye that any kind of enlightenment will come, if at all. And it's in that moment where the trepidation lies. It's not being dead I fear so much as the final approach.

Perhaps I'm getting it wrong. Perhaps I should regard growing old as a privilege. Not that I should feel blessed by the prospect of its torments – the slow decay, the indignities, the increasing powerlessness and debilitation that beset the unfortunate – merely that, lest I forget, there are many who don't get the chance. Perhaps they're the lucky ones, cut off in their prime before the rot sets in – preserved for ever as healthy, vigorous, whole people, the future a blank canvas. What might have been. The famous – Mozart, Hendrix, Winehouse – or not – Andrew, Sheila, Olivia, Stacey, Charlie, Bill, Stephanie, whatever their names might have been. We all knew one. Oh, she was so talented, such a life force – impossible to think she's gone. Imagine what she might have gone on to achieve.

And if that thought is designed to make me feel guilty for each wasted minute, then perhaps it's the spur I need to remain young at heart, to retain the youthful vigour I admire so much in those older people who, from where I'm standing, are the ones looking old age in the face and giving it a loud raspberry and a defiant 'V' sign.

Or is that just denial? Does it feel as if I'm protesting too much? Should I just sit back in that armchair, accept the decay, the stiff joints, the inevitable slowing down and increasing difficulty of everything from walking to dental hygiene? After all, there are few things sadder than an older person desperately trying to be young – squeezing into jeans and using expressions like 'chillax' and 'down with the kids'. That's no way to be – not in my book, anyway. By all means I shall try to retain some sense of vigour and zest for life, try to make light of such problems as might beset me. I'll probably fail, and turn into one of those people incapable of holding a conversation without steering it to kidney stones and strangulated hernias, but at least the intention is there.

In an ideal world, old age – at least in its pre-collapse stage – should confer some element of respect. Old people should be lauded for their experience and wisdom, and it should be called on, added to the sum of human knowledge. Instead, they're shoved to one side, ignored, put out to pasture – society's invisibles, rotting in obscurity.

Except when they're made president.

Perhaps there should be a caveat: respect does not automatically come with longevity. A twenty-five-year-old idiot doesn't necessarily become a seventy-year-old sage simply by living for a long time.

But vanity, my constant companion from cradle to grave, leads me to believe I'll be in the other category, the category of old people to whom the young look and think: 'That's the way to do it. That's how to be old.'

Just as long as they don't talk down to me. I'd be happy with that.

'All right, Grandad? I SAID, HAVE ANOTHER CUP OF TEA (deaf old git).'

Grandad. Ye gods. What a prospect.

What a bastard old age is. You see what it does to people: the hurt, the struggle, the sheer difficulty of even the simplest things. The mundane ugliness of it, robbing people, bit by bit, of the things that made them, that defined them. Energy, wit, life. Great minds diminished, betrayed by their own longevity.

Old age, proper old age, is not for the squeamish. Sod it, with its Zimmer frames and Stannah stairlifts, mobility scooters and dentures. Sod the falling apart, the slow decline, the mute acceptance, tame submission, the withering and fading and, eventually, the slipping away, unnoticed except by the nurse whose job it is to deal with what's left when the soul moves on to oblivion.

Sod them all. I won't be one of those people. I should probably stay fit, stay active, stay flexible. Yoga, brain games, walking. Floss daily and go easy on the fats. And sugars. And empty carbs. And booze. And everything I've loved all my life, all those things that haven't exactly made life bearable, but have certainly added zest to it, made food and drink a positive pleasure rather than survival fuel.

But while I do try to do those things, and am not in any case drawn to complete indolence by natural inclination, I draw the line at things that will make me actively miserable. I'm at the age where people apparently think they can postpone the effects of ageing by leading a healthier lifestyle – exercise, diet, the usual gubbins – as if those modifications can make a significant impression on the one thing that really controls our lifespan, and over which we have no control: our genes. Anyway, what kind of trade-off is it? A few years of self-inflicted misery on a treadmill to buy yourself a little more time sitting in a chair with piss running down your legs waiting for Kevin – or is it Trevor? – to bring you your plate of mince.

No thanks. I'll carry on as I am, if it's all the same with you. But best not have any more tea, or I'll be up all night.

And as the years of dodder approach, I'm determined not to be one of *those* old people. You know the ones. Shadows of their former selves, the walking dead, proper geriatric.

Easy for me to say, of course, from the perspective of so far relatively healthy middle age. Easy for me to say how old age – merciless, cruel, not for the squeamish – should be embraced, regarded not as a foe but as a friend. Easy for me, who has never known it, to anticipate that for me, somehow, it will be different.

Fast-forward ten, twenty, thirty years. Then we'll see.

For much as I joke about Stannah stairlifts and Saga cruises and mobility scooters and retiring to Eastbourne and communities for the aged and losing my marbles and 'If I were an old person I wouldn't be able to open that' and 'Young people today don't know they're born' and 'Why do they have to play their music so loud? It's not proper music anyway' and 'All that time they spend on the computer – it's not right' and 'Tuck your shirt in, young man, pull your trousers up – you look ridiculous', it's a fragile and fearful humour at best, because there will be a day when it's no longer a joke, when I'll be properly defeated by a jam jar or a tin opener or a plastic seal, or I'll want to pick up that knife that fell to the floor, but the hips will hurt, and the knees won't bend, and I'll be beyond the stage of laughing about it, and I'll stand by the fridge, desperate for help but too ashamed to ask, shaking with frustration and shame and fear and rage rage rage at the dying of the light, or maybe I'll be sitting on the sofa, shouting at the television, hating everything, railing at the indignity of senescence, because I'll know it's all going, deep down I'll know, and at some level I'll be watching myself decline, shoving the thoughts to the back of my mind but knowing anyway, trying to laugh it off but failing, because at heart, no matter how much I might want to jeer at it, to mock it, to stick two fingers up in its face, it will come.

It will come.

And so I must savour life while I can. Taste that apple, smell that jasmine, listen to that goldcrest – and I mean properly listen to it. Allow that piping song, thin and insubstantial, to pervade the brain, to nourish it, to put a spring in the stride and a smile on the face, and to keep going for just one more day. And then another, and another, and another still.

Because when it's gone, it's gone, leaving not a rack behind, save ill-held memory.

SPACE TRAVEL

3,300

Subject provided by Charlotte Cunningham

'My battery is low and it's getting dark.'

Poignant and poetic stuff, especially from a robot.

Those words constitute the last message from Opportunity, or MER-B (Mars Exploration Rover – B), or 'Oppy' to its friends. Oppy had been on Mars since 2004, its original three-month mission extended to fifteen years* by judicious recharging of its batteries with solar power, and tactical hibernations to save energy during dust storms. It was sent there to find out stuff about the Red Planet, and this it did, knowing no better than to collect, analyse and send back data, soldiering on until it could soldier no more.

We loved that, the idea that Oppy was plucky and resourceful, defying the odds. The Little Rover Who Could.

And we loved Oppy's last words, too. When it became clear that this was to be its last communication with the

* To be precise: 5,498 Earth days, or 5,352 sols (Mars solar days).

unfeeling world that had sent it millions of miles* in the service of mankind, there was a bizarre outpouring of grief. Social media was filled with the sound of sobbing and wailing and gnashing of teeth, as if it wasn't a machine that was about to die on that distant rock, but a human being.

Such is the egotism of the human race that we'd anthropomorphise a pebble if it made us feel better about ourselves.

Those moving words weren't spoken by Opportunity, of course. It just transmitted data, as it had done for fifteen years, as it was programmed by us to do. The raw data of those final transmissions would have meant nothing to the average observer. It took a human to translate it for the layperson to understand, and so it was that millions of people read those words and constructed a narrative of a hard-working and brave robot dying a lonely death on a rock far from home. Oppy was one of us, the latest casualty in the continuing quest to explore the unknown. We cared for Oppy, even if belatedly, because we could imagine ourselves in its place, and having seen the footage from its predecessor Curiosity, we wondered what it would be like on that bleak and distant planet.

Oppy gave us insight into the loneliest reaches of the human soul.

* The distance from Earth to Mars varies according to the two planets' orbits round the Sun. At its closest, Mars is the trifling matter of 34.8 million miles from Earth; at its furthest, it's the considerably more significant distance of 250 million miles away. These are numbers to boggle the mind, especially when you consider it's our closest neighbour in the solar system.

It started with Tintin. Tintin and Captain Haddock and Snowy and the hare-brained Professor Calculus, plus of course the hapless Thompson Twins (stowaways on the rocket because they didn't know the difference between 1.34 a.m. and 1.34 p.m.), off on a two-book adventure* that grabbed me by the imagination and didn't let go. At the age of ten I didn't particularly go for the 'laser guns and little green monsters' type of sci-fi, and Hergé's typically rigorous approach, with illustrations blending precision with imagination,† gave the world an authenticity and realism that chimed with the pedantic side of my nature.

I came to it all in retrospect, reading the books in the 1970s, when the race to the Moon had already been won. And at this point I should probably insert my own memories of watching the Moon landing, recalling how my parents let me stay up late to watch those indistinct images travelling as if by magic from 238,000 miles away, perhaps with a mug of Ovaltine and a digestive biscuit as I sat bleary-eyed in my jimjams, dozing on my mother's lap as the unfolding drama held us entranced from the corner of the room.

Nah. I don't remember it. I was four. I don't even know if my parents stayed up to watch it. For some people it's a core part of their earliest memories, fundamentally shaping how they see the world. For me it's something that happened to other people, merely one piece in the vague jigsaw puzzle of

---

* In English, *Destination Moon* and *Explorers on the Moon*; the original French titles were *Objectif Lune* and *On a marché sur la Lune*.

† The moonscapes and views of space that played such a large part in the success of the books were in fact the work of Bob de Moor, one of the first recruits to the newly formed Studios Hergé to help lighten Hergé's workload.

world events that happened while I was too young to remember: Vietnam, The Doors, Derek Underwood spinning England to victory on the rain-affected last day of the Oval Test in 1968.

If anything, while the names Armstrong and Aldrin* resonated strongly, I identified more with Laika, the dog who in 1957 became the first animal to orbit the Earth. For a child, a cuddly dog represented more than a random American ever could. I imagined Laika as a hero pet, returning triumphantly from her mission and living out her days in luxury. It simply didn't occur to me that she was never intended to survive.

But I didn't need these manifestations of the real thing. Not when I had Tintin.† The details of Hergé's extraordinarily prophetic creation‡ were so convincing that, if I thought about it at all, I assumed the books were inspired by the real-life Moon landings. Only many years later did I come to the belated realisation that the Tintin Moon books pre-dated not just the Apollo programme, but Sputnik, Laika, Gagarin, Tereshkova and all the rest of them. When

---

* It's tempting to feel sorry for Michael Collins, the third member of the Apollo 11 mission, who went all the way to the Moon without setting foot on it – tempting, but I suspect misguided. He described his emotions as he orbited the Moon waiting for his colleagues to return as 'awareness, anticipation, satisfaction, confidence, almost exultation'. And there is a photograph, taken by Collins, of the lunar module with Earth in the background, the significance of which is that he is the only person, alive or dead, not in the frame. That's a decent legacy.

† *The Muppet Show*'s 'Pigs in Space' feature also had its influence, albeit a slightly different one.

‡ He portrayed deep crevices on the Moon containing vast ice sheets, an idea thought fanciful at the time; recent discoveries show that there is indeed ice on the Moon, though perhaps not quite to the extent that Hergé imagined. Still, one in the eye for the naysayers, which is always nice.

the first Moon adventure appeared in *Tintin* magazine in March 1950, the idea of people actually walking on the Moon was still fantastical, rather than something in the public consciousness as a looming reality. That such giant leaps were made so quickly was thanks to human ingenuity prompted by the reliable spur of international rivalries. Looking back, history often seems inevitable, but one can't help wondering just what resources the Soviet Union and the United States might have devoted to space exploration without the incentive of running the Space Race as a proxy for war. There's little doubt that mankind has been the ultimate beneficiary of this monumental display of willy-waving, but perhaps the spirit of international cooperation that led to the building and launch of the International Space Station (ISS) represents a better model.

This habitable satellite, made up of various modules, bays, ports and solar arrays, has been in low Earth orbit since 1998, circling the Earth every ninety minutes or so, and in that time has played host to over 200 people from eighteen countries. Its creation and continued viability would have been the stuff of science fiction forty years ago, yet now people live on it for months at a time.* This has normalised the miracle† of space travel to such an extent that astronauts who have spent significant time there have to remind themselves that what they're doing really isn't normal, that it's outside the experience of all but the tiniest proportion of humanity.

* Cosmonaut Gennady Padalka holds the current record, having spent 879 days in space.
† Word provided by David Barnett.

Another common experience shared by ISS astronauts is a benevolent version of the one foreseen by Douglas Adams in *The Hitchhiker's Guide to the Galaxy* – the Total Perspective Vortex, a Tardis-like box that shows you, terrifyingly and in excruciating detail, exactly how tiny you are in proportion to the universe.

According to Commander Chris Hadfield – probably the most recognisable face of the ISS, thanks to the series of entertaining and informative videos he posted during his stay there, not least his rendition of 'Space Oddity', which garnered 7 million YouTube hits between the time of his recording it and his return to Earth two days later – astronauts in the ISS start by finding and pointing out their own local landmarks, and gradually expand outwards until they're looking at the planet as a whole, understanding and appreciating, from their daily view of the blue marble floating in space, the commonality of humankind. We're all the same, and we're all in the same boat.

Astronauts and cosmonauts, as far as I can tell, tend towards pacifism.

I try to imagine what it's like, how it must feel.

I close my eyes, placing myself in the module. Never mind that I'm sitting on an enormous canister containing an unimaginable amount of fuel, ready to blast me an unimaginable distance at unimaginable speed. Never mind that I am completely untrained, unprepared, unsuited for the experience ahead.

Never mind that. Just think of the views.

Think, too, of weightlessness, the freedom it must bring,

the closest thing to unassisted flying a human will experience. Think of looking out into infinite space and feeling able to touch it all at once and yet at the same time further from it all than ever before.

Think of Earth, our only home, seen from that kind of distance. Everything that has ever been, reduced to the size of a porthole window, yet infinitely enhanced, understood, appreciated.

A life-changing experience, no doubt. If only I weren't so terrified of flying.

The story goes that a NASA scientist was showing a Russian counterpart the advanced life-support equipment NASA had developed to deal with cardiac emergencies in space. The Russian scientist looked at him pityingly. 'Steve, in Russia we just send healthy astronauts.'*

Exceptional physical fitness might seem a prerequisite for anyone contemplating a journey into outer space, but things move on. The average age of the 600 customers who signed up for a suborbital trip with Virgin Galactic in 2013 was fifty-five. These trips will last about two and a half hours, and the passengers will be subjected to pressures up to 4 *g* as well as experiencing a few minutes of weightlessness. That is assuming the trips will happen – we are, at the time of writing in 2019, still waiting for them to enrich the lives of those wealthy and daring enough to shell out for them, although there have been several non-professional

* Sadly, the popular story according to which the Americans spent millions developing pens that would work in space while the Russians just took pencils turns out not to be true.

space travellers, mostly self-funded. While potential travellers do have to pass a physical (as well as a financial) before being allowed to fly, the fitness of the individual for such short forays is of far less importance than you might expect. Human physiology hasn't changed in the last forty years; the change lies in our ability to cloak that physiology in ever more sophisticated layers of protection in order to mitigate the effects of space travel.

Things are different, of course, if you're planning a longer trip. The biggest challenges facing those interested in developing space for human habitation (apart from finding the extraordinary amounts of money required to fund such missions) are to do with its habitability. We have evolved for life on Earth, and when we spend any significant time away from it, stuff happens to us. Muscles atrophy; skeletons deteriorate. Cardiovascular function is impaired, body mass decreases, immune systems function less efficiently. And the longer you spend in weightlessness, the more significant the effects. Throw in the dangers naturally associated with propelling the human body upwards at great velocity while strapped to a massive tank of high explosive, and it's clear that long-term space travel is not for the faint-hearted.

But it's not for the reckless either.

The early years of development of any new mode of transport are fraught with danger, and as these methods have become more technologically advanced, the risks have become greater. Astronauts go into each mission knowing the dangers – as Chris Hadfield puts it, 'What's going to kill me next?'

And yet they still volunteer, the balance of those two

fundamental human characteristics, curiosity and fear, skewed strongly in favour of the former.

To the layperson it seems like extraordinary bravery, even recklessness. Astronauts, naturally, don't see it that way at all. They even say that the nature of their job necessitates a heightened awareness of its risks.

But then nearly all of them are test pilots. They have a different normal.

At some point, like Sputnik and Salyut 1 and Skylab and Mir before it, the International Space Station will be decommissioned and consigned to history. Newer, more advanced projects will replace it, and the astronauts of tomorrow will look at it and wonder how we managed to get it up there with such primitive technology, much as we look at Apollo 11, with its minuscule computing power,* and think, 'They went to the Moon in *that*?'†

They did, of course, and then they did again, and then, after twelve people had set foot on it, Moon exploration stopped. Been there, done that. The focus shifted to yet more ambitious projects. The thought that the two Voyager probes, launched in 1977, are still out there, ploughing their way into interstellar space, quite boggles the mind, as, frankly, do most things related to this incessantly bewildering subject. The famous *Pale Blue Dot* photograph sent back by Voyager 1 in 1990, our home planet barely visible in

* Equivalent to what it takes to make a greetings card play 'Happy Birthday' at you when you open it. I gather from those who know that this is an unhelpful and inaccurate analogy, but I'm using it anyway.

† There are those who think they didn't. What a sad way to live your life.

the vast sweep of space, had a profound impact on our understanding of the enormity of it all. Cognitively, if we'd been paying attention, we would have understood how big the universe is, and the obscurity of our place in it, but to have it laid bare for us, in an image of our own creation, brought it home more forcefully than even the famed *Earthrise* photo taken by William Anders from lunar orbit during the Apollo 8 mission in 1968 or *The Blue Marble* of Apollo 17 in 1972.

Space is huge; we are tiny.

At the time the photograph was taken, Voyager 1 was 3,762,145,929 miles* from home. Travelling as it is, at about 39,767 mph, it will reach the Oort Cloud (the outermost region of our solar system, so just next door in interstellar terms) in 300 years, and will have passed through it 30,000 years after that. And then it will wander the Milky Way, hoping someone will pick it up and miraculously have some means of playing and understanding its cargo: a gold-plated audio-visual disc, with photographs of Earth and its inhabitants, greetings in fifty-five languages, whale sounds, and music ranging from Mozart to Blind Willie Johnson.

What their reaction would be can only ever be a matter for conjecture.

Those numbers – the 6 billions, 30,000 years and so on – are relatively small fry when you consider that the Local Group of galaxies in which we find ourselves has a diameter of 3 megaparsecs, or 10 million light years.

After a while these numbers cease to have an impact. Whenever I try to get my head round the distances involved,

* It helps if you say the word 'billion' in Carl Sagan's voice.

it does a sort of spinny turn, collapsing under the sheer weight of zeros, and I have to have a bit of a lie-down.

Because space isn't just, as Douglas Adams pointed out, really big; it's cold and empty as well, inhospitable and unwelcoming, not fit for human habitation.

And yet the urge to explore drives us towards it.

But these distances are shrunk by our progress in space travel, as the globe was shrunk by air travel. Already Mars seems closer than it did twenty years ago. And at some point in the not-too-distant future (in geological terms, of course, which work to similar ridiculous scales) the same will happen to the next place we decide to visit, whether it's Europa – one of Jupiter's seventy-nine moons, which has icy seas spewing geysers into space – or Titan, Saturn's largest moon – those crazy guys at NASA are thinking of sending a helicopter mission there – or Enceladus, another Saturnine orbiter, also with salty geysers.

And then what?

Well, to infinity and beyond.

There are already seemingly outlandish ideas for interstellar travel. LightSail, for example ('Solar sailing uses reflective sails to harness the momentum of sunlight for propulsion'), or Breakthrough Starshot ('a ground-based light beamer pushing ultra-light nanocrafts to speeds of up to 100 million miles an hour').

I mean, come on.

It's so easy to mock what you don't understand. I read those words and they seem like the most preposterous science fiction, and then I have to remind myself that pretty much any great idea (and many patently nonsensical ones, to be fair) was roundly mocked at its inception. The main thing is that space travel will get easier. Things tend to. The invention of the motor car might have led some naysayers to warn of the dangers of high-speed travel, but within a few decades it was widespread and normal; just half a century after the Wright Brothers' famous and revolutionary flight in 1903, commercial air travel was commonplace; and within a century of Scott's journey to the inhospitable wasteland of the Antarctic, deep ice-core samples have had a fundamental effect on our understanding of the planet's history, thus helping us plan for its future.

And that is why space travel is important. It's not just the exploration, the expansion of human endeavour, the reaching towards and beyond what is known. It's not that we might one day find another planet capable of supporting human life – a prospect both pleasing and dismaying, given the mess we've made of this one – nor even that we might stumble upon absolute confirmation that we're not alone in this vast and unfathomable universe whose secrets we have barely begun to unravel.

You just never know what's out there until you go.

Impelled by nostalgia, I reread the Tintin Moon books, cherishing every panel, marvelling at the vision and imagination that produced them.

I'm struck, this time, by one moment in particular.

The mission has successfully cleared Earth's atmosphere, and the journey to the Moon is underway. Professor Calculus calls Tintin up to the observation periscope. They look through it at Earth, the Blue Marble, the Pale Blue Dot. Hergé's representation of it is beautiful and striking. Earth, seen by humans in all its magnificent tininess for the first time.

Imagine that. Imagine being the first to see it. Imagine being anyone seeing it. You'd look and you'd look and you'd look. I would, anyway. I suspect I would never stop.

THE INTRINSIC LINK BETWEEN CHOCOLATE, THE WOMBLES AND MUSICAL THEATRE IN POST-MILLENNIAL BRITAIN

3,200

Subject provided by Jack Bennett

There was always going to be one. I knew it from the start. Ask forty people to think up subjects for you to write about, and sure as guillemots are small, cliff-edge-nesting members of the auk family, someone will try to be clever, perverse, or an irritating mixture of both.

Thanks, Jack.

But while this subject has caused consternation and eye-rolling at various points in the process – and more than the average amount of procrastination to boot (and that, let me tell you, and as any writer of even moderate experience will attest, is a lot of procrastination) – I confess a sneaking admiration for it.

Chocolate, Wombles, musical theatre.

My reluctance to roll up the sleeves, elucubrate,* and hew

* Word provided by Angela Dickson. It's an obsolete word meaning 'to work into the night', with particular reference to writing. It derives from the Latin word *'elucubrare'* – 'to compose by lamplight'.

finely honed prose from the wordface has nothing to do with any aversion I might have to those subjects. I am, in fact, well disposed to each of them.

Chocolate is obviously great – I am, as I type, allowing a square of Lindt Excellence Caramel with a Touch of Sea Salt to melt on my tongue and fill my senses with chocolatey joy, and I enthusiastically recommend the experience; when it comes to the Wombles I yield to few in my admiration for those snouty little eco-warriors whose endearing antics did so much to enliven all those dreary 1970s television afternoons; and musical theatre, at its best, is an entrancing spectacle bringing together two of the greatest art forms known to humanity.

I could, in fact, expand volubly on any one of those subjects, well beyond the prescribed 3,200 words.

But finding a link between them, apparently unrelated as they are – well, that's a snorter, and no mistake. And not just any old link, mind – an *intrinsic* link.

Difficult, no doubt about it.

Very difficult.

Tough tough tough. Toughie toughie toughity-tough.

Yes, I am – you guessed it – playing for time, filling paragraph after paragraph with padding, delaying the moment when I actually have to knuckle down and do it.

So here I am, 364 words (no, tell a lie, 370 – oops, make that 374) into the piece, and no closer to an explanation of the subject than at the beginning.

Right. Get down to it, Parikian. You've put it off too long.

It occurs to me that I have three options:

Option A: I could ignore the given subject altogether and write about a subject of my own choice, rounding off the piece with a throwaway line like, 'Oh and by the way, the real intrinsic link between chocolate, the Wombles and musical theatre in post-millennial Britain is that they're all things Jack Bennett asked me to write about in this piece.'

Option B: I could write extensively about one of the subjects, mostly ignoring the other two but shoehorning in the odd reference to make it look as if I've taken the subject seriously.

Option C: I could actually take the trouble to look for a genuine link between the three subjects.

As it happens, I'm going to have a bash at all three.

But first let me tell you briefly about Max Robertson. Because if I can link these things not only with each other, but also with one of the other pieces in this book, I reckon I deserve a bonus point or two.

Sports commentary, as already touched on,* is difficult. Tennis commentary on the radio especially so. Max Robertson – and if you're British, interested in sport and older than fifty, you might already know this – was a tennis commentator of what we'd now think of as the old school. He was capable of extraordinary speed of speech, but unlike those cattle auctioneers, with their simply impenetrable 'HUMMmezeeerveneerbedooomeneberzeve-ZUMBenoodelooze-doobeHUPPerdoodevender-SOLD' delivery, Robertson was able to marry that speed with impeccable enunciation. He also, as a sidebar, made history by not only going down the infamous Cresta Run but also commentating coherently on it as he went. In a fifty-year career that also took in the early

* Go back and read 'Where's the Cue Ball Going?' if you haven't already. I'll wait.

editions of current affairs programme *Panorama* and the Queen's Coronation, he earned an enviable reputation as a safe pair of hands.

But his relevance to the matter in hand is this: he was married to Elisabeth Beresford. And Elisabeth Beresford, as students of 1970s children's literature and television will know, created the Wombles.

The idea for the Wombles came from a childish mispronunciation – one of Beresford's (and Robertson's, come to that) children, on a Boxing Day walk one year, said, 'Isn't it great on Wombledon Common?' Amusing enough for the parents at the time – the kind of thing that might slip into family folklore, like the one time, ONE SINGLE SOLITARY TIME, I took all the gravy when I was seven, but have I been allowed to forget it? Oh no, of course not. Every time we have gravy, here it comes: 'Don't let Lev have the gravy first, ha ha.' Oh yes, VERY amusing. Well, let me tell you something – wait, what?

Right. OK. Sorry. Off-topic.

It's said that Harry Potter and his world jumped straight into J. K. Rowling's head fully formed, and so it was with Beresford and the Wombles. They were strange, furry little creatures, with faces verging on the ottery,* whose mission in life was to womble around the common, tidying it up and turning their finds into things that came in useful about the house.

There was Great Uncle Bulgaria, the venerable head of the clan – Dumbledore with a furry snout, rather stern and forbidding but with an underlying kindness; Tobermory, in

* Word provided by Alastair Simpson.

charge of the workshop, brilliant at making use of the things the other Wombles brought home; Madame Cholet, the cook, whose specialities were things like elmbark pie and double buttercup ice cream; and then the young Wombles, Tomsk, Orinoco, Wellington and Bungo – each with their own characteristics and idiosyncrasies.

The Wombles became known and loved by millions through their televisual incarnation – five-minute stop-motion films broadcast at peak kids' time, the meat in a *Play School/Jackanory* sandwich – but they started as books. The first one appeared in 1968, but it wasn't until its broadcast on *Jackanory* – a programme whose concept, an actor reading a book direct to camera, now seems impossibly quaint – that the Wombles began to reach a wide audience. The commissioning of an animated series proved the breakthrough. Ivor Wood did the animation, Bernard Cribbins the narration, and Mike Batt the music.

The message at the heart of the Wombles – their motto was 'Make Good Use of Bad Rubbish' – remains, it hardly needs overstating, pungently relevant to this day, but it's easy to forget just how revolutionary an idea recycling and general 'greenness' would have been in the early 1970s. Beresford was years ahead of her time. The programme's popularity led to worldwide fame for the cuddly little snouters, and the production of a wide range of Wombles merchandise, a lot of which *HEAVY IRONY KLAXON* no doubt went on to contribute to the littering of public spaces all over the world.

So. There you are. The Wombles. Lovely, heartwarming stuff. But how am I going to segue to chocolate? Or musical theatre? Or both?

It's at this point that I find myself trawling through Wikipedia on the hunt for connections, no matter how tenuous. It was serendipitous enough that Beresford was married to Max Robertson, which makes a nice little counter-link to another part of the book, but what about all the people involved in creating the Wombles?

The most obvious would seem to be Mike Batt. It was Batt who wrote 'The Wombling Song', a catchy, lilting little number with a homespun feel to it – the kind of thing you accidentally find yourself singing under your breath over and over again while doing the dishes one autumn day forty-five years later, and which resolutely fails to leave your head for two days, thank you SO much, Mike.*

Batt's list of credits is, to say the least, extensive: he's collaborated with Art Garfunkel, Cliff Richard, Steeleye Span, Elkie Brookes, Barbara Dickson, David Essex, Alvin Stardust, Hawkwind, Justin Hayward and many more – at this stage it almost becomes simpler to list the people he hasn't worked with – as well as conducting concerts of light music all over the world, and launching the careers of Vanessa-Mae, Katie Melua and the string quartet Bond.

The guy's a music machine, and has been for more than forty years. It's hard not to admire someone who just keeps on producing material. And, pleasingly for the project at hand, he has links to musical theatre. Not only did he co-write the title song for *Phantom of the Opera*, but he mounted an ambitious stage production of his album

* Never underestimate the importance of a good TV theme tune. Their composition (and I'm talking about the really good ones) takes as much skill and craft as a symphony – if not, I grant, the time investment.

The Hunting of the Snark, which, in his own words, 'was mercilessly pounded by the critics'.

So there we have it. From the Wombles to musical theatre in one easy step. All that remains is to identify a link between Mike Batt and chocolate and we're home and hosed. It occurred to me briefly to get on Twitter and ask him if he liked chocolate, but I'm not sure that's qualification enough to fulfil the brief. The vast majority of people like chocolate – we need something a bit deeper than that. How marvellous it would be if he had an ancestor who had been involved in the setting up of Valrhona, or if he turned out to be a majority shareholder in a cocoa plantation in Costa Rica. These things may yet turn out to be true, but so far my researches have yielded nothing of the kind.

To the others, then.

Bernard Cribbins, who provided the narration for the series, is famous for many things,* but it's the realm of musical theatre that interests us for this particular exercise, and there he boasts as impressive a list as on the rest of his CV: Nathan Detroit in *Guys and Dolls*, Moonface Martin in *Anything Goes*, Dolittle in *My Fair Lady*, and Watkins in *Lady Be Good*. These credentials are, if anything, yet more glowing than Batt's, but again my time-wasting research into the Cribbins/chocolate connection takes us only to dead ends.

* I knew him from the superb novelty single 'Right, Said Fred', which I now discover was produced by George Martin, whose oboe teacher was Jane Asher's mother, which is just one more example of the way the world is full of irrelevant connections that make you incline your head and go, 'Oh yeah, right. Interesting.'

You can take it as read that the same applies to David Tomlinson, Frances de la Tour and Bonnie Langford, the stars of the 1977 film *Wombling Free.*

I am defeated and deflated. And still another 1,340 words to go. Sorry, make that 1,333.

What all this means is that while I wait for Mike Batt to reply to my question about his connections with the chocolate industry I can fill some space with a small confession.

I hesitate, because it's the kind of confession that's likely to step on toes, ruffle feathers and put backs up, which is certainly an impressive feat of acrobatics, if nothing else, but not something I like to do.

Ah well, here I bloody go.

I didn't like the Wombles very much.

Confessions are cathartic – I think I feel better already.

It's not that I hated them. You can't hate the Wombles. They're a national institution. It's like hating Michael Palin. Just not possible.

I said earlier that I yield to few in my admiration for them, but admiration isn't love. I thought they were, you know, fine. No more than that.

I suspect that had they appeared on the telly when my son was at a Womble-watching kind of age, I would have pressed them on him like John Cleese pressing a wafer-thin mint on Mr Creosote in *The Meaning of Life* – assiduously, politely, not taking no for an answer. 'Dad' me would definitely be on the side of the Wombles, with their litter-picking and do-gooding and generally gentle and uncontroversial whimsical goodness.

But young me wanted something a bit more surreal. Something like, for example, *The Magic Roundabout.*

Ah, *The Magic Roundabout*. Now there was a programme. Quite insane, in the best possible way. The French original, *Le Manège Enchanté*, was the work of Serge Danot and Ivor Wood – the stop-motion animator, coincidentally, who would later work on *The Wombles*. They created a set with a distinctive visual style – brightly coloured and dreamlike, with the eponymous roundabout featuring at the beginning and end of each five-minute episode. Against this backdrop would whizz a legless dog, a daisy-chewing cow, a rabbit with a guitar, a gormless snail and a moustachioed springy thing of indeterminate species, genus, family, order, class and, frankly, phylum. And we mustn't forget the girl, whose role was to inject a level-headed note of reason.

I don't know what the French names of these creations were (and on this occasion am strangely averse to looking them up on Wikipedia), but in the English version familiar to my generation they were Dougal, Ermintrude, Dylan, Brian, Zebedee and Florence.

The bright look of the programme was attractive enough, but what set *The Magic Roundabout* apart, what converted amusing strangeness into sheer absolute ruddy genius, were the characters, voices and storylines. And those were the work of a man called Eric Thompson. What I didn't realise at the time – why would I? – was that the English version had nothing to do with the French original. The images were the same, and delightful in themselves, but the freewheeling narrative* that gave the programme its joyous quality was all Thompson's work. He watched the programmes on an

* The word 'zany' – one of my least favourite, along with its confrère 'antics' – is hovering on the edge of this paragraph, hoping to be let in. No chance.

old-school editing machine with a tiny screen, and made up stories to fit the pictures. The size of the screen is a partial explanation for some of the programme's weirdness – he would simply get things wrong, once writing a story that revolved around a house that on closer inspection turned out to be a sugar lump.

If the plots sometimes seemed loose, the characters deranged and the dialogue nonsensical, then as far as I was concerned that was the whole point of it. But plenty of people – possibly projecting their own experiences of the 1960s – were quick to assume that the whole thing was some kind of drug-fuelled hippy fantasy, filled with references to various narcotics. I don't buy this; I just think that these people – Danot and Wood and Thompson – had imaginations and wanted to entertain children. To a rational adult *The Magic Roundabout* seemed strange,* but to a child the programme made perfect sense. Of course a daisy-chewing cow wearing a hat would sing old music-hall numbers to a disgruntled train; of course a legless dog would scuttle about the place talking to himself and being mildly annoyed by everything; of course a rabbit with a guitar would lope gently onto the screen, say, 'Like, yeah, not cool,' then fall asleep. It was the most natural thing in the world.

Like many people, I suspect, I identified most with Dougal. His Tony Hancock-like mutterings ('I don't know – the world's going to the dogs. Wait a minute, what am I saying . . . ?') were not only endlessly entertaining, but

* Although I should note that when they changed its time of broadcast there was a deluge of complaints from adults, not necessarily acting on behalf of their children.

chimed with something in me – an innate feeling, perhaps, that if only people would realise they were doing everything wrong and that my way was better, the world would be a vastly improved place.

It didn't bother me that Dougal had no legs – a decision made by the producers because it made the stop-motion filming simpler – in fact, I didn't notice the lack of legs until someone pointed it out to me as an adult. Talk about slow on the uptake. But 'twas ever thus. In a related incident years later, I didn't realise until she was very well established as one of my favourite actors that Emma Thompson was Eric Thompson's daughter.

Ah, Emma Thompson. An actor so beyond reproach that I would cheerfully submit to having the phone book read at me as long as it was her doing it. Looking at her CV, I remember now that she has musical-theatre credentials of her own – she appeared in *Sweeney Todd* at English National Opera, but if you go even further back, one of her first roles was in *Me and My Girl*, the production at the Adelphi Theatre revised by Stephen Fry that played its part in the launching of his spectacularly successful career. So there's more musical theatre right there. If only I could find some sort of connection between her and bloody chocolate. Someone please tell me that the Thompson family is descended from Bendicks or Cadbury or that Emma's grandfather was the first person to bring a Toblerone into the country.

Hang on a minute. Stephen Fry.

At this point I'm dredging something from the depths of my faulty memory. Just let me pop off and check it. Hang on a tick.

YES. Found it. I knew I was right. In your face, synapses.

Stephen Fry, in case you've lived on another planet for the last thirty years, is one of the central figures in post-millennial Britain – writer, actor, broadcaster, comedian, audiobook reader, voiceover artist, adverts guy, and general all-round Stephen Fry. In one of his many books, the deeply confessional memoir *Moab is my Washpot*, he writes of his great-uncle George's book *The Saxon Origin of the Fry Family*, in which George takes a snobbish swipe at another branch of the family, the branch best known for (and I can hardly believe this has worked out so neatly) making chocolate.

Get in, as I believe idiots sometimes say.

The Wombles – Ivor Wood – *The Magic Roundabout* – Eric Thompson – Emma Thompson – *Me and My Girl* – Stephen Fry – Fry's Chocolate.

And so there we are. There were a few diversions on the way – Max Robertson, Elisabeth Beresford, Mike Batt, Bonnie Langford and Bernard Cribbins, none of whom turned out to be necessary to the investigation at hand – but it turns out, with a sort of magnificent inevitability, that the intrinsic link between chocolate, the Wombles and musical theatre in post-millennial Britain is Stephen John Fry.

It would be disappointing, frankly, if it were anyone else.

(Oh, and by the way, the other intrinsic link between chocolate, the Wombles and musical theatre in post-millennial Britain is that they're all things Jack Bennett asked me to write about in this piece.)

ICE HOCKEY

3,100

Subject provided by Keith Ashby, who was there

The river burst its banks every year. It didn't take much. A few days of rain and the surrounding meadows would be inundated, the surface of the water dull under Tupperware skies, groups of lapwings huddling on the occasional island of grass poking up between the gently rippling expanses.

For me it was drama, the daily car journey to school enlivened by seeing how far the water had advanced, how much of the meadows it covered. One year, thrillingly, it came to within feet of the road. Would it rise enough to make the road impassable? Would I get – oh, the joy – a DAY OFF SCHOOL?

No.

The floods subsided, the meadows returned to normal, and I had to get my daily excitement from counting the rooks' nests in the trees or pretending I'd seen a curlew.*

Several years later, the Holy Grail. Floods, followed by a Big Freeze, the words capitalised because it was a

* I was, as a child, a magnificent liar.

Significant Occurrence. Which, to be fair, in the low-lying and relentlessly temperate Thames Valley, it was.

I was home from London, mooching as only a student on holiday can mooch. Telly, book, mooch. Mooch, book, telly.

Someone in the village had an idea. They'd been down to the meadow, seen the extent of the ice, tested it with their not insignificant weight. It was solid, flat, glassy. The river remained unfrozen, of course, potentially treacherous if you went too close. But there was a lot of ice, a broad expanse of it. Plenty of space for skating, or sledding.

Or ice hockey.

We didn't need any further encouragement. The next morning a group of us went down there, as motley a gang as ever played the game. A gallimaufrey* of hockeyisers. We didn't have proper equipment – the citizens of Oxfordshire in the 1970s were as likely to own a pair of skates or an ice-hockey stick as a weasel is to own a chainsaw – so we improvised. Gumboots and cricket bats were the order of the day. A puck was fashioned from a block of wood, jumpers laid out as goalposts in time-honoured fashion, and the game began.

It seemed such a good idea at the time.

Ice hockey is a hard game.

Not hard as in difficult, although I'm sure that's the case too. Sports, at least the ones worth talking about, are difficult. Why would you bother otherwise?

No, it's hard as in ice, hard as in physical, hard as in cold

* Word provided by Josephine Leak.

and brutal and definitely not for the faint-hearted. Scrimshankers* need not apply. Broken teeth, noses and jaws are routine. The puck, famously, is propelled at speeds of up to a gazillion miles a second.† Spectators watch the game from behind Perspex to avoid maiming and disfigurement.

I stood behind the goal, keen to experience the physicality of the game at close quarters, but also keen to escape the insistent batterings of two drummers, cheerleading for the home team, who had taken up their positions five yards away from my first vantage point up in the terraces.

Streatham Redhawks‡ vs Basingstoke Bison. A game, even to my inexpert eyes, of honest endeavour and occasional skill, one side (Basingstoke) superior to the other and gradually exerting their control as the game progressed. A slow application of authority, an inevitable goal, then another halfway through the second period. Early in the third, home hopes sprang as Streatham pulled one back, but it was a false dawn, quickly snuffed out by an immediate and brutally efficient reply. As a spectator at countless lower-division football matches in my youth, it was a story I knew well.

The players, even at this level, displayed an ease and grace on the ice I can barely comprehend, changing direction at will, and accelerating to chase the puck with lithe and powerful efficiency. The falls and body checks were wince-inducing, the tactics fascinating, the guidelines for

---

* Word provided by Nick Hely-Hutchinson. It means 'shirker' and I like it very much indeed.

† I might not have done all the fact-checking I should have on this one.

‡ They used to be Streatham Redskins, but changed the name for, well, obvious reasons.

what constitutes an infringement, at least to my ignorant eyes, unfathomable.

Spare a thought for the referees. They share the space with the padded and helmeted players, potentially caught in the same firing line of both puck and large human barrelling towards them at great speed, yet they wear no protective equipment at all. Maybe they're just adept at dodging things. They're definitely good at skating backwards.

It was a game of gradually dwindling excitement and interest. Once the result was beyond doubt, it lost its appeal. I left, thinking vaguely that I'd like to return sometime, that there was definitely something about ice hockey I could get excited about. I just didn't quite know what it was.

We don't do ice hockey in Britain. Not really. There are leagues and cups and clubs all over the country, and there's a steadily growing fan base, but it's not in the blood. What I learned about the sport in my youth came from *Peanuts*.* Snoopy and Woodstock playing on the frozen water fountain; the human characters – equipment far too big, skates flat to the ice – playing out the daily interactions of childhood† that were the staple diet of the strip; Charlie Brown, occasionally close enough to success that he could smell it, but never able to grasp it. Life in microcosm, seen through a sporting lens.

For this young Brit, it was a lens tinged with romance of a particularly elusive kind. Like all the sports represented in that peerless comic strip, it felt familiar yet remote. Baseball, basketball, American football, ice hockey‡ – I knew of

* What I learned about *everything* in my youth came from *Peanuts*.

† And, of course, adulthood.

‡ Americans: football and hockey, as distinct from soccer and field hockey. You're welcome.

their existence, came to understand broadly how they worked, but they remained alien sports. Perhaps that was part of their appeal. A British Schulz, had there been such a thing, would have drawn football, rugby and cricket, and it wouldn't have been quite the same. Reading and rereading those strips, I could let my imagination conjure images of the sports beyond the confines of the four panels, and they were images tinged with mystery and wonder.

The reality of ice hockey, when it came to our television screens once every four years in the Winter Olympics, was more mundane. It wasn't the last resort – any sport was better than none – but nor was it the first choice.

The skiing events, familiar from weekly viewings of *Ski Sunday*, had a certain glamour, enhanced by the theme music,* the remoteness of Alpine slopes from flat and unsnowy Oxfordshire, and David Coleman's commentary – apparently shouted through several pillows and a wash of static from inside a distant telephone box.

Swish, swoosh, swash.

'An' 'e's GONE!'

And then, after Franz Klammer had won, it was over to the Schitzentwattensaal, where the USSR were thrashing a hapless Poland 17–1 to the sound of skates on ice, clacking sticks, and a breathlessly awestruck Alan Weeks.

'And they REALLY are all OVER them! This Russian machine is UNSTOPPABLE!'

Cold War analogies aside, these uneven matches made for pretty desperate viewing to my untutored eye. While my

* The theme music for all sports programmes in the 1970s seemed to me superb. *Sportsnight with Coleman*, *Grandstand*, *Match of the Day* – harbingers of excitement.

mother's focus was inevitably on the losing side – 'it's their mothers I feel sorry for' – and while there was a grim fascination in any one-sided contest, and a hope for this statistics-obsessed observer that some sort of record would be broken, that kind of one-sidedness is rarely brimming with tension, and my lack of knowledge and understanding of the finer details meant that engaged viewing was more or less impossible. When watching sports I'd played myself, I had at least some grasp of tactics, albeit necessarily a childish one. And while the concept of ice hockey is simplicity itself – propel hard rubber thing into goal – there are presumably all sorts of subtleties to do with angles, puck control, opponent marking, strategies and so forth that sail right over my head like a Chris Waddle penalty.* To my fledgling eyes it was difficult to discern the comparative merits of the players' puck-handling skills, mostly because a lot of the time it was difficult to discern the puck.

Look, I know it's the easiest thing in the world to mock what you don't understand and can't be bothered to find out about. Easy, lazy and supremely irritating to those who actually have some knowledge about it. I've seen people do it to my great love, cricket. The attitude is: 'I don't understand it, and can't be bothered to look into why people find it fascinating, so I'm just going to kick it.'

Bill Bryson did this well in his book *Down Under*, in a passage that had me simultaneously cheering the effortless flow of the prose and screaming, 'Take the trouble to learn

* Or, as the man himself insists on saying while commentating on the radio, 'pelanty'.

something about the game, why don't you, Bill, before you rip the piss out of it?'

And I've just done it with ice hockey. 'Oh look, you can't see the puck, ho ho, don't they just beat each other up, hee hee.'

It's lazy, and I apologise. But that's what it looked like to me when I was young.

If a single game was ever going to fire me with enthusiasm for the sport, it was the 'Miracle on Ice'.

Unstoppable the Soviet ice-hockey team might have seemed, but even the apparently invincible are susceptible to a surprise vincing, and in 1980 they got theirs, at the hands of an American team who were no more expected to win than Dulwich Hamlet would be if they were playing Manchester United.* It seems strange to cast any sporting team representing the USA as plucky underdogs, but in this case they truly were, a group of comparative amateurs holding off the onslaught of the mighty Soviet machine to record as unlikely a victory as you could ever wish to see. The closeness of the result (coming back from 1–0, 2–1 and 3–2 down, and holding onto a slim 4–3 lead as the clock agonisingly ticked down the slowest minutes in American history) made for thrilling viewing, even for this ignorant viewer. And if we in the UK missed out on the American commentary ('Eleven seconds, you've got ten seconds, the countdown going on right now! Morrow, up to Silk. Five seconds left in the game. Do you believe in miracles? YES!') that presumably represents that moment of collective euphoria as surely as Richie Benaud's 'it's gone straight into

* At any sport, I suspect, but particularly Association Football.

the confectionery stall and out again' a year later represents Ian Botham's mullering of the Aussies for the English cricket fan, it was more than made up for by the visuals: ecstatic Americans piled up in a bundle at one end of the arena as shell-shocked Russians looked on in a disbelieving group from the middle of the ice.

It was their mothers I felt sorry for.

How long had we been playing when it happened? Had I made a significant contribution to the game? What was the score?

I don't remember.

The general memories of the morning are still there. Banter, bonhomie, general goodwill; a childish excitement among grown men, born of the unusualness of the activity, and the feeling that this was something we wouldn't ever get to do again.

We were right about that part.

Looking back, with the benefit of thirty years of steadily accrued health and safety wisdom, it's easy to see the flaw in our plan. Taking a flat-footed clumsy bundle onto the ice without any protective equipment is tantamount to lunacy, and I was that F-F CB.

Hindsight is 20/20.

I'd been skating once in my life, on a school exchange to Germany when I was sixteen. Photos of the occasion suggest that after an initially tentative start, I developed enough confidence to engage in the activity in a borderline competent way, while at the same time wanting it to be over as soon as humanly possible. While I am, in those photos, skating on an expanse of open ice and not clinging to the side railings like a gibbering poltroon, the set of my body and legs suggests a rigidity not entirely compatible with a natural skating technique, and the look on my face tells its own story. Call it concentration, call it nervousness, call it abject fear – ice and I were not, and never would be, natural partners.

Bearing that in mind, it's possible I wasn't experienced enough to undertake a full-on game of cricket-bat-and-gumboot ice hockey on a frozen meadow. My skill set was severely lacking. But so, I imagine, was everyone else's. I don't remember any discussion of how best to stay upright on the ice – people just seemed to do it. So I felt it incumbent on me just to do it as well. I suspect, knowing me, that I was quietly nervous, but on seeing other people's confidence, assumed an air of nonchalance. Of course it would be fine. Of course I wouldn't fall over. And if I did, it would be in a Norman Wisdom comedy kind of way, arms and legs flailing before measuring my own length face down on the freezing ice and ruefully picking myself up again to the derisive hoots of my colleagues.

I have since learned that the best way to keep your balance in icy conditions is to walk like a penguin. Weight forward, small movements, restrict the risk of falling.

These simple precepts, it seems, I singularly failed to observe.

I remember the 'puck' sailing past me; I remember the expanse of ice between me and it; I remember voices encouraging me to go and get it.

And that's it.

I was unconscious, we think, for about twenty minutes. That is, so I'm told, a very long time to be out.

And when I think of those lost minutes, my recovery, the assessment at the hospital, the overnight stay 'for observation', the convalescence at home, the return to normal with no ill effects,* I now think of actress Natasha Richardson.

Natasha Richardson, who incurred a head injury while skiing; Natasha Richardson, who shrugged it off in good spirits and joked with her family; Natasha Richardson, who died of an epidural haematoma two days later.

How fragile, our hold on life. How fleeting our stay.

I woke to the smell of exhaust fumes, the sound of worried voices, the feel of cold hard metal on my cheek. A headache – a hard pain, throbbing, blocking thought. It was enough just to feel, to be aware, awake, alive. Understanding could come later.

Dimly, I knew who I was. A few seconds later I knew the where and the what. Then, slowly, groggily, I worked out why I might come to be in this cold and smelly vehicle with a dry mouth and a strange sense of detachment. The thought popped into my head that I might be dying, and that if I were, then it might not be such a bad way to go, apart from the headache. It has occurred to me many times since that if I'd fallen at a slightly different angle or with greater force, I might have died without knowing a thing about it. From on to off without a flicker.

Or maybe it doesn't work like that. Maybe at the final approach there is a liminal† awareness: the white tunnel, the

---

* People who know me: THANK YOU FOR YOUR HILARIOUS COMMENTS.

† Word provided by Roger Miller.

bodily detachment, the sense of peace and acceptance. We don't know. And that's the point. We don't, can't, mustn't know. Knowing about our death, how could we properly live?

Hands in my armpits, grasping my feet. The transfer from farm pickup to ambulance. And there, my mother's voice, the worry leaping out at me, piercing the fug.

Impossible to truly comprehend, at the age of twenty, that permanent undertow of parental anxiety. I know it now, have felt that same panic, sprinting across a cold and windy velodrome towards the sprawled shape of my own son, his bicycle sliding down the treacherous banking to clatter against his still form. I know that surge of anxiety, the tardy urge to protect, the relief at the first stirrings, the continued worry, the surreptitious monitoring, not wanting to nag but desperately searching for signs of anything untoward. And I know the selfish anger, too. Don't do that to me, don't make me worry, don't be in danger, don't break out of the cocoon.

Don't grow up.

She told me later that she knew, at the first ring of the phone, knew for stone-cold certain that something had happened, and that it had happened to me.

No mobile phones, of course. Not in 1985. Someone had sprinted back to the nearest house, dialled the number – 6-0-3, clicks and whirrs and the static crackle as it waited to connect – and somehow found the words.

And while I lay unconscious in the back of the farm pickup, she sprinted through the village to be by my side, powerless and terrified; and at the hospital there will have been pacing and waiting and sitting and worrying, and when the specialist did his rounds and said, 'So you've been in a car crash, then?' and I had to correct him and he checked his notes again and took my pulse and gave me a cursory examination and airily announced the all-clear, perhaps the relief was tinged with a suspicion that maybe the authority of his reassurances was undermined by his inability to identify the patient correctly.

And then it was back home, driving slowly, and a precautionary day in bed with a Dick Francis or maybe two, and no doubt she resisted the urge to check on me every five minutes, and tried to match my nonchalant mood, and for all this parental worry and love and care and support and soft-boiled eggs with toast soldiers, all she got in return, I have absolutely no doubt, was a grunt of thanks and, 'What's for supper?'

It's the mothers I feel sorry for.

THE BEST MUSIC I KNOW AND WHY IT MATTERS

3,000

Subject provided by David Pievsky

It is 114 seconds long, and whenever I listen to it I start welling up.

A lone player, exploring the possibilities of the keyboard. Two notes, rising – a clarion call, the resonance hanging in the air, full of expectation; then single notes, crystalline, picked out of a limpid silence; momentum builds, a slightly clumping gait, the rhythm almost aleatorically free but subtly discernible; the gestures become larger, intervals more widely spaced, building to a climax; and then, a magical surprise – a break from the original pattern, ecstatic trillings in the upper register, unrestrained joy, dissolving gradually until the opening clarion call is repeated in the highest reaches of available sound, transfigured, left to decay, twin question marks.

Dinosaur Suite – Triceratops, a work of high art recorded by my son Oliver at the age of five.

Richard Wagner – *Der Ring des Nibelungen*
Frank Sinatra – 'My Way'
John Lennon – 'Imagine'

That list isn't quite what you think it is.

There is a list, somewhere in my head, of music. It's not massive, and it soon dissolves into grey areas of vagueness and doubt. To qualify for inclusion on the list, music must meet two basic criteria.

It must be Great Music, revered by millions, enshrined in the Hall of Fame. Music for the ages.

I must hate it.

I'm exaggerating. I don't hate *The Ring*. I just . . . can't be doing with it. I can think of many ways to spend fifteen hours of free time – experiencing the *Ring* cycle is not one of them.

It's not that I haven't tried. I have listened to it. All of it. Several times. Each time I've wondered whether the magic so obvious to many people will make itself apparent to me.

Nope. Not a sausage. Barely even a chipolata.

It's my fault. I acknowledge the music's greatness, its importance in the development of musical language in Western classical music, its pivotal role in the history of musical theatre. I am not worthy. Oh woe, oh woe. Don the hair shirt.

I can see its appeal: the grand scale, the massive orchestra masterfully handled, the complex harmonies, sprawling drama, mythology bundled into a four-evening experience of gripping intensity. I can even hear its appeal, usually when the orchestra is given free rein, without – and at this point I must break off to plead with singers, and especially Wagnerian singers, not to take this personally – the encumbrance of the voices.

But if I recognise and acknowledge its importance and greatness, I cannot feel it. Not deep down. Where some music hits me in the solar plexus, Wagner mostly washes over me, leaving no lasting emotional effect, merely a little dampness behind the ears.

Sorry, everyone.

It's not the same with 'My Way'. I don't need to give that a second chance. I hated it on first hearing. The lumpen, slow-motion sentimentality of the music is one thing, but pair it with the lyrics and you have an infallible formula for instant retching. What yer man is basically saying in this song is that while he deigns to acknowledge the possibility that he might have done some regrettable things in his life, they are so pifflingly insignificant that he's not going to tell us about them, but he's going to go out of his way to tell us how few and how pifflingly insignificant they were. Would you like fries with your breathtaking arrogance, sir?

And not only that, he mentions his regrets, and then in the very next line he says he's not going to mention them? I'm afraid the beaver has very much already been released into the wild on that one, Sunny Jim. Now off you pop, you slathering egomaniac, and leave me with my Otis Redding.

As for 'Imagine', that limp, inane, vapid, trite, toe-curling, buttock-clenching, poorly constructed lump of simplistic harmony, bland melody and bad poetry, it's just plain awful and that's all there is to it. A piece of music so obviously bad that mere mention of it makes my teeth itch.*

By the way, perverse as it may seem to start a discussion

* Other opinions are available.

of the best music with an evisceration of the worst, you have no idea how cathartic it is.

My point is – and I'm aware I'm making it in a bizarrely vindictive way, although I console myself that none of the people in my firing line are still alive – that everyone's musical *Weltanschauung*,* their kaleidoscope of preferences, their private mixtape of the very best of the very best, is different. Mine is different from yours is different from hers is different from theirs. As individual as DNA, and entirely subjective.

And now, having addressed the subject by answering exactly the opposite question, let's try to answer the question itself.

Dinosaur Suite – Triceratops, despite my assertion above, isn't high art. It's the curious noodlings of a small child, recognisable as such within a few seconds.† If I were to transcribe it and present it as a work of contemporary music by a promising young composer, few would be fooled. And play it to anyone but three specific people, and the reaction would most likely be dismissive. But for those three people (me, my wife and the auteur himself), it packs an emotional punch of some power. Admittedly, in the case of one of the three of us, that emotion is extreme and agonising embarrassment, but that's irrelevant: music's value lies in its effect on the listener. Nothing else. If you

* Word provided by Tim Milford. In case you don't have any German, it means 'outlook on the world'.

† It does, however, finish with the same two notes it started with, so we should give Oliver some credit for grasping the concept of thematic unity.

want to argue that the benign charms of 'How Much is that Doggie in the Window?' are superior to the monumental greatness of Beethoven's Ninth Symphony, I am powerless to contradict you. I could come up with all sorts of arguments, citing the symphony's unprecedented stature in the canon of Western classical music, the universal humanity of the values it expresses, its ability to encompass all human emotion and experience, but it all comes to naught in the face of 'I prefer the other one – you can hum it, it's nice and short, and it reminds me of my mum'.

It's this subjectivity that makes all comparisons of art ultimately futile. Who is to say that one creation is 'better' than another? How insufferably arrogant. And better at what, exactly? Sure, Mahler's *Das Lied von der Erde* is magnificent at expressing joy, despair, love, angst and the eternity of loss, but you can't live your whole life on that particular emotional rollercoaster – you'd be dead by the age of twenty-six. Much of the time you're not in a Mahler mood, and what you need is some AC/DC or Herbie Hancock or Vivaldi or Louis Armstrong or the Carpenters or Metallica* or Martha Reeves and the Vandellas or David Bowie or Whitney Houston or Bernstein or Gordon Goodwin's Big Phat Band or Debussy or Duran Duran or John Cage or Björk.

This is why my list of favourite music changes as often as I feed the cat. There are so many factors at play. So when David† gave me this subject, my heart sank just a bit. But it soon bobbed to the surface again. And then, without dwelling on it, I wrote down a list of music. Here it is, verbatim.

---

* Word provided by Fenella Humphreys.
† Hi, David.

Stravinsky – Rite of Spring *but also* Firebird *and also* Petrushka *and also* Apollon musagète, *oh crikey*
Sibelius – Symphony No. 7 or 5 or 2 or 6, or maybe all of them
Mozart Figaro? Così? Don Giovanni?
Mozart Clarinet Concerto *and quintet, last three symphonies*
Mozart – a whole pile of other stuff, e.g. piano concertos, chamber music, agh
Brahms all four symphonies but especially 4
Reich Sextet
Earth Wind and Fire 'September', 'Boogie Wonderland'
Stevie Wonder Hotter Than July *or* Innervisions
Otis Redding and especially '(Sittin' On) The Dock of the Bay'
Janelle Monáe Dirty Computer
Something big-bandy – in fact, quite a lot big-bandy
Buena Vista Social Club
Mozart violin concertos played by Dad
Beethoven Violin Concerto *ditto*
Oh, go on then, yes, the late quartets if you insist
Some Mahler if in the mood
Bartok. Music for Strings, Percussion and Celesta? Concerto for Orchestra?
Not Bruckner, sorry, nor Wagner
Some Britten, definitely
Ravel Piano Concerto, Mother Goose
Strauss Four Last Songs – *how could I forget?*
Ooh! Prokofiev!
Schubert!

Ruben Gonzalez
Bowie Blackstar *if not too depressing*
Scott Bradley, but prob only with the actual cartoons

I could have gone on, but it was time for a break, so I put the list away and got on with things. And now, looking at it again, all I can think is 'Where, in the name of absolutely everything that ever lived and breathed, is Bach? And Dvořák, Astor Piazzolla, Keith Jarrett, Verdi, Marvin Gaye, John Coltrane, Korngold, The Divine Comedy, Gershwin, Dionne Warwick and Oscar Peterson? What do Shostakovich, Miles Davis, Art Tatum, Donald Fagen, Janáček, Chick Corea, Ella Fitzgerald, the Beatles, Berlioz, Billie Holiday, Frank Zappa and Prince have to do to get on this list?

Haydn, for fuck's sake.

All of which merely serves to demonstrate the enormity, even impossibility, of the task.

Six pieces. Let's just try to pick six pieces.

You'll be able to see, from the artists I've already mentioned, the general trajectory of my musical tastes – to a great extent you could concoct a shortlist of your own using the materials provided and I'd probably give it a little nod of approval. All of those creators (and a hundred, a thousand more) have produced music that at various times has moved, entranced, uplifted, motivated or thrilled me. Some of them have even made me want to dance, which is quite the miracle, given the flappiness of my feet and ineptitude of my hips.

It's at this point that I realise how relieved I am not to be famous enough to be invited on to *Desert Island Discs*. What a miserable choice to have to make. Elisabeth Schwarzkopf famously skirted the issue by narrowing it down just to recordings on which she was the performer – a pragmatic, if mildly egotistical decision. When my father was interviewed on local radio in a similar format he wisely selected representative pieces from favourite composers that he thought would make a varied and interesting programme. Unfettered by such restrictions, here are the six pieces/albums I would choose right now, at 10.07 a.m. on Wednesday, 9 January 2019:

Sibelius – Symphony No. 5
Mozart – Violin Concerto in D, *K. 218*
Reich – Sextet
Stevie Wonder – Innervisions
Ravel – Piano Concerto
Otis Redding – '(Sittin' On) The Dock of the Bay'

Right, so that's that done. Rest assured it'll be a different list in ten minutes. But while we have it, let's try to explain why those examples matter. To do this, we first have to imagine a world without music.

Ugh.

For some people this might seem a delightful prospect. For them, music of any kind is an irrelevance – it barely touches their lives, they can't tell the difference between Minkus* and

* A ballet composer of, let's be absolutely honest about this, the second rank. Word provided, cheekily, by Nigel Bates.

Mingus,* and they'd happily spend the rest of their lives surrounded by silence. If pushed they might select, well, 'How Much is that Doggie in the Window?', say. Can't fathom it myself, but then there are loads of things in this world I can't fathom: hedge funds, quantum physics, the appeal of desiccated coconut.

But let's say that you like music, and on arriving home of an evening you like to sit and listen to something to help slough off the cares of the day. You activate the music source of your choice, sit back and wait.

Nothing. Instead of sounds to soothe the soul, there is silence.

And now I feel the spirit of John Cage stirring.

'Aha! The silence! That's where it all is. Listen to the specific silence of the room, its own rhythms and creaks and breaths and—'

Yes, yes, John, OK. We're up to speed with the concept. But while *4'33"* was a groundbreaking and important experiment, and a constant reminder of the importance of true listening, in music, silence still needs something after which, before which, between which to exist. Those vibrations of air which, when organised in certain ways, do so much to make our existence on this planet that much more worthwhile. Take them away and we are bereft.

Of course, if you know it well enough from repeated listening, there's nothing to stop you hearing the music in your head, but it's not the same. There's no substitute for

---

* A jazz musician of, let's be absolutely honest about this, the first rank. Word provided by me.

those vibrations. It's a physical thing, music. And, as anyone who has ever been annoyed by any music anywhere will know – muzak in a shopping centre, thrash metal from a teenager's bedroom, a bad saxophonist busking on the Tube – it gets inside your head and affects you in ways that defy explanation.

Let me pick three of the six pieces above and try to explain how they got into my head and what they do when they're there.

I was four or five, I should think, and a favourite way of passing a morning was to sit quietly and listen to my father practising the violin. If he were still alive, I reckon I'd still be doing it today, because, to put it mildly, he was good at playing the violin.* This memory, while precise enough in its content (I can remember the texture of the carpet, the smell of the room), doesn't carry details of specific repertoire. I'm sure he practised all manner of pieces while I sat there, depending on what he was due to perform. But the main thing I remember is his sound – clean, strong and always in tune. In later years, as I learned more about music, I discovered that he was noted for the quality and distinction he brought to his performances of Mozart. Repeated listenings to his two commercial recordings of Mozart concertos revealed this to indeed be the case.

I cherish these recordings. They're a way to keep him alive.

And that, Kirsty, is why I've selected this Mozart.

A few years later. My fifteenth birthday. My brother,

* Some readers, familiar with my father's playing, will no doubt regard this as the understatement of this or any other century. I couldn't possibly argue with them.

knowing I have developed a passion for hitting things,* gives me an album with the instruction 'listen to the drumming'. I listen to the drumming. It is superb. Even I, usually more interested in hitting things in an orchestral context, can hear that. I can hear the crispness, the bounce, the accuracy and irresistible oomph of the rhythm section. They drive the music, give it life, all the time without drawing undue attention to themselves. There's nothing particularly flashy about the drumming on these songs, but substitute an inferior musician and their impact would be lessened.

But if I heard the rhythm section and appreciated their work, and if the horn section gave equal pleasure and satisfaction, it was the man himself who caught the ear and the heart. Still does.

That voice. That magical combination of youth and age, pain and joy, exuberance and melancholy. What a quality it had. In the upbeat numbers he's there, front-manning it up with the best of them, but it's in the ballads where he comes into his own, gets to the heart of the song.†

When I hear Otis Redding sing '(Sittin' On) The Dock of the Bay' now, it does have those associations – I think of my brother, which is always nice, and I think, nostalgic fool that I am, of the dusty smell of record players, of placing the disc on the turntable,‡ the needle on the disc, of hearing the light scratching that prefaced the music, and listening to the WHOLE ALBUM, pausing only to turn it over.

---

* Purely in a controlled, musical environment. No humans or animals were harmed.

† Get me, the middle-aged white classical musician guy, explaining about black soul singers of the 1960s.

‡ Word provided by Rupert Smissen – a tribute to a turntable I borrowed from his father twenty-five years ago and am still to return. Sorry, Bob.

Music can be a time machine, triggering memories good and bad. But its emotional impact isn't just nostalgic. Some music invades you by force and holds you against your will.

Hello, Steve Reich.

There's no particular association with *Sextet*, no trip down memory lane or soggy wallowing in nostalgia. It's just a cracking piece of music. The whole bee, not just the knees. From the opening chords (*djum-djum-djum-djum djum-djagga-djagga-djagga djagga-djagga-djagga-djagga dja-dja-dja-dja-dja-dja-dja*) to the final precipitous rush over the cliff's edge, it has me in its grip. Every single time. It's almost a demonic possession. I find it impossible to listen to merely an extract of it – it's all or nothing. And every time I hear it, it's a reminder that I'm alive, and that this is a good thing.

The best music does that. It tells us what it's like to be human, and it does it in a way that other things can't. This isn't to be dismissive of other art forms, because they can do the same thing in reverse – find me the musical equivalent of a late Rembrandt self-portrait and I'll happily listen to it, but good luck finding it in the first place.

And that is why it matters.

So go now and listen to some music. For it is the stuff of life.

Dammit, if you ask nicely I'll even let you listen to the *Ring* cycle, 'Imagine' or 'My Way'.

THE 1681 'FLEMING' STRADIVARIUS

2,900

Subject provided by Sarah Too

I thought I was being funny. I thought I was being clever. I thought I was being funny and clever, but I was being nothing of the kind, just an overenthusiastic and thoughtless eight-year-old who took parental approval for granted and understood little of the adult world.

We had a teacher. He was a funny man, keen to keep the class amused. Nowadays, what he did would probably be a sackable offence, but this was the 1970s. *Autres temps, autres mœurs.*

In our class was a brainy boy, a bookworm, as often as not oblivious to the intrusion of the outside world.* And so it was, one morning, that the teacher played a trick. Arriving a little late for class, he noticed our brainiac boy, reading, as was his wont, a book. Absorbed, ensorcelled,† oblivious to anything outside the magic world within its pages. So

* He once beat me at chess in, I think, four moves – I maintain to this day that my ability to lose so quickly was an even more impressive feat than his ability to win in the same time.

† Word – an archaism meaning 'bewitched' – provided by Richard Robbins.

naturally Mr ———— did what any tone-deaf teacher with no proper regard for the welfare of his charges would do: he crept up close to the boy's desk and jumped onto it.

How we laughed. Never mind that it was bullying; never mind the mental anguish caused. We were eight, and we laughed.

And then the germ of an idea popped into my head.

'I know,' I thought, 'I'll do that to Dad when I get home.'

Once hatched, it was only a matter of time before I put the plan into practice. That Saturday, my mother sent me to fetch my father for lunch. The execution of the plan couldn't have gone better. My father was practising the violin in his room. I crept, I waited, I pounced, adding a resonant 'Boo!' to inject potency and hilarity to the practical joke.

If I have any advice for a young child setting out in life and keen to do well by their fellow humans, it is this: avoid surprising someone while they are engrossed in playing Bach on a Stradivarius.

In an alternative universe, he drops it. I shudder to imagine that universe.

He didn't drop it – the violinist's instinct for instrument preservation is entrenched and unshakeable. And while he did forgive me (I think), it felt like a close-run thing at the time.

Parental disappointment has a potency very few emotions can match.*

* Honestly, I can still hear his voice as he explained what I'd done. 'I nearly dropped the Strad.' The kind of thing your mind dredges up to torment you at three in the morning.

Travel south-east from Milan for about forty miles and you will reach Cremona, the city on the River Po that for a couple of hundred years was the home of violin-making. It was in Cremona, in the second half of the sixteenth century, that Andrea Amati came up with the design that is still, with various modifications and improvements, in use today; it was in Cremona that his descendants – sons Antonio and Girolamo, and then Girolamo's son Nicolò – continued the tradition, producing fine instruments and passing their knowledge on to many pupils; and it was in Cremona that one of those pupils, Antonio Stradivari, devoted the best part of seventy years to developing his craft, becoming, by common consent, the greatest of them all.

Between 1666 (when he was twenty-two years old) and his death in 1737, Stradivari made over 1,000 violins, of which about 600 survive.* Talk to people who know about these things – players, makers, dealers – and they will tell you that he reached the absolute peak of his achievement at some point in the early 1700s. The instruments he made between his sixty-fifth and seventy-fifth birthdays are particularly sought after for the quality of their sound, but even from his earliest attempts there were signs that he had outstanding ability. And his productivity – and the quality of his output – continued unabated until his death.

The name Stradivarius is known beyond the world of music, as reliable a signifier of quality as Rolls-Royce, Leica,

* There are also thirteen surviving violas, sixty-three cellos, five guitars, two mandolins and a harp.

or Faber-Castell.* When the makers of the *Pink Panther* films gave Inspector Clouseau a violin to show up his Holmesian pretensions, they didn't make it a Guarneri or a Vuillaume.

Quite aside from the headline potential of an expensive musical instrument at auction, there is undeniably a mystique surrounding Stradivari's violins. What is it, the average punter would like to know, that makes them so special?

Theories abound. Some focus on the quality of woods available to the makers, the result of the Little Ice Age that prevailed at the time; others cite the particular chemical treatment applied to the wood by the Cremonese masters; yet others attribute great importance to the varnish applied to the wood (the recipe of which has been lost); and, of course, one shouldn't belittle the importance of spending a lifetime perfecting a craft. My conducting teacher, Ilya Musin, was once asked where his immense understanding of the craft of conducting came from. He gave the questioner a pitying look. 'I've thought about little else for seventy years.'

What exactly separates Stradivari from the rest is a matter for the experts. Certainly, listening to a fine violinist in the concert hall or on a recording, I and most others would be hard pressed to identify the instrument being played. Indeed, periodic experiments are conducted, 'blind listenings' comparing different makes of violin to see if experts can distinguish one from the other. My father took part in such a test in the 1970s, playing four violins – a

* No money or goods were solicited or received for these endorsements, which in retrospect was a missed opportunity, because I could do with some free pencils.

Stradivari, a Guarneri, a Vuillaume and a modern instrument – to a panel of experts from behind a screen. Unsurprisingly, none of the experts identified all the instruments correctly. It was a contrived exercise, from which we learned little more than that we had learned nothing. Whenever these tests are conducted, with the inevitable accompanying lack of certainty, it gives fuel to the notion that the supposed superiority of the Cremonese instruments, and especially of Strads, is hype, a construct, a figment of the imagination.

Yet for the most part, the world's top players still aspire to play Strads and Guarneris.

Perhaps the listener isn't best placed to judge the difference. Perhaps we should trust those who have the most intimate relationships with these instruments, those who play them week in, week out, who over months, years and decades build a relationship as close as is possible with an inanimate object.

Perhaps they know something we don't.

In 1957 my father relinquished his job as leader of the Philharmonia to pursue a career as a soloist. It was a bold move, but one, I suspect, that had been on the cards for a while. What he needed, though, was a suitable violin – one that had the requisite fullness of tone and projection to fill the larger concert halls. No doubt he tried quite a few. That kind of violin doesn't grow on trees,* and it took him a couple of years to find the right one.

* You're right. Violins don't grow on trees – they're made of them. Apart from the strings.

The violin he acquired in 1959 and that he played for the rest of his life was made at the beginning of Stradivari's maturity. The date attributed to it is 1681,* and it is known as the 'Fleming'.

A lot of Strads have names – 'Messiah',† 'Firebird', 'Vesuvius' – perhaps reflecting the history of their ownership, or connected with some anecdote in their past. In this case, the name refers to Evelyn Beatrice Sainte Croix Fleming, widow of Valentine Fleming, the MP for Henley in the early twentieth century. An accomplished amateur violinist, she inherited her husband's estate when he was killed in World War I, and acquired the violin from renowned dealers of stringed instruments W. E. Hill & Sons two years later.

That Eve Fleming was the mother of Amaryllis Fleming, the cellist with whom my father played in a piano trio for over a decade near the end of his life, is one of those neat coincidences with which life is littered; that she was also the mother of Ian Fleming, writer of the James Bond novels, is of no relevance at all to our current story, but will at least be of interest to fans of trivia.

What was it that my father found in that violin that he didn't find in others? It would, no doubt, have had all the qualities for which Stradivari's instruments are known: a full and rich sound, easy response, a pure singing tone.‡ But

---

* I'm hedging my bets here, simply because my father held a different view. The ins and outs of attribution are way beyond my pay grade, so I'll leave it at that.

† Supposedly the only Strad in existence to remain 'as new', it lives in the Ashmolean Museum in Oxford.

‡ One recent study in Taiwan showed that, for whatever reasons, Amati and Stradivari instruments produced acoustic signatures closer to those of the human voice than other contemporary instruments.

there would have been something more, a personal and instinctive feeling that the instrument was somehow 'right'. This bond will only have grown over time, as player and instrument became gradually more attuned to each other.

And at no time would he have considered replacing it with something else. Such is the strength of connection between the player and their chosen instrument. And to lose it, or for it to be damaged in any way, would have been a grievous setback, akin to a bereavement.

No wonder he was so upset when I nearly made him drop it.

I have photographs of the violin, taken when it was sold after my father's death. A violin is made to be played, but it's only natural to pause for a minute and contemplate the beauty of a good one. And this is a good one. Even I can see that.

The back, made of two pieces of matching maple joined in the middle, has a subtle glow that owes much to the varnish but also to the grain, the slightly asymmetrical flashes of darker wood lending visual interest. The front, one piece of softer spruce, is darker, the narrow grain lines more prosaic. The interest here, to this observer at least, is in the f-holes, symmetrically carved either side of the bridge. They have a slender elegance that quite defies scientific analysis but no doubt nonetheless conforms to acoustic and structural ideals, allowing the sound to escape and enhancing the resonance of the instrument, while not compromising the violin's structure. Stradivari's f-holes are a signifier, to an expert, of the authenticity of a Strad – violinistic philistine that I am, I just think they look beautiful.

And then the scroll, an ornament to which the eye is naturally drawn, like the escutcheon* on a ship's prow. It's an opportunity for the maker to display their wood-carving skills. This one, so I'm told†, is not the original, but a later replacement also by Stradivari. It opens out from a tight coil at the centre, spiralling outwards towards the fingerboard and body of the violin with the elegance of a swan's neck. Archimedes would approve.

I try to picture Antonio Stradivari working on this violin in the attic of No. 2 Piazza San Domenico in Cremona, the house he had bought the year before and where he would live for the rest of his life. I imagine the violin taking shape, from the creation of the internal mould, a flat piece of wood that acted as a template for the outline of numerous instruments, to the final application of varnish. A series of painstaking steps, patient and thorough, each stage guided by that mixture of innate understanding and learned processes that combine for any work of art.

A violin like this represents two weeks' work, more or less. Three hundred years later, the evidence of his craftsmanship and skill is plain for all to see and hear.

A violin is a robust and delicate thing. Robust because it is designed to withstand intense pressure from the tension of the strings; delicate because it is sensitive and susceptible to

* Word provided by Kat Stephen.
† My thanks to Charles Beare for sharing his copious knowledge.

nuances of heat and especially humidity[*] (and of course to nuances of being dropped because the user has been shocked out of his wits by a well-meaning but disastrously muddle-headed eight-year-old).

And delicate things need adequate protection. We're not talking here of the curvy cases like the ones handled so clumsily by the gangsters in *The Ladykillers,*[†] the contours of the instrument clearly visible in the shape of the case, but of something a bit more luxurious.

I can visualise my father's violin case. An oblong box with a pale green, sun-bleached cover. Open the lid. There are accoutrements – at least two bows, clipped into place on the inside, a pocket for rosin and pencils and rubbers, spare strings coiled in little paper envelopes – but you don't see those at first. Of course you don't. The violin, that's the main event.

It sits in a bed of library-coloured velvet, wrapped in a large patterned silk handkerchief. There is an element of ritual about all this: the opening of the case, the unclipping and tightening of the bow, the application of rosin – too much and the bow becomes gritty across the string, making a harsher sound, too little and the sound is hollow and the bow moves skittishly, harder to control – and the sounding of the open strings in a particular sequence and rhythm[‡] as preface to a practice session.

---

* A sensible violinist keeps a humidity indicator in their case, either in the form of a piece of card with moisture-sensitive spots or a more sophisticated hygrometer, which shows the percentage of humidity with a dial or digital display.

† I couldn't write this piece without mentioning that film, one of my father's favourites.

‡ Most musicians have their own way of saying hello to an instrument, as individual, I suspect, as fingerprints.

That sound was deeply embedded in my head from an early age, when I would sit cross-legged on the floor and listen to my father as he practised. It seemed, I think, like some kind of miracle, and in a way I suppose it was. No wonder my own foray into the bottomless pit of misery known as 'learning the violin' was brief and ill-fated. How unattainable such perfection must have seemed.

That my father was really very good at the violin only dawned on me some years later, when people kept on telling me. Of course he was good at it; he was my dad. And then, when he died, they kept on telling me even more. But by then I was on the path to a musical career myself – and if I lacked the phenomenal patience and application required to master such a recalcitrant and fiendish instrument as the violin, I did at least have some understanding of the sound of good playing.

And, come to that, the sound of a good violin.

Sixty years after my father acquired it, and thirty-two after his death, I meet the 1681 'Fleming' Stradivarius again.* If I'd thought about it at all, I'd imagined it elsewhere. I knew it had gone to Germany after the initial sale, but had no knowledge of its subsequent movements. But it is, to my surprise, in London.

I meet Cecily Ward one bright spring morning at her house in north London. She gives me coffee, talks about the violin, about what it is to play a Strad, to fall in love with it, to know that with this instrument you will be the best

* Thanks to Sam Blade for joining the dots and making introductions.

violinist you can be. She talks about what the instrument gives her: a simultaneous blend of exhilaration – as if walking a tightrope – and security; the sense that she can do anything, but also that the drop is precipitous.

And then she shows me the violin.

I've been expecting a moment of recognition, a sense of reunion, but no. I never knew it well enough, not at first hand. This violin is both familiar and unfamiliar. I wouldn't, I don't think, be able to pick it out in a line-up.

It's strange, though, to look at it in different hands, to know that I am looking at something that was part of the background to my childhood, that was part of my father, that no doubt has his DNA all over it.

Cecily plays a few phrases on it. It is fine playing, and the sound, rich and full, fills the small room – it would no doubt fill bigger ones. For a moment I have an urge to sit cross-legged on the floor and listen, but luckily it passes.

And the thought of jumping up and shouting 'Boo!' – praise the Lord – never even enters my head.

THE ART OF THE SANDWICH

2,800

Subject provided by Gwen Nathan

Consider this: a chilled food cabinet in a faceless shop in a faceless town somewhere in today's England. A row of cardboard and polythene cartons, each containing a sandwich marginally less appetising than its neighbour – a neat trick if you can pull it off. Typically in these cartons, two slices of mass-produced tasteless pap masquerading as bread encase a thin smear of bland paste devoid of redeeming qualities; or perhaps the filling comprises a sickly concoction of pig and poultry products calling themselves 'the all-day breakfast sandwich'; or a pasty mush with flecks of yellow, only identifiable as 'tuna and sweetcorn' on close examination of the label. They stare balefully at you from the shelf, demanding you cough up £4.50 to wade through their insipid ghastliness, an encapsulation of the myriad horrors of fast food – sans sweet, sans salt, sans sour, sans bitter, sans umami, sans character, sans love, sans everything.

And breathe.

It needn't be like that. For while it's true that at its worst the sandwich is among the most abhorrent things it is possible to inflict on the human palate, at its best . . . ah, at its best the sandwich is one of the glories of world cuisine.

Ever since John Montagu, 4th Earl of BLT, called for some sort of snack to be brought to his table so he could continue gambling without interruption, this deceptively simple idea – something enclosed between two pieces of bread – has seized the human imagination. The machinations of popular folklore being what they are, it's unclear whether the specific combination was in fact his idea, or whether he just barked, 'Valet, get me a snack and look snappy about it!' If the latter, we should pause for a second to acknowledge the contribution of that nameless servant to the history of gastronomy. Because if there's a more universal and democratic food type, we have yet to find it. From the childish pleasure of the sugar sandwich* to the grotesque and uniquely American magnificence of the Dagwood† and touching on all the stops in between, the sandwich has conquered the world.

Such is the infinite variety of sandwich species, genera and phyla, not to mention human taste, it's almost impossible to be prescriptive about what constitutes a good one, but we can at least attempt to define our terms and set out what a sandwich is – and, crucially, what it isn't. It might seem an obvious question, and one to which we all think we know the answer, but it addresses a point I'd like to make in an overly pedantic manner in a couple of paragraphs, so off to the dictionaries we go.

* Admit it, you used to eat them when you were a child. Maybe you still do.
† Its guiding principle appears to be 'pile everything up until it falls over'.

Here's Chambers: 'Any sort of food between two slices of bread.' Succinct and to the point, as is their wont. The *Shorter Oxford English*, not unexpectedly, goes into a bit more detail: 'A set of two or more (esp. buttered) slices of bread with a usu. savoury filling between them.' For the sake of balance, here's the Cambridge version: 'Two pieces of bread with cheese, salad, or meat, usually cold, between them.' Across the pond, Merriam-Webster goes for: 'Two thin pieces of bread, usually buttered, with a thin layer (as of meat, cheese, or savory mixture) spread between them.'

And so on.

You might have guessed where I'm going with this.

No?

'Two slices of bread' . . . 'two or more . . . slices of bread' . . . 'two pieces . . . ' . . . 'two . . . '

Two.

Two.

TWO.

Yes, 'open sandwich', I'm looking at you. You might think you can slide in here wearing a false moustache and comedy glasses, and you certainly seem to have Scandinavia fooled, but you're no more a sandwich than a weasel playing a ukulele is Jascha Heifetz, so off you hop.*

While I'm giddy with the power of pedantry, let's dispatch all notion of wraps, tortillas, pittas and such like as belonging to the sandwich family. They are all delicious, magnificent, bathed in the golden sunlight of culinary excellence.

But they're not sandwiches.

* Sorry, Scandinavia.

OK then. Battle lines drawn, let's engage.

What is 'the art of the sandwich'?

How long is a piece of chewing gum? How green is my valley? How many roads must a man walk down?

What is the meaning of life?

Try as we might to pin it down, the definitive answer eludes us. Let's say you want to lay down guidelines on the subject of the bread. It constitutes, after all, two-thirds* of the elements of the snack in question, so might be considered of the utmost importance. You can make the best filling in the world – moist, balanced, toothsome – and all your efforts will be dashed to the ground by flabby, tasteless, lifeless, not-fit-for-purpose bread. Whether it's white, brown, granary, ciabatta, focaccia, roll, bap, bun, bagel, teacake, baguette, rye, pumpernickel, soda, sourdough, brioche or zwieback, if it's not of the highest quality you might as well chuck it in the bin.

Or so you'd think. Because, for all that the sentiment in the last paragraph is worthy, its heart firmly in the right place, there's something indefinably wrong about it.

In contradiction of all wisdom about the importance of quality ingredients, when it comes down to it, we all know that the Queen of Sandwiches is the bacon sarnie on cheap white, moistened with a careless smear of slightly too much ketchup. It's a truth, as people too often say, universally acknowledged. Look into your heart of hearts, delve deep into those memories, cast aside all thoughts of wispy rocket leaves, exorbitant chutneys and relishes, fougasse, challah or lavash. White bread. Crispy bacon. Butter. Ketchup. No

* Yes, OK, three-fifths in a club sandwich.

need to overthink it. The ultimate manifestation of the magnificence of cheap food.

Game over, then, surely? We crown the bacon sarnie on cheap white the winner and leave it at that.

Maybe.

Or maybe you think about it some more, and remember the sublime joy of thick slices of rare roast beef coated with sinus-clearing horseradish sauce on roughly sliced white bloomer; or the pure hedonism of slightly too much chicken and slightly too much avocado, bound together with slightly too much mayo and squeezed between two slices of multigrain, the filling oozing slightly out of the sides, but that's OK because you can always hoover it up afterwards; or perhaps, more refined but no less enjoyable, thin slices of smoked salmon, a good spreading of smooth cream cheese, lashings of lemon juice and matching quantities of black pepper?

Life is rarely simple.

But while we might, under the right circumstances, admit all the above to an imagined pantheon of Sandwiches of Great Repute, we have to be careful. One false step and the sandwich becomes somehow suboptimal. Maybe the beef is overcooked, the horseradish bland, the chicken dry, the avocado either too rubbery or too mushy, the salmon's flavour lacking depth, or the pepper ground too enthusiastically – all these factors can readily derail an otherwise worthy sandwich.

So how do we ensure that our sandwich comes up to scratch? Perhaps we can take as a starting point the sage words of Max Beerbohm, in a letter to his friend Reggie*

* People, by and large, aren't called Reggie any more. Shame.

Turner in 1893. 'When I ask for a sandwich,' he wrote, 'I do not mean a loaf with a field in the middle of it.'

And so say all of us.

What we're after is balance. Bread of the requisite density, moisture and taste; the filling, whatever its provenance, to be succulent, bursting with savour, and complemented by some accompanying element, maybe in the form of a sauce or chutney. Contrasts work well: bland plus tangy, smooth plus chunky, light plus firm.

The matching of bread to filling is key. Only a lunatic would make a fried egg and ketchup sandwich using those tiny crustless squares of white bread more suited to tea with the Duchess of Devonshire. And you're not going to layer your finely sliced peeled cucumber, unaccompanied save for a delicate layer of soft butter, between two chunks of brown sourdough and call it fit for human consumption.

There is a danger, in our quest for perfection, that we will overthink it, and thus produce something that is, although it might fulfil its obligations as per the official description, somehow unsandwichy. Perhaps there will be one or two ingredients too many; the bread will lack oomph; lettuce will be pointlessly inserted; the tomato slice too damp, rendering the bread slightly pappy; the ingredients might well be individually perfect, but their assembly somehow wide of the mark – ill-matched combinations, or unbalanced quantities, or wait a minute, you're going to put THAT in it?

And while it can be good to plan the sandwich, to give due consideration to each of its constituent elements, is there greater satisfaction to be had than the unexpected, unrepeatable success of the spur-of-the-moment improvisation? I once made a sandwich of two slices of granary toast, a tin of tuna, some thickly sliced cucumber, grindings of black pepper and a hastily knocked-up mustard mayo. Average, everyday, slightly wrong. I ate it leaning against the fridge, listening to Earth, Wind & Fire, and even now, thinking about it, I come over all Proustian. It was an entirely unspecial meal, but somehow it sticks in my mind as a template for the unexpectedly glorious culinary experience. I needed lunch, I made it, and through some alchemy I created a moment of perfection. I've tried to replicate it since, always without success. Perhaps I was just very hungry.

Cometh the hour, cometh the sandwich.

Occasion is also important. Imagine the aforementioned formal tea. And now imagine being offered the kind of sandwich you might make yourself at 1 a.m., fresh from the pub and suddenly assailed by an attack of the yearning hunger that comes with drunkenness. It simply doesn't compute. Whatever you make on those nocturnal forays (and if it contains cucumber, it will either be a terrible mistake or in the form of a gherkin foraged from the forgotten jar at the back of the fridge), it's not going to be something appropriate for polite company. You'll stand there in the kitchen, swaying slightly, choosing ingredients. You'll slice a pair of misshapen doorstops from the crusty loaf, shave some Cheddar from the block with great care, slather it with some of that chunky chutney you got from the farmer's market, a grinding of pepper, a sprinkling of salt, maybe a squirt of mayonnaise, ooh and perhaps a bit of mustard for sharpness, and then you'll stagger across to the table and eat it, thinking strange thoughts, and it'll be the embodiment of greed and gustatory indulgence, and it'll only be the next morning that you'll realise that half the sandwich filling is on the kitchen floor and your face is smeared with mayonnaise.

Well, you might not. But I certainly will.

Now then. Some details. All entirely personal, and therefore by definition all entirely right. You will, if you have the remotest capacity for independent thought, disagree with some of them. That's as it should be, but I'm also hoping that somewhere along the line there will be something in the following that will have at least one person nodding in agreement and murmuring a reverent 'Ah yes!' under their breath.

Here's hoping, anyway.

The bread: I'm partial to something seeded. Less so, it has to be admitted, as I get older and my teeth offer more opportunities for the sequestration of those seeds for later use,* but partial nonetheless. A good seeded bread won't stint on the quantity or variety of seeds, but nor will the weight and texture of the bread be compromised by their presence. Heft, that's what we're after. Heft and weight and a pleasing nuttiness.

But let's not dismiss the satisfaction to be derived from the chewy blandness of a well-made white loaf, vehicle for many a successful sandwich. Not the kind you get in the supermarket that collapses on itself in a squishy disaster when you try to cut it, the crust flaking all over the place. No, a solid, crusty-but-sliceable white made with good strong flour.

* See also: bits of cold roast lamb.

And are we at home to thinly sliced rye bread as vehicle for the deep dark taste of good pastrami, like we're in New York or something?

We emphatically are.

This could go on for ever. So many breads, each with its own qualities and ideal partners. Luckily the next element of the sandwich won't detain us for long.

The spread: whatever you choose, whether it's butter, butter or butter, you'll spread it right to the edge, won't you?

WON'T YOU?

Very well, then. On to the filling: right this second, as I type these words, I would commit heinous crimes for cold roast lamb, slightly fatty, in thickish but not unmanageable chunks, embellished with some of the scrapings from the roasting tin and a generous allowance of redcurrant jelly (not excessive, though – no more than half the jar). There are those who would sully this exquisite combination with leftover roast potatoes – I urge you to shun these people as you would a rabid dog.

While that cold roast lamb is my utopian ideal at this precise moment (and I must say that my lascivious* yearning for one has only been exacerbated by writing about it), come to me tomorrow and I'll purse my lips and wax lyrical about the joys of Cheddar and tomato, or steak and onion, or (yes yes yes!) fish fingers and ketchup.

Have you ever had a sandwich of white bread and dark chocolate? No? What the hell have you been doing with your life? Go! Don't hesitate – just go!

It's all a matter of taste, but there is one thing that has

* Word provided by Christian Halstead.

come up in the course of my researches on which I stand firm: there are those who lobby for the inclusion of a layer of potato crisps* in a sandwich. What strange people they are.

Before we finish, we mustn't forget the residuals, the things that can make your sandwich experience† more enjoyable. A ham sandwich (the ham will be sliced thick, it will be moist, it might easily have been cooked in Coca-Cola, and there will be good mustard unstintingly applied) is, in my view, happiest when wrapped in greaseproof paper, the edges folded over so as to make an enticing bundle, the contents perhaps just discernible through the opacity of the paper. Mock all you like, but it's those marginal gains (to borrow from the parlance of international professional cycling) that can raise a sandwich to a different level. Tupperware is good for many things, but it sure sucks the romance out of a sandwich.

So where does all this leave us? You might argue that I'm making too much of it, that the quality of a sandwich matters little as long as it provides you with fuel for the afternoon, but let's reflect for a moment. Say you live for seventy-five years. Setting aside a couple of years at the beginning, when sandwiches aren't likely to be on your agenda, and maybe another couple at the end (likewise), that's seventy years of sandwich eating. Say one a week, for a total of around 3,500 sandwiches in a lifetime.

---

* America: chips. We will never agree on this, so in the interests of transatlantic brotherhood I have made myself bilingual in this and many other matters of apparently minor importance. 'Pavement' is another point of contention, leading as it can to actual death if the difference between the side of the road and the middle of it isn't made crystal clear.

† I'm sorry. I'm so very sorry.

That's a lot of sandwiches, you'll say, but is it really that many? Given the variety of breads and fillings and garnishes and flavours out there, is 3,500 really enough sandwiches for you to be splurging your allocation on dried-out edge-curling fish-paste-besmeared monstrosities from a chiller cabinet?

No. No, it is not. Life is far too short for bad sandwiches.

Go then. Make your sandwiches. And whether you choose chicken, turkey, beef, ham, lamb, pork, bacon, salmon, corned beef, pastrami, salami, hummus, guacamole, roasted vegetables, liverwurst, pâté, Brie, Cheddar, Lancashire, mozzarella, provolone or Stilton; whether you slather it with mayonnaise, mustard, salad cream, tapenade, salsa, pesto, chutney, onion jam, hoisin, hot chilli, peanut butter or any of a thousand more, bear one final thing in mind, as expressed by the ineffably wise Nigel Slater – 'only the generous can make a sandwich worth eating'.

RED-WINE STAINS

2,700

Subject provided by Alan Grant

There is an argument, it hardly needs saying, for not spilling it in the first place. Pace yourself, don't drink too much, don't overfill the glass, avoid sudden movements.

But we all know that won't work.

Spread salt liberally over the stain, allow to dry; wash with cold water and detergent or baking soda.

It all starts so promisingly. A sweeping drive, a group of fallow deer watching warily from under a tree. A kestrel, Gerard Manley Hopkins's dapple-dawn-drawn falcon, hovering motionless, an aerobatic miracle ignored by 200 people. An old stone doorway framed by tumbling wisteria, porch opening out to the hall, broad staircase ahead. Dark wood, soft furnishings. An atmosphere of muted luxury.

Not cheap, but then it's Chantelle's big day, a special, unrepeatable occasion.

Unrepeatable? Whisper it soft, but it will be repeated, and sooner than even the most cynical of observers might have imagined. Not like this, though – it'll be an altogether more low-key occasion. Fifteen people at the registry, then the room over the local pub. Steak and chips and a barrel of beer.

Here, today, a glass of bone-dry champagne, presented on a silver platter. Waiting staff walking round with crab puffs, salmon-and-dill parcels, olive-and-feta dainties. Polite conversation with people you barely know, nor entirely want to. '. . . used to be flatmates with Serena's cousin . . .', '. . . mostly working out of Singapore these days . . .', 'Beautiful service, I thought, despite the vicar . . .', '. . . slightly relieved she turned up of course, ha ha – eh?'

That first sip, bubbles fizzing on your tongue. The crab puff, feather light. The taste of sophistication, or so you tell yourself.

You find yourself on the fringes, next to a woman. Aloof, reserved, starchy.

'And you are . . . ?'

'Held loosely together with gaffer tape and string. How about you?'

She doesn't get it. Oh well. Ten more words each, the definition of desultory, and then she's had enough. Her eyes dart, slightly panicked, looking for someone else. Anyone else.

'Go,' you want to say. 'Go to your people. I'm happy with my thoughts. Me and my empty glass.'

Full glass. You don't mind if you do.

Mix three parts hydrogen peroxide with one part dish soap. Pour over the stain, and let it sit for a while. Add more solution occasionally. Do not rub or scrub – just wait.

'The Axbridge Ballroom is able to seat 300 guests and as such is ideal for conferences and weddings, offering a unique ambiance with lots of character, outdoor patio area and stunning views across the grounds.'

The stories in that room. Just scratch the surface and they'd bubble up, spilling out over the thick carpet, climbing the mahogany-panelled walls and showering the assembled company with the curdled vitriol simmering within. Parents, siblings, aunts, uncles, cousins, in-laws, ex-boyfriends, ex-girlfriends, colleagues, acquaintances, strangers, secret crushes, not-so-secret crushes, jilted lovers, brooding haters, octogenarians, teenagers, babes-in-arms, toddlers, millennials, Gen Xers, Baby Boomers, dashing blades, crashing bores, snowflakes, shitflakes, hipsters, office drones, bigots, sexists, racists, homophobes, transphobes, you-phobes, them-phobes, absolutely-bloody-everything-phobes, Brexiteers, Remoaners, liberals, fascists, communists, wishy-washy middle-of-the-roaders, and at least one person who just wants to sit in the corner talking to nobody and getting quietly smashed until it's over – all thrown together because it's Chantelle's big day and she wanted to include everyone. It is, after all – as she has reminded everyone at every possible opportunity – the best day of her life.

Which doesn't say much for the days to come.

There are people here who haven't spoken to each other

for years. Others who once made oaths to love, honour and cherish, then three years later realised it wasn't worth the candle. Lifelong friends who are still friends only from force of habit, couples who have run out of conversation, and at least five people who everyone else is praying they won't be sitting next to.

You don't know this; but, extrapolating,* you know it. And if that makes you less than generous, then lay the blame firmly at the feet of weddings past.

The champagne really is rather good. Suffused with mild goodwill, you look for your name on the seating plan.

Nope. Don't know any of them. Probably for the best.

This is what happens when you live abroad for ten years.

Absorb as much of the spillage as possible with paper towels. Sprinkle bicarbonate of soda over the stain. It will change from deep red to pale grey. Don't overdo it. Wring out a cloth with white vinegar, wipe, leave to dry and vacuum the affected area.

Standard wedding tables, standard wedding chairs. Embossed name-cards, the names handwritten in curlicue script. Swagged curtains, plush carpet.

Crisp white linen tablecloths.

Gleaming cutlery, smudge-free glassware, perfect flower arrangements.

---

* Bernard Hughes kindly gave me the word 'extrapolate' to include in this book. I used it earlier, but I am throwing in its present participle just for the hell of it.

Treat bags for children and adults alike.

Menu cards.

You decide to amuse yourself with a little rewriting.

Pointless Slivers of Smoked Trout, Textures of Air, Foam Mousse.

Vegetarian option: Inevitability of Goat's Cheese with Sun-Toughened Tomatoes.

Leg of Cornish* Lamb Eight Ways, Harassed Potatoes, Tired Vegetables au Beurre Congelé, Not Enough Rowan† Jelly.

Vegetarian option: Roast Cliché of Portobello Mushrooms with Port Disapparition, Invisibility of Fines Herbes.

Quincunx‡ of Chocolate Desserts with Coffee-Bean Cream Smear, Ill-Advised Raspberry Blob, Crumble Topping Gravel.

Wines, both white and red, carefully selected to be not quite right with the food, but not quite wrong either. Characterless, inoffensive. Liberal-Democrats-of-the-1990s-type wines.

The round table is just too big to allow conversation with anyone except your immediate neighbours. The portents aren't good.

You turn to the lady on your right. She's older than you, wearing a classy cream number that by all appearances cost more than your flat. She looks terrifyingly aloof and condescending, but you've had two glasses of champagne so you're emboldened. You introduce yourself with a smile. The look she gives you, honed by years of unconscious

* Word provided by Karenza Passmore.
† Word provided by Aisha Memon.
‡ Word provided by Tom Gauterin.

practice, has shrivelled greater people than you. You are, it tells you, no larger than a muon, a mere speck on a speck on a speck – of less importance than dandruff.

She leaves a pause of just the right length to indicate her utter indifference to you and everything you have ever found interesting or important, then murmurs a barely perceptible 'Oh', and turns away from you to talk to the neighbour on the other side.

Probably just as well.

Waiters are bringing chilled bottles of white wine. Manna, pure manna. You're all over it like a mongoose* attacking a snake.

Take a clean cloth and blot as much of the stain away as possible. DO NOT SCRUB. Dab with white wine. Blot again. If any of the stain remains, dab with club soda. AGAIN, DO NOT SCRUB. If the stain persists, try talcum powder.

Even the worst white wine is improved by proper chilling. Not too much, not to set the fillings tingling, just enough to induce a cool film of condensation on the glass.

And this isn't the worst white wine. You take a sip. More than a sip, if truth be told, probably closer to a quaff.

You are now ready to address the man on your left, who seems to consist entirely of an intimidating combination of flesh, sweat and beard.

* Word provided by Ailsa Forsyth.

He offers you a large hand. You take it. His crushes yours like an elephant treading on a nut. This has happened to you before, more than once. You have, you think, a normal handshake, delivered with normal hands. It's never occurred to you to squeeze the lifeblood out of a new acquaintance on first meeting.

What you want to do is scream: 'AAAAAAHHH! JESUS, WHAT THE HELL ARE YOU DOING, YOU UTTER BASTARD? IT'S JUST A FRIENDLY GREETING AND YOU DECIDE TO INFLICT MULTIPLE CONTUSIONS. WHAT KIND OF ARSEHOLE DOES THAT?'

What you actually do is tamp down your inner shriek of agony, smile wanly, and settle in for what promises to be the worst forty-five minutes of your life.

We love first impressions. We might deny it, might consider ourselves non-judgemental, but there's no stopping us. It's human nature. Meet someone new and there we are, judging away.

You're boring. You're nice. You're acerbic. You're sweet. You're weak. You're strong. You're my soulmate. I loathe you.

Your first impression of this man – you just catch his name, Geoff, mumbled through a forest of beard – is that he's the kind of person who takes great pleasure in telling people that he speaks his mind, doesn't suffer fools gladly, calls a spade a digging implement, and doesn't have any truck with nonsense. You sense that the words 'it's political correctness gone mad' tremble permanently on his lips. Geoff is, in other words, a colossal, crashing, magnificent bore of a man, a behemoth of the genus, capable of stopping a rhinoceros in its tracks with the irresistible power of his fatuous and offensive tedium.

You know this beyond all doubt before he's opened his mouth.

Six words in, you sigh a silent sigh and take another quaff of the Argentinian Torrontés. You were right. Of course you were. You have the unerring instinct of a seasoned bore magnet.

He opens with a question – 'Come far?' – but it's not a question, more a gambit. Your answer – 'London' – is an irrelevant detail. He sweeps it aside like a horse flicking its tail at a fly. Even if you had said 'Betelgeuse' it would have had no effect. He wasn't listening, not really. It was just a preliminary to his own tedious soliloquy. And now he's off, detailing his own journey – 'Terrible around the roadworks at Chobham' – and executing the deftest of segues from traffic to cars to the manufacturing industry to, inevitably, immigration. All done in about a minute, the years of practice worn lightly. And once on the subject – 'I mean, I don't mind within reason, but there is a limit; nothing against them, our neighbours are Polish, and we have this Romanian builder, he gets the job done quicker than you can say Jack Robinson, strictly cash of course, but if it keeps the price down a nod's as good as a wink, say no more, but here's my question, I mean where do you draw the line, and not being funny, but how do you know who's coming in?' – he settles in for the long haul like a hippo at a watering hole.

You make a vow. Five more minutes of this and you will in fact kill him. It would, in its own way, be a victimless crime. The world wouldn't miss Geoff, not really. There would be pretend outrage, of course, but deep down everyone would know you'd done the world a favour. An image flashes before you of his family, queuing up to thank you at the trial with tears in their eyes.

A swift defenestration* might do it – but Geoff is large and the windows distant. You look at the table. You have three forks and three knives to choose from – you're pretty sure you could muster enough force with the largest of them if you found the right point of entry. All those rereadings of *Modesty Blaise* might just have been worthwhile after all.

You start plotting an escape route, just in case.

But first, just one more quaff.

Pour milk in hefty quantities over the stain. Let it soak in, but do not rub. Once all the wine has been absorbed, wash in the usual way.

Somehow, without realising it, you've eaten the trout, and now the lamb is in front of you. It looks, against all expectation, rather good. Moist, pink and adorned with just the right amount of a gravy that owes its richness to judicious reduction rather than artificial enhancement.

The red wine is good, too. You're not naturally inclined towards flowery descriptions of wine. If pressed, you'll distinguish 'rich' from 'thin', 'fruit' from 'vinegar', 'yummy' from 'execrable'. Wine is for drinking, food is for eating – like jokes, they are ruined by overanalysis.

But Geoff is still boring on – 'What I don't understand is

* Word provided by Jackie Steinitz.

why we went into the damn thing in the first place' – and you've got to keep yourself amused somehow.

You take a sip. 'Nutty.' Another sip. 'Blackberries – no, hold on, black*currants*.' One more. 'Autumn woodsmoke, with a waft of echinacea.'

'I mean, we're beholden to the whim of unelected bureaucrats with their snouts in the Brussels trough!'

You find that, like spinning plates, a judiciously placed 'Uh huh', 'Oh yes, right' or 'I see' is enough to keep Geoff going without any further contribution from you.

You're feeling your way in to this glass of wine, pacing yourself, but now it's time for a proper quaff. 'Definitely chocolatey, perhaps with a hint of nutmeg. A positively bumptious little number, this, bounding energetically onto your palate with a cheery "what ho!" and without so much as a "by-your-leave".'

You are now, without any semblance of doubt, thoroughly pissed. It's all you can do to stop yourself from standing and declaring, at the top of your voice, 'David Durose is a mighty god! All hail David!* Now join me, one and all, in a lusty bacchanal!'†

Oh dear.

Apply cat litter to the affected area, pressing down softly with your hands. When the stain has been fully absorbed, vacuum thoroughly.

* David paid good money for me to include these words. I hope he doesn't mind that I've put them into the mouth of a desperate drunk.

† Word provided by Charlotte Woodward.

It doesn't start as an extravagant gesture. It just turns into one halfway through.

The intention was to reach for your napkin so you could dab at the stain the red wine made on your shirt because the glass slipped in your hand and you caught it just in time but nevertheless some of it slopped over the side and it was kind of inevitable because you're at the exuberant stage of pissed.

But while moving your left hand towards the napkin you forget you still have the glass in your right and somehow they get tangled and then you're not sure how it happens, but suddenly, against all the odds, you have the undivided attention of Madame la Haughty-Knickers. Her former disdain has been replaced by a sort of horrified disgust, like a dowager duchess discovering two scorpions shagging in the sock drawer. Her classy cream number is cream no more.

Stretch the stained area over a bowl and pour copious amounts of boiling (or nearly boiling) water over it, making sure not to leave any area untreated.

In equal parts horrified and thrilled, you stand.

The short-term effects of alcohol on the human body are well documented. You're not quite clear whether it's the lack of fine-motor coordination or the impairment of judgement that causes what happens next. Perhaps an unhappy combination of the two. All you wish anyone to know is that you mean well.

A lunge, a sweep of the arm, an ill-aimed grasp, and now your plate – lamb, gravy, potatoes, vegetables and all – is somehow lying in Mme la H-K's lap, and the red-wine bottle – recently opened at your behest – is falling and rolling and the wine is glugging out onto the crisp white linen and there's a red slick spreading across the table and people are pushing their chairs back to avoid getting red-wine stains on their posh wedding gear and all you can think of is oh shit this looks just like that scene in *The Untouchables* when Robert De Niro smashes that guy's head in with a baseball bat and then there's that overhead shot, crimson blood on white linen.

On the upside, Madame la Haughty-Knickers's day is quite ruined. And it's shut Geoff up good and proper.

Apply a dollop of shaving cream, then work it evenly over the stain using the curved side of a spoon. Dampen a sponge with warm water and wipe up the foam, gently scrubbing if necessary.

Well, only if you insist.

HOW NOT TO CURE HICCUPS AT MIDNIGHT ON RYDE ESPLANADE

2,600

Subject provided by Dudley Pritchard

Take a glass of water – the bigger the better. Drink it quickly. Down in one. No sipping.

We usually get on so well. Seventeen years we've known each other. Seventeen years of cricket, beer, music, board games, meals, walking, more beer, more music. Nothing controversial, no bust-ups, no dramas. That's not Dudley's style.

He is – and I'm not just saying this because he's asked me to write this piece, nor because he's my brother-in-law – a thoroughly decent and civilised person.

But at approximately 12.20 a.m. on 6 May 2018, I could cheerfully have throttled him and chucked his lifeless body into the Solent.

Strong words, I'm sure you'll agree. Words that require some context. Let's take it back to the beginning.

Fill a glass with water and drink from its far side, being careful not to spill any, but also drinking as fast as is practical.

I like walking. It's always seemed a civilised way of getting about the place. Running is too sweaty, too knee-pounding, too much like hard work; cycling is great, but there are hills and traffic and drivers hating you; swimming is good, but either you're not going anywhere except up and down the pool, or you are going somewhere but swallowing gobbets of seaweed and salt water and susceptible to gull attack.

I remain unconvinced by rowing.

Walking, however, allows you to take exercise while retaining a semblance of dignity, lets you examine things up close, gives you a sense of scale, and affords the option of getting out of breath should you so wish. I even like going up hills – they disrupt the monotony of the flat, your thigh muscles get a good workout, and there's a view at the top.

In short, give me a nice long walk, preferably along a route with plenty of birds and other wildlife, and I'm happy.

And that's how I found myself walking round the Isle of Wight on the first May Bank Holiday weekend in 2018. Not just sauntering aimlessly for a couple of hours before retiring to the pub, but actually walking all the way round the outside of it – sixty-six miles. At three miles an hour – a steady pace for a man of my age, fitness and leg length – that's twenty-two hours of walking, more or less. With the necessary stops, a pre-Saturday-breakfast start should see you breasting the tape for elevenses on Sunday morning, having walked through the night.

That's the plan, anyway.

But plans, as the poet Burns sagely surmised, 'gang aft agley', and agley this one most emphatically ganged.

Pull hard on your tongue.

The Isle of Wight is available for walking round at any time. We didn't need to share our adventure with hundreds of others as part of an 'Ultra Challenge'.* But there's something enticing about the collective experience, plus the undoubted attraction of organised pit stops every fifteen miles, with tea and biscuits and massages. And of course it's all for charriddee.†

And so I find myself outside a large tent near Chale at eight on Saturday morning, refusing to do the Zumba warm-up despite the compère's cheery exhortations. Enforced joining-in makes my teeth itch, so I opt for some gentle stretching instead. This pre-walk hoo-ha is a hoo-ha I could well do without. I'm keen to enter the fray.

The south-west coast of the Isle of Wight is almost insultingly picturesque. It's a scene to incite even the most apathetic observer to poetry: rolling land, distant cliffs, pewter sea contrasting with a bright blue sky.‡ Throw in a buzzard riding a thermal overhead and the rolling skirl of

---

* 'Ultra' is the biggest, no? Or is 'hyper' bigger? Or maybe 'mega'? We urgently need clarification.

† You could give the money to the charity without the palaver, but this is apparently an unfashionable view.

‡ I damn nearly wrote 'cerulean' there – that's how potent this view is.

a skylark and you have the definition of idyllic. God, should you countenance His or Her existence, is in His or Her heaven, et cetera and so forth.

The cast list: me; my aforementioned brother-in-law Dudley; his younger brother Peter. We have abundant time ahead of us, sixty-six miles to walk, and the world to set to rights. We're good at that, chatting an awful lot of shit about politics, science, music, nature, religion, cricket, art, philosophy, literature, the coats of arms of the House of Plantagenet,* the relative merits of the flat back four versus the continental 'libero' system, and the strengths and weaknesses of local authority recycling schemes. It's just as well anyone within hearing distance is focused either on walking or on chatting their own brand of shit.

At this stage the walking is easy, partly fuelled by our shit chat, but also because we've only just started. Full of energy and enthusiasm for the task ahead, we feel as if we could go on for ever.

Ha.

Eat powdered cocoa off a spoon. Careful when swallowing.

Of all the memorable sights on the walk, the jewel has to be Tennyson Down. It's a magnificent whale's back of a climb, setting off steepish but not daunting, and gradually levelling out as you near the monument at the top. To the right, the charms of the island gradually reveal themselves, a

* Word provided by Catherine Lee.

patchwork quilt* of the natural and the man-made: rolling hills, farmland, the seething metropolises of Yarmouth, Newport and Cowes, villages dotted about the place like dirty socks on the bedroom floor, and in the distance the pale gleam of a large solar farm. Beyond that, the Solent, glistening in the spring sunshine. And further, the mainland, somehow prosaic compared to the island's charms.

On days like this, sunshine throwing everything into sharp definition and a light breeze ruffling our collars, it's sensational no matter where you look, a view that should be prescribed on what's left of the NHS.

We stand at the top, drinking it in. On a normal day, we might go straight back down to Freshwater for a pint. But today is not a normal day, and the temptation doesn't even register. Today, we're on a mission.

Forty-eight miles to go.

Place a half-teaspoon of sugar on the back of the tongue.

Eat little and often. Energy foods, easily digested. Keep hydrated. Wear a hat. Pace yourself.

I do it all, ever mindful of just how far sixty-six miles is, of how long it will take, and that the first real challenge will come under cover of darkness.

I did the first half of this walk last year. Thirty-three miles – a good day's walk, ending at dusk and delivering the satisfaction of a good night's sleep.

* Word provided by Victoria Nowell.

But we like to stretch ourselves, don't we?

Don't we?

Hold your breath and count to one hundred.

At about twenty miles, two small girls have set up a stall from which they sell glasses of lemonade, cannily reckoning that the combination of winning smiles and chattiness will make us forget for the moment that the next stop, with its free drinks, is just half a mile away.

They're right.

Chew a teaspoon of dill seed to stimulate the vagus nerve.

The final approach to the halfway stop, along the promenade on the outskirts of Cowes, is longer than I remember. Frustratingly so. I'm still full of walking, but also ready for a break.

A common tern flits past. Its cousin, the Arctic tern, has the longest migration of any bird, covering 14,000 miles in single-minded pursuit of perpetual summer.

Fucking lunatic.

Stick your fingers in your ears and drink a glass of water through a straw.

The trouble with a prolonged stop at halfway is that you seize up. I can feel it happening. We've been walking for nearly twelve hours – our bodies have got used to activity. And it's dusk, the sudden drop in temperature doing strange things to my limbs. I'm keen to crack on, but I'm also keen to eat.

We're met by eager and concerned wives, partners, children and friends. Homemade pasties are offered and consumed. In my case, in a dour, contemplative and trepidatious silence.

Eat little and often. Energy foods, easily digestible.

Ah.

Get someone to tickle you.

I'm not hiccuping as we wait for the chain-link ferry to take us across the River Medina; I'm not hiccuping as we start the uninspiring trudge along the A3021 out of East Cowes – the least attractive part of the walk, a far cry from the glories of Tennyson Down half a day and a lifetime ago; I'm not hiccuping as we cross Wootton Bridge and begin the climb up to the ferry terminal.

It starts somewhere between Fishbourne and Binstead. A sense of unease in the upper chestal area, a feeling that something's stuck, an inability to take proper breaths. And then they have me.

Stride stride *HIC* stride stride stri-*HIC*-de stride stride st-*HIC*-ride.

Bugger.

For a while I blame the pasty, but deep down I know this is an excuse to cover up my lack of stamina. The pasty is blameless. Homemade and delicious, it offered vital sustenance at the halfway point. I could have eaten it more slowly.

The confidence of twelve hours earlier is a distant memory. Now, engulfed in darkness and beset by a weariness of body and soul, I contemplate what still remains with foreboding, and perhaps just a bit of swearing.

The conversation has moved on to driverless cars and the future of the internet. My contribution is scant.

HIC.

Have someone give you a surprise, perhaps by jumping out at you unexpectedly with a loud accompanying noise. 'Boo!' is standard – other noises are available.

Doubtless he means well; doubtless I make a meal of it; doubtless we're all fatigued and not operating at peak levels of reasonableness.

Nevertheless, what the blinking fuck?

If there's anything positive to be said for having your brother-in-law jump out at you without warning and with a loud 'BOO!' in your right ear, it's this: it certainly helps quicken the stride.

The next pit stop is half a mile away, about 800 metres. I remember watching Sebastian Coe run this distance in 1:41.73 one dark night in 1981, exhorted by an overexcited David Coleman – an astounding piece of running on a track barely fit for a local recreation centre, the last 300 metres undertaken entirely alone as Coe broke his own world record by over half a second, leaving his nearest rival, Billy Konchellah, floundering behind him. The record lasted for sixteen years, testament to its status as one of the most remarkable pieces of athletic brilliance in history.

I assume this astonishing burst of speed was caused by Konchellah shouting 'BOO!' in his right ear.

I reach the stop first. There's a tinge of furious reproach to my hiccups now. I fill a cup with water, try to drink it the wrong way round, fail, hold my breath, count to one hundred, and wait for the inevitable harbinger of disappointment.

Fuck–*HIC*–ing he–*HIC*–ll.

I lie on the damp grass and ponder the futility of human existence.

Twenty-four miles to go.

Pinch your nose, then spin round in a clockwise direction singing 'Row, Row, Row Your Boat'.

All *HIC* I need to do is stop *HIC* hiccuping. How diff–*HIC*–ult can it be?

It can be imp–*HIC*–ossible.

Take a large sip of water, leave it in your mouth, tug your earlobes downwards and tilt your head back.

Three a.m.

I've walked fifty miles, and I know the game is up. Hiccuping for four hours is debilitating. You should try it. It's the grim inevitability of it – every ten seconds a false dawn. Maybe this time they'll sto–*HIC*–p.

Bugger.

And then, a magical thing.

We've reached the island's lowest point, by Bembridge Harbour. The others have gone ahead at my behest. I don't want to hold them back. I feel like Captain Oates or that guy in *Terminator 2* or someone like that.

The soundtrack to this part of the walk has a strange rhythm to it, the swishing of my trousers combining with the soft tread of my shoes and the hiccups to produce a mesmerising pattern.

Swish-plop swish-plo–HIC–p swish-plop swish-plop sw–HIC-ish-plop swish-plop swish-p-HUUUC–lop (hooomb) swish–HIC–plo—

Hang on. Hooomb?

I stop, my birder's instinct attuned to every sound, not daring to believe it. It's an aural hallucination, surely? It must be the exhaustion and the hiccups playing silly buggers with me. I haven't heard that sound since the last time I (*hooomb*)—

It's not close, but this sound travels far on still air. And to my right is a solid expanse of reed bed, just the thing for hooombing from.

Hooomb.

No doubting it this time. This eerie noise, like blowing across the top of a milk bottle, is the sound of a booming bittern.

Take a heron, shrink it slightly, paint it with streaky brown camouflage and bung it in a reed bed – you have, more or less, a bittern. Almost extinct in this country a few decades ago, their numbers have increased, but this sound is still rare enough to elicit a flurry of excitement.

What do bitterns do at night? They hooomb.

Place a layer of paper towel over a glass and drink water through it.

The bittern has a magical effect on me. A burst of optimism pricks me into an increase of pace. I can do this. Just three miles to the next stop, then on to the last quarter. I've done fifty miles – how hard can those last sixteen be? Just put one foot in front of ano–*HIC* oh, shit it all to fuckarse and back again, you bollocking twatmonger.

And at that point I know the game is up. Four hours of non-stop spasming of the vagus nerve really takes it out of you. This isn't just the weakness of exhaustion. I'm beginning to feel on the verge of actual illness. The hiccups, I fear, will never stop. I have a concert the day after tomorrow, and there comes a time when you have to be sensible about things. I can't conduct from a hospital bed.

Dudley and Peter have stopped to take photos of each other at the fifty-mile marker. I surge past them, determined for it all to be over now, thanks very much. A few hundred yards later there is a bench. I lie down on it, hoping that five minutes in a prone position will somehow do the trick and that dawn will bring a final burst of energy to see me through to the end.

A forlorn hope.

The approach to the last pit stop is a stiffish climb through a copse and then out onto the open expanse of Culver Down. Rosy-fingered dawn is doing its bit, and I'm accompanied by the first stirrings of the dawn chorus – a skylark, as it happens, the sound that put a spring into my stride eighteen long hours ago.

I shamble into the tent. My wife, primed in any case to meet me here and cheer me on for the final push, takes one look at me, links her arm through mine, and leads me gently out of the tent, across the grass to the car. It's a noble failure. Fifty-one miles isn't sixty-six, but it's not bad.

It's only when I'm back in the comfort of the cottage, have tottered upstairs and collapsed onto the bed, engulfed by exhaustion, that the hiccups finally subside, and I drift off to a deep sleep, dreaming of skylarks and pasties and hooombing bitterns and things that leap out and go 'boo' in the night.

WHY DIDN'T ANYONE TELL ME THIS EARLIER?

2,500

Subject provided by John and Sally Isaacs

Life is a voyage of discovery. Even before we're born we start to develop our own world view – sketchy, muffled and lacking in detail though those first impressions may be.

Then, at the moment of our birth, we learn very quickly that life is agonising and frightening and lonely and – ow, stop doing that and what the hell is *that*? Get it away from me! Bloody hell, NOBODY TOLD ME IT WOULD BE LIKE THIS. I might just go straight back inside. Oh, hold on, though, ah, that's better *num num num*, think I might sleep now but first *gnnnnnnhhhhh* a poo.

The early years are all about exploration. The world is fascinating, and we want to learn about it. In doing so, we also learn some important life lessons: cuddles are nice, water is wet, whacking yourself on the head with the TV remote control is painful. And of course we learn from other people – parents, siblings, relatives, peers, teachers. The world bombards us with information and we soak it up, our spongy brains apparently insatiable.

The years pass and we accrue experience, each morsel adding to the sum of our knowledge and wisdom. Sometimes we have to experience things many times before their lessons sink in; sometimes once is enough and we bury the memory so we don't have to relive the trauma; and sometimes we just forget things, because that's how our brains work.

As we broaden our horizons we begin to realise how much there is to learn. Stuff to do with money and Cicero* and red wine and ham sandwiches and Sibelius and blacksmiths and cricket and jigsaw puzzles and DIY and loyalty and dental floss and love and steam trains and particle physics and tax returns and hiccups and French irregular verbs and tectonic plates and wheelwrights and Pythagoras and friendship and bassoons and dogs and dishwasher salt and photosynthesis and betrayal and chainsaws and *Calvin and Hobbes*† and murmurations and how to roast a chicken and all that kind of caper.

Our reaction to this new knowledge is most often low-key. We just nod and carry on with our lives. The information we've just accrued, whether it's how to shift red-wine stains using white wine‡ or Kevin Pietersen's ODI batting strike rate,§ either sticks or it doesn't, but there's nothing particularly revelatory about the learning experience. The information might pop up years later without explanation, just when we least need it, but most often it gets subsumed into the general accumulation of stuff in our head that fogs it up and makes us forget how to think clearly.

* Word provided by Ailsa Forsyth.

† Words provided by Steven Pallett.

‡ Not nearly as effective as it's often made out to be.

§ 86.58, stats fans.

Some of it we might dabble in and then choose to ignore for the rest of our lives – Wagner, Quorn and morris dancing, to pick three entirely random examples – but other stuff might pique, tickle and float our interest, fancy and boat respectively, and so we find ourselves knowing more about those things than other people would consider reasonable or decent. But other people can go hang – these harmless obsessions are the stuff of life and absolutely to be encouraged and applauded. There's everything to be said for a life spent becoming the world's foremost expert on, for example, storm petrels, because what you're doing there is adding to the sum of human knowledge, and that's a Good Thing.

But however much we might learn about storm petrels or West Ham FC or the tone poems of Antonín Dvořák,* there will always be moments in our life when we realise how little we know. There we are, quietly trundling down the slow road to our inevitable decrepitude and death, and from nowhere comes the realisation that we don't know how to make a really good hollandaise or how to dismantle a motorbike engine or the meaning of the word 'polysyndeton'† or whatever it might be, and it stops us in our tracks just a bit. Often they're things that have been hidden in plain sight, so our ignorance is just a question of our own failure to observe, and the revelation brings about a minor crisis of self-worth. We question ourselves. A scintilla of doubt forms, lodges, grows. How have we managed to function as a human being for all these years without acquiring

* Thoroughly recommended, by the way.

† Polysyndeton means using lots of conjunctions to make long sentences. I used it in the paragraph before last. Asyndeton means using no conjunctions. I am using it in this footnote.

this basic knowledge? Have we, in fact, been going about this life business in the right way? What else is out there that we don't know?

Ooh, loads of stuff.

- You can put a lit match to a dandelion clock and it disappears in a quick 'poof'.
- A blue whale's tongue weighs the same as an elephant.*
- The word 'helicopter' isn't divided 'heli' and 'copter', but 'helico' (Greek: *helix* – spiral) and 'pter' (Greek: *pter* – wing). If you want to be completely up yourself, you can display this knowledge by pronouncing it 'helicoPTER'. But I wouldn't if I were you.
- The Harry Warren song 'Chica Chica Boom Chic', sung by Carmen Miranda in the 1940s, anticipated the opening chords of John Coltrane's 'Giant Steps'.
- The quack of a duck, contrary to a popular myth that circulated the internet a few years ago, *does* echo. I mean, of course it does. Duh.
- While on the subject of that awkward 'pt' juxtaposition, the silent 'p' in 'ptarmigan'† was added by Robert Sibbald in 1684, apparently to give it a faux-Greek appearance. It actually comes from the Gaelic *tàrmachan*, meaning 'croaker'.

---

* My thanks, respectively, to @ShotShy, @CranbrookIron, @RichlyEvocative and @KirkdaleBooks for these gems.

† Word provided by John Mitchinson.

- Boxes of kitchen foil and cling film have little tabs that you can push in to help stabilise the roll inside.*

- An abecedarian insult is one given with the words in alphabetical order. Example: 'Sir, you are an abysmal, barbarous, craven, dyspeptic, egregious, fulminating, glumpish, hectoring, impudent, jackassified, knuckle-headed, lumpen, micturescent, numptyish, offal-gobbling, puerile, quacksalving, ruffianish, solipsistic,† thriftless, uppity, virulent, wanton, xylophobic, yam-loving zygomorph.'

- You can work out how much the American 'cup' measure is by chanting the following simple mnemonic: 'Why the hell are you measuring solids by volume, not weight? By the way, it's approximately 8.45 fluid ounces.'

- You can tell the difference between Asiatic and African elephants by looking at their hind feet: Africans have three nails, Asiatics have four. Also, the Asiatic elephant has one finger-like projection on the tip of its trunk while the African has two. And yes, to appease those of you (and that's all of you, I'm pretty sure) who are right now screaming, 'WHAT ABOUT THE EARS? WHY DON'T YOU JUST LOOK AT THE EARS?' you could just look at the ears, which are significantly bigger on the African variety. Or you could just look at your GPS

* THANK YOU, ISABEL. MY LIFE IS CHANGED FOR EVER.

† Word provided by Cath Ricketts and Ken Knussen. I'm trying not to take it personally.

> and work out which continent you're in. Unless you're looking at the elephant in a zoo, in which case there'll be some kind of information board nearby. And if the elephant is charging towards you with rage in its eyes, none of this is relevant or useful, because you probably haven't got long to live, and won't want to spend your last seconds on Earth worrying which kind of elephant is going to be responsible for your untimely demise.

Now, at this point you might be sitting there with a mixture of smugness, pity and exasperation, rolling your eyes and thinking, 'Well, duh, I thought everyone knew these things'; or, like me, you're experiencing a sort of explosion of 'Oh crikey, YES, I am for ever transformed and shall henceforth tackle the travails of twenty-first-century life with renewed vim and gusto'. Or you might belong to a third subset, thinking, 'Well, I suppose those facts are interesting enough, but they're not going to help with world peace, famine prevention in developing nations or finding a cure for cancer, are they?'

It's a fair point, well made. But let's not underestimate the importance to humanity of being distracted by apparently unimportant things. Take penicillin, for example. It's not widely disseminated, but the reason Alexander Fleming allowed his petri dish to go neglected was because someone had told him that the only station on the London Underground that doesn't contain one of the letters in the word 'mackerel' is St John's Wood, and he was looking for a Tube map so he could check.

But even if they don't lead to discoveries that change the course of history, you never know when these apparently inconsequential morsels of information are going to come in handy. The catch being, of course, that you also never know which of the thousands of similar titbits you're going to need at any time, and the second catch being that you will inevitably forget the important one just when you need it.

So, in the public interest, and bearing in mind that the universe works in unfathomable ways, here are a few more. You never know – just by reading this list you might be kept from doing something you thought was more important but in doing so might stumble upon a discovery that proves in the long run to have a profound impact on the future of humanity.

And even more importantly – from the 'covering my arse' point of view – in the future you won't be able to ask 'Why didn't anyone tell me this earlier?' because I'm telling you now. Don't say I didn't warn you.

- There are no cats in the Bible.

- The way David Bowie sang the word 'starman' in 'Starman' was meant to sound like the 'somewhere' in 'Over the Rainbow'. (This one is so staggeringly obvious, now I've been told, that I'm almost embarrassed to admit it had never previously occurred to me.)

- There are only three words in English with all the vowels in the order in which they appear in the alphabet. They are 'abstemious', 'arsenicous' and 'facetious'.

- If you're the kind of person who is adamant that 'y' is a vowel, just add '-ly' to those words. Thanks for your input.
- The Everest family, after whom the mountain was named, pronounced their name 'Eve-wrist', so we've basically been getting it wrong all this time.
- Talking of which, the Beatles album *Abbey Road* was nearly called *Everest*, but *Abbey Road* was simpler to get to for the cover photo.
- The inward curvature of the upper part of your car is called 'tumblehome',* a word borrowed from naval architecture, where, in the context of boats, it is far more widely used.
- There is a word in Finnish, *myötähäpeä*, for the embarrassment you feel on behalf of someone who is making a fool of themselves.
- The petrol-pump icon on your car dashboard has a little arrow next to it that tells you which side the petrol cap is.
- If you hang a rubber band on a hook and then add a series of small weights to it, then take them off again one by one, the rubber band will be longer at each step of the unloading phase than at its equivalent point in the loading phase. This is an example of elastic hysteresis.†

---

* Word provided by Laura Pritchard.

† Word provided by Amro Gebreel, and boy did I have trouble finding a place for it.

- A synonym for the word 'synonym' is 'poecilonym'.
- If you ever meet my wife Tessa, say 'Gazzer'* to her with an exaggerated West Country accent and she will be forced to explain its significance.

These are all fine things, but in the grand scheme of everything, they amount to little more than pussyfooting around. What about the big stuff? What about love? What about death? What about herons?

Ah, well, if it's arcane facts about herons you're after, you've come to the right place. Did you know that some birds, the grey heron (*Ardea cinerea*) and its cousins among them, have comb-like serrations on one toe, known as pectinate claws, which they use for grooming and cleaning?

You are now ready to proceed with your day.

The astute reader will have noticed that I skipped over those first two subjects, love and death, with a speed that we can only ascribe to an unwillingness to address them. They are big subjects, arguably the biggest of them all – yes, even bigger than herons – and I, like most of humanity, find them daunting and mysterious. Terrifyingly so, if I'm honest.

Love is as large as the universe. No force on Earth has its effect, enabling us to move mountains one moment and make complete prats of ourselves the next. It is, like all worthwhile things – Mozart and hummingbirds and chocolate† and *Detectorists* and bacon sarnies and David Gower's

* Word provided by wife Tessa, who's stitched herself up good and proper with that one.

† You will have recognised already that I'm now embarking on another bout of polysyndeton.

cover drive and Rembrandt and gelato and the sun glistening on a mirrored sea and Winnie-the-Pooh and the chattering of swallows and the soughing of the wind in the trees* and oxbow lakes and *Some Like It Hot* and, let's be honest, like all life itself – ultimately pointless. We need sex to ensure the survival of our species; love is the luxury adjunct. But aren't we lucky to have it? (We're lucky to have sex too, but that's a different story and a different book, almost certainly not written by me.)

As for death . . . well, no matter what anyone tells you, no matter how much you ready yourself, no matter how often your brain, your senses, your intelligence tell you that it will happen, that it's inevitable and that no amount of jogging or clean living can change that fact, nothing can prepare you for it, whether it's the loss of a loved one or your own shuffling off the mortal coil.

Nevertheless, on we plod, not knowing whether this is the last of it or if there's a really good stretch just round the corner. And right at the back of my mind is the latent fear that if there is to be a moment of enlightenment, a blinding revelation that allows us to understand what all that activity, all that breathing, eating, drinking, sleeping, loving, fucking, thinking, working, reading, singing, laughing, dancing, shitting, pissing, farting, wanking, caring, nurturing, admiring, crying, studying – just all that living that makes up what we call human existence – was all about, when that moment of understanding comes, it will be my penultimate thought, and the last one will be 'Why didn't anyone tell me this earlier?'

* A lovely sound, which enables me to include its German equivalent, *Rauschen*, as requested by Rebekah Drury.

PEDANTS AND PEDANTRY

2,400

Subject provided by Paul la Planche

Hello.

Hello there, Inner Pedant. How are you?

I am well, thank you. How are you?

I'm good.

Oh dear. Please don't.

What?

You know perfectly well.

I know. Sorry. I'm just teasing. How can I help? What's bugging you today?

Well, firstly, your use of the word 'bugging' to mean 'bothering' or 'troubling' is an Americanism and has no home in British English, our language of preference.

Duly noted.

But to answer your question: a great deal.

Really?

Yes. I am beset by ignoramuses and doofuses.

Shouldn't that be 'ignorami' and 'doofi'?*

* Word supplied by Rachel Scott, who I fear will be disappointed by my treatment of it.

No it should not. 'Ignoramus' comes from the Latin, meaning 'we do not know'. It's a verb in Latin, but a noun in English, so we pluralise it like any other regular English noun.

OK then.

And as for 'doofus', whether it has its origins in the Low German word doof, *meaning 'stupid', or as an alteration of 'goofus' – which in turn is a variant of the 1920s slang word 'goof', meaning an idiot, which will be familiar to readers of the great comic novelist P. G. Wodehouse – or whether it is even from the Scottish word* doof, *meaning 'dolt', it is not a Latin word. So to treat it as such, even in jest, is pure nonsense.**

That's me told. Who are these ignoramuses and doofuses, anyway?

Nearly everyone I encounter, apparently.

Poor you. Let me guess – is it a language thing?

It is a language thing.

'Could of', 'literally dying', 'the proof is in the pudding', 'going forward', 'very unique', 'expresso', 'panninnis', 'pacifically', 'eckcetera' – that kind of thing?

You've managed to select some of the more heinous examples. It's almost as if you already knew.

I am familiar with the workings of the Inner Pedant. I wish I weren't, but I am. I sometimes think, by the way, that we'd both be better off if you were to just buzz off and leave me be.

Thank you.

No offence, obviously.

By way of response, let me say two things: firstly, I cannot

* Sorry, Rachel.

'buzz off' because, as your Inner Pedant, I am part of you. You have me for life.

I feared as much.

And secondly, I don't think 'no offence' means what you think it means. In my experience it is almost exclusively used as a pretext for saying something offensive. The logic seems to be that it's fine to say, 'You're an odious human being and I loathe you and the air you breathe,' as long as you affix a quasi-humorous 'no offence' afterwards. But it's not fine; it's horrible.

Point taken. Setting the offence thing aside for the moment, and returning to the pedantry: you do understand that your obsessive need to find fault in every little thing that doesn't conform to your vision of an ideal universe makes you seem hectoring, nitpicking, po-faced, priggish, smug, superior and really not much fun, don't you?

What on earth makes you say that? All I want is for people to get things right.

And to tell them they're wrong.

It's the only way they'll learn.

Learn what, exactly?

To get things right.

Such as?

Well, to take just one example, why do so many people start their sentences with the word 'so'? They're asked a question, and the answer always starts with 'so'. It's meaningless.

But isn't that 'so' merely an introductory particle, what's known as a 'discourse marker', equivalent to the Italian *allora* or *dunque*? It serves a purpose. It paves the way for what they're about to say.

Well, I—

Sorry, what did you say?

I didn't get a chance to say anything. You interrupted me.

No, you said something. What was it?

Well—

Exactly. 'Well.' And what does that 'well' mean?

Well, it—

Hmm?

I—

Is that 'well' possibly an introductory particle that you use to pave the way for what you're about to say? And is it not meaningless?

I see what you're doing. But it's different.

How so?

It . . . just is.

Because, and I'm just conjecturing here, it's what you grew up with, and everyone should just knuckle down and speak the way you want them to speak – namely, the way English was spoken in your small circle of acquaintances sometime around when you left school?

No!

OK then. As long as you're sure.

Well, how about this, then? The appalling ubiquity of 'Can I get'? You remember when we were in that café this morning?

I do. We asked for a *caffè latte*, the barista said, 'A latte?' and before I could stop you, you made me say, 'No, a *caffè latte*', with a prim emphasis on the Italian pronunciation, and she gave us this withering look, as if to say, 'Really, though? On top of everything else I have to put up with?'*

---

* Some people would like me to write 'up with which I have to put', which tells you something about the evil of pedantry.

Then she made the coffee and it was clear from the set of her back that she hated us.

Latte *is the Italian for 'milk'. Go into a café in Italy, ask for a* latte *and see what they bring you.*

That's not the point though, is it? We're in England, not Italy. And everyone knows what you mean when you say 'latte'. It's entered the language as a synonym for excessively milky coffee that makes you feel slightly queasy. You may not like it, but there's nothing you can do about it.

Yes there is. I can chunter away inside your head, stoking the fires of indignant rage and rendering you grumpy and irritable – a job, incidentally, to which I am well suited. Anyway, I didn't say it. You said it.

You're right. I said it, but only while under your malign influence, O Inner Pedant – He Who Must Always Be Chuntering. You don't get to say anything out loud yourself, but when you're particularly exercised by something you have this magical ability to make your words come out of my mouth. I'm getting better at resisting it, partly because I'm more relaxed about such things than I was, but you're still in there, observing and judging, aren't you? And you pop up at the most inconvenient and annoying times. Like, for example, immediately after the *caffè latte* incident.

That man had an annoying beard.

That's your opinion. But the beard wasn't the real problem, was it? Not really. It might have exacerbated the situation, but it didn't lie at the heart of the matter, did it?

He said, 'Can I get a flat white?'

It's a good job I keep you suppressed most of the time – you could make me quite unpopular. Go on then, tell me what's wrong with 'Can I get a flat white?'

Everything.

Come now. You'll need to be more pacific than that.

STOP IT STOP IT STOP IT.

Sorry.

It's the barista's job to get the coffee, not the customer's. 'Please may I have' is the correct form.

OK, so I'm with you on the 'please' thing. It's more polite. And 'may', while quite old-fashioned nowadays, is preferable to 'can' – you're asking permission to do something rather than questioning your own ability to do it – even if 'can' is so entrenched in the language as to be inextricable.

We agree then.

Not so fast, man cub. It's the 'get' that really gets you, isn't it?

It is.

Well, I'm afraid on that one you're just plain wrong.

Don't do this to me.

No, you really are. I mean, if you're going to pedant—

Did you just use 'pedant' as a verb?

I did. And unrepentantly. As I say, if you're going to pedant, it's self-evident that you have to pedant well. Of all human activities, pedanting is the one thing you mustn't do badly. So: the word 'get' has several definitions in the dictionary, as I demonstrated with the phrase 'that really gets you'. Shall I read some?

No.

Well, I'm going to anyway. 'Get: to obtain; to acquire; to procure; to receive; to come to have.' So I'm sure you'll agree that it's OK to ask a barista if you might obtain, acquire, procure, receive or come to have a coffee.

Huh.

In fact, it's frankly perverse to wilfully* misunderstand someone, purely so you can seethe with indignation while at the same time patting yourself on the back for being better at English, better at life, better at humanity than them. Because that's what you're doing, isn't it? You wouldn't think, when a child says, 'I wonder what I'll get for Christmas,' that they intend to travel to the North Pole to fetch the presents themselves. So why would you think that a customer in a coffee shop, whether they be annoyingly bearded or not, is intending to go behind the bar, shove the barista – whose job, as you correctly point out, is to make the coffee – out of the way, and then make the *caffè latte* themselves? It's perfectly obvious, unless they are actually moving in the direction of the coffee machine as they speak, that they don't mean 'get' in its alternative sense of 'fetch' but in the sense of 'receive,' so why would you think otherwise?

Nice use of the subjunctive there.

Thanks. I was quite proud of it. You know, dredging it up in the heat of battle and all that. But you haven't answered my question.

Nor do I intend to, because your argument is specious in the extreme.

You're just too stubborn to acknowledge its merits.

Why do you hate me?

I don't hate you. Far from it. I need you.

Really? That's the first I've heard of it.

Certainly I need you. In my professional life, in partic-

* Yes, a split infinitive! Next up: ending a sentence with a preposition and running with scissors.

ular. A conductor has to be obsessed with small details and prepared to correct people, whether they like it or not. It's part of the job. Left to myself, without the guiding light of my Inner Pedant, I'd just say, 'Oh fuck it, that'll do – let's go to the pub.' But with you on board I have to make sure I do the job properly, or at least to the best of my ability, otherwise I'd have to suffer your tutting all night long. And it's the same with the writing. For the first draft I lock you, bound and gagged, in the cellar – I have to or I'd never be able to start. But when I've splurged the first draft onto the screen, in all its sesquipedalian[*] glory, with unnecessarily long words like supercalifragilisticexpialidocious,[†] dichlorocyclopropanation[‡] and *Donaudampfschifffahrtselektrizitätenhauptbetriebswerkbauunterbeamtengesellschaft*,[§] I untie you and let you loose, perched on my shoulder like some overcritical parrot, picking holes in everything.

I can't sit on your shoulder and pick holes in things at the same time, unless they're within reach of my beak.

They're metaphorical holes, as well you know. And you're a metaphorical parrot.

Very well then.

The point is this: I need that parrot. It makes things better. But much as I admire your work in the professional sphere, I do wish you'd lower your head below the parapet when I'm engaged in the discourse of everyday life. People don't like it.

---

* Word provided by Clare Beck. When applied to words, it means 'long or polysyllabic'.

† Word provided by Adrian Charlesworth.

‡ Word provided by Stephen Kenny.

§ Word provided by David Prosser. Yeah, thanks.

They need to be told.

They really don't.

I do it for their own good. Life is an education. In any case, they should already know better. Imagine confusing 'their', 'there', and 'they're', for goodness' sake!

How's your skiing these days?

My skiing?

Your skiing.

Much the same as yours, I should imagine. Unexplored since that traumatic day thirty years ago. But what relevance does our skiing have to the matter at hand?

Well, perhaps these people – the ones you dismiss so readily as jabbernowls* because they're either confused by a point of grammar or indifferent to it – are fiercely intelligent in other ways. They might be brilliant with numbers or a paintbrush or a bassoon or a lathe; maybe they can make the perfect sandwich, or the smoothest gelato you've ever had; or they might be amazingly good at snooker or gardening or, as it happens, skiing. Words might not be their medium, but imagine how dismal you'd look if attempting to keep up with that brilliant skier on a black run; and imagine how chagrined you would be if they turned on you with a patronising sneer and said, 'You do know you're supposed to stay upright, don't you?'

The two are not comparable.

I think they are. And I think you know it but are too stubborn to admit it. That's fine, by the way. It's part of you.

A gracious admission.

* A lovely old word meaning numbskull, nincompoop or blockhead. It was provided by Rebecca Wood.

Hmm. By the way, do you know the dictionary definition for 'pedant'?

'A person who parades or reveres excessively academic learning or technical knowledge; a person excessively concerned with trifling details or insisting on strict adherence to formal rules or literal meaning.'

Setting aside for the moment my lack of surprise that you know that definition word for word, do you know what I find most interesting about it?

I suspect I do, but you're going to tell me anyway.

It's the use of the word 'excessively'. Never a good thing, excess. Take that over-milky *caffè latte*. Yuk.

I prefer a flat white.

Me too. Anyway, it's a far cry from the good old days. Back in the seventeenth century 'pedant' could also mean a schoolmaster or pedagogue; someone who helped people by educating them, but – and this is the key point – in an appropriate manner.

You have made your point. Hammered it home, even.

Sounds painful. So, what have we learned?

Not to be pedantic.

Absolutely. Because pedantry is, as Holbrook Jackson (1874–1948) so pertinently pointed out . . . ?

The dotage of knowledge.

Well done. The good news is, however, that you're allowed to be a stickler. Stickle away all you like, especially when I'm conducting Sibelius or profreading books.

That should read 'proofreading'.

There you go, you see? I do need you after all.

JEAN SIBELIUS

2,300

Subject provided by Richard Vodden

There are those who like James Bond. I'm one of them. But ask me to choose a series of books to represent the 1960s world of espionage, and I'd pick Peter O'Donnell's *Modesty Blaise*.

Ah, Modesty. Beautiful and dangerous, but also tender and vulnerable. Expert in unarmed combat, marksmanship, strategy, and a host of other villain-thwarting skills. Able to kill with a single stroke of the kongo, her preferred weapon, but only inclined to use it as a last resort. You could lock her blindfold in a car boot, take her on a circuitous 200-mile journey, and she could tell you within half a mile where you'd ended up. A female role model written by a man, she paved the way for *The New Avengers*' Purdey, Buffy the Vampire Slayer, Lara Croft and many others.

And, as if all that weren't enough for teenage me* to have a massive crush on her, she loved Sibelius.

Ah, Modesty.

In the first of the thirteen books, while on a stakeout,

* Yes, and adult me too. Fair cop.

Modesty and her sidekick Willie Garvin are discussing music. Willie likes Mozart. Fair enough, so does Modesty. But she urges him not to be deterred by Sibelius's apparent unapproachability.

It's a passage simultaneously surprising – Action-Packed Spy Thriller in Sophisticated Classical Music Talk Shock! – and entirely natural. Of course Modesty knows about classical music. It's consistent with her character. She's that kind of badass heroine.

You would never catch James Bond talking about Sibelius. Sums it up, really.

Why Sibelius?

Why not Mahler, Mozart, Shostakovich, Brahms, Stravinsky, Haydn, Ravel, Gershwin or Debussy? What about Clara Schumann, Hildegard of Bingen, Ethel Smyth, Judith Weir, Thea Musgrave, Nadia Boulanger, Rebecca Clarke and Grace Williams?

Well, they're all excellent too.

But there are some people, whether they're creators or performers or sportspeople or just good eggs, for whom there is a 'reserved' sign on the Table of Especially Good and Meaningful Things. P. G. Wodehouse, Seve Ballesteros, Piero della Francesca, David Gower, Rubén González, William H. Macy, and dozens of others whose names aren't leaping into my head right now but when you mention them later I'll go, 'Oh yes, of course.'

And Jean (born Johan Julius Christian) Sibelius.

Sibelius's corner on the T of EG & MTs is small but clearly delineated. Squashed into it with him, in a box marked 'Influences and Associations', are his wife Aino, a cigar or two, the lakes and forests of Finland, a flock of whooper swans and staggering quantities of alcohol.

The Table of Especially Good and Meaningful Things is quite the table.

Sibelius's music stands apart. This isn't to say he is 'better' than anyone else (I cover my thoughts on that concept in 'The Best Music I Know and Why It Matters', p. 142), merely that his voice is distinctive – it sometimes takes barely a nanosecond to identify a snippet as positively by Sibelius.

If you're new to his music, it's difficult to know where to start. Do we ease you in with his most famous composition, *Finlandia*, a hymn to Finnishness written in protest at creeping Russian censorship? Or do we plunge you into the deep end with, say, the Second Symphony, which, although dismissed as 'vulgar, self-indulgent, and provincial beyond all description' by American composer and critic Virgil Thomson, somehow manages to endure in the public's affections by being AMAZINGLY GOOD, THANKS VERY MUCH, VIRGIL, YOU JUDGEMENTAL SNOB.

Ahem.

Where we won't start is with his light music. I have no problem with light music per se – this isn't a snobbery thing. One of my favourite pieces is Leroy Anderson's 'Serenata', an expertly constructed and sassy bit of quasi-muzak that ticks all my boxes. It's just that Sibelius's light music is comparatively insignificant – why spend time on it when he was capable of producing music of depth and beauty, drawn from his soul at great psychological cost, and obsessively reworked until he could do no more?

Three moments. That's what I'll pick. Three moments

from a hefty output – about 400 works in a variety of genres, spanning eight decades. Three moments that do things to the soul.

You know what I mean when I say 'moments'. They happen when music touches places not accessible to anything else. It might be in the music of Stevie Wonder or Bach or Janelle Monáe or Aretha Franklin or Billie Holiday or Perry Como or maybe even Ed Sheeran. They will make you go, 'Ah – that,' and they will have a physical effect on you, and you'll close your eyes for a second and savour it, and maybe somewhere behind them a tear will pop out and say 'gotcha' before you give it a firm rebuke and with a shake of the head and a tut you'll be back to your normal, presentable self.

Or maybe you'll succumb to the moment and let yourself dissolve in what people sometimes call 'a really good cry', because that music has put its finger on your barest nerve, held it there for a second, and twisted.

Or maybe the effect will just be a sense of wellbeing, a gentle release inside, the relaxing of muscles you didn't know were tense.

Whatever, these moments are to be savoured. Sibelius provides me with a lot of them – here are just three.

MOMENT NO. 1

A bit of a cheat, because this is in fact two moments. But they're quite close to each other, and one kind of leads to the next, so I'm conflating them.

On 21 April 1915, Sibelius saw sixteen whooper swans and made an entry in his diary.

> One of the great experiences of my life! They circled over me for a long time. Disappeared into the solar haze like a gleaming ribbon. Their call the same woodwind type as that of the crane, but without tremolo . . . a low-pitched refrain reminiscent of a small child crying. Nature mysticism and life's angst! The Fifth Symphony's finale theme: legato in the trumpets!

The swans of Sibelius take to the air at letter E in the last movement of his Fifth Symphony, and twenty-five bars later comes my first moment. Because at that point the swans, having taken off from the lake in the pine forest, shift their angle of bank and veer towards you, and the sun, shining from a clear blue sky, catches their plumage in such a way as to reveal the majesty of the wotsit high atop the thing in all his, her or its glory.

Seeing it on the page, cold ink on dead paper, is enough to set me off; hearing it in my mind's ear, I have to sit for a second; standing in the middle of it, air vibrating around me, I'm done for. Which, if I happen to be conducting it, simply won't do. Because not only must I guide the players through that moment and the treacherous musical waters ahead, but I have to gird my loins for the end of the symphony – Moment 1b, if you like.

MOMENT NO. 1B

'The music is not in the notes, but in the silence between' – a quote attributed to both Mozart and Debussy. Miles Davis said something similar. Like many such sayings, it's both true and not. The music is in the notes, but the silences let it sink in.

Sibelius knew this. His silent moments invite you to look into the abyss, or place you in a boat on a Finnish lake, pine scent in your nostrils, surrounded by eternal sky and about to be engulfed by swans.

And the silences at the end of the Fifth Symphony are more potent than any music.

Loud chords, like musical pillars, progressive exclamations of the approaching ending, the culmination of thirty minutes of vibrating air, linked by a musical trembling, as if coaxing the listener towards exultation.

'Here it is,' it's saying. 'Do you feel it?'

Pillar.

Nothing.

Pillar.

Nothing.

Pillar.

Nothing.

Pillar.

Nothing.

Pillar. Pillar.

But they weren't always silences. In early versions of the piece these bars consisted of what you might call 'your average bells and whistles' – agitated string tremolo, a loud held chord from everyone else, those pillars bursting through the texture.

But Sibelius was a serial reviser, and at some point he must have understood the power of silence.

Genius is the infinite capacity for taking pains.

MOMENT NO. 2

If the Fifth Symphony is all about the noble Nordic swans, then the Sixth is all about the 'pure, cold water' on which they swam.

How different it is – ice to its predecessor's fire.*

The mood of this symphony is far from the 'wild and impassioned' music he originally envisioned when he started work on it. But in among the reserve there is turbulence, and it's out of this, about four minutes from the end of the symphony, that Moment no. 2 emerges. Storm clouds have gathered, and the main theme of the movement returns over a jumping, repeating pattern played by the cellos and double basses. It's a moment that takes a deep breath and says, 'Right, here we go.'

And what Sibelius does then is quite extraordinary. Having stoked the music into fervour, he eschews the conventional 'blaze of glory' ending, chooses not to wind up to an artificial climax, but instead winds it down, draws it back to where it came from, allowing it to drift away on the wind.

If you've inadvertently left your player on 'repeat', the symphony will start again without a pause, a move I thoroughly recommend. This is cyclical music – I like to think there is a peaceful place where it is played on a loop for you to experience when you wish, like heavenly muzak.

If you don't fancy that, you could, as is sometimes done in concert, allow the Seventh Symphony to rise from the silence without a pause.

* In this analogy, there is no 'lukewarm water'.

MOMENT NO. 3

Conventionally, a symphony has four movements – individual pieces of music linked by related themes to form a coherent and satisfying whole. Haydn did it, Mozart did it, Beethoven, Brahms and Tchaikovsky did it.

Mahler did it too, sometimes, but was also fond of throwing in extra movements and choirs and vocal soloists and off-stage cowbells and HONESTLY, GUSTAV, KEEP A HOLD OF YOURSELF FOR ONE GODDAMN SECOND.

Sibelius was no exception to the four-movement symphony rule. In the beginning, at least. But in his Third Symphony his subversion of symphonic form began – two movements overlapping, joined into one. He called it 'the crystallisation of chaos', and that's good enough for me.

He repeated the trick in the Fifth Symphony, the fusion of movements this time subtler, more gradual, an acceleration whereby you find yourself, almost without realising it, no longer wallowing in melancholy but skipping through the snow.

The Seventh Symphony takes this process to its logical conclusion, transfiguring the form to such an extent that it was originally entitled *Symphonic Fantasy No. 1*. But a symphony it is, four movements condensed into one – kaleidoscopic, seamless and endlessly evolving from one thing to the next. To this listener at least, it's one long, twenty-two-minute 'moment'.

But for me the moment of moments comes five minutes in, and involves a trombone.

You know the trombone. Oompah-roompah slidey-slidey whoops, Mrs Wisdom, your son's just taken a pratfall.*

Not with Sibelius. Sibelius trombone moments are nuanced and layered. They can be affecting in their sparseness – the Third Symphony contains fewer than a hundred notes for each of the three trombones, but what notes they are – or lean and powerful, underpinning those passages when Sibelius seems to make the music come towards the camera across a frozen lake.

The trombone in the Seventh Symphony doesn't occupy centre stage, but that only intensifies its effectiveness. The backdrop is an orchestral sound like no other – kaleidoscopic, cosmic, a sound to lose yourself in. And through this shape-shifting wall of sound come five notes.

Five. That's all he needs. It's music of such concentration it should come with a hazard warning. In the score, there is one word above it: 'Aino'. His wife and lifelong support, who bore his alcoholism and deepening torment with patience and love.

The Seventh Symphony is often seen as the ultimate symphonic statement, not least in light of Sibelius's ensuing musical silence. He lived another thirty years, writing little of note and, eventually, nothing at all. There were sketches for an eighth symphony, but they perished when he burned a number of his manuscripts on the fire at Ainola, the house where he lived with Aino for fifty years.

Perfectionism is a double-edged sword.

Despite the ravages of alcohol, Sibelius was made of sturdy stuff, and lived to the age of ninety-one, remaining

* I am oversimplifying. Trombonists may choose not to forgive me.

physically active until the end. One September day in 1957, he saw a flock of cranes on his morning walk.

'There they come,' he said to Aino, 'the birds of my youth.' One of the birds broke ranks, did one circle of Ainola, then rejoined the flock. Two days later, Sibelius died of a brain haemorrhage. At the time of his death, his Fifth Symphony was being broadcast from Helsinki.

So that's Sibelius. And I, Modesty to your Willie, urge you with gentle insistence to give him a go. Allow yourself to fall into his music for a bit. Don't think. Immersion, not analysis. For the hard core this could take the form of a day devoted to the symphonies. It's just under four hours of listening time: numbers one and two in the morning, three, four and five in the afternoon, six and seven in the evening. Accompany them, if you wish, with some Finnish vodka.

It's what he would have wanted.

HAS CRICKET EVER BEEN 'CRICKET'?

2,200

Subject provided by Mark Allen

South Africa, March 2018.

Australia, not used to losing, were losing. Behind on the first innings, and making scant inroads into South Africa's batting line-up in the second, they faced a large deficit, and the likelihood of going 2–1 down in a four-match series.

Desperate times call for desperate measures, and few things can be as desperate as what followed.

It was, when you think about it for a minute, laughably inept. A discussion among the 'leadership group'* led to an impromptu plan to tamper with the ball. Cameron Bancroft, a junior team member, was chosen as the fall guy. And oh, how he fell.

At first it was thought he'd used sticky tape to pick up dirt from the ground and rub it into the ball; then it turned out to be sandpaper. The ridiculousness of this ruse was highlighted by his hasty attempts to hide the offending paraphernalia down his trousers while in full view of the dozens

* How sick of those words we all grew in the days that followed.

of television cameras that attend any international cricket fixture nowadays.

And so began the saga, which resulted in the banning of the three protagonists – two of whom happened to be the captain, Steven Smith, and vice-captain, David Warner – and a bout of national soul-searching quite out of keeping with our expectations of macho Australian culture.

Inevitably, the whole thing played out to head-shaking, hand-wringing and endless commentary. And you didn't have to look far to find a stinking wodge of *Schadenfreude* from the non-Australians, who rushed to highlight the hypocrisy. One minute the Australians were trumpeting their credentials as ethical leaders of the game, with endless talk of their ability to identify the exact location of the mythical 'line' of acceptable sporting behaviour without once crossing it; the next minute they were vaulting over said line with all the élan of a peak-form Yelena Isinbayeva.

While it's tempting for the impartial cricket fan to find it all very amusing, the whole affair was rather sad, not least because it unnecessarily took a year out of the careers of Smith and Warner, two of the world's finest batsmen, and deprived us of the pleasure of watching them while they were in the form of their lives.

A spectator from Victorian times might have looked on with pursed lips and a disapproving frown. This, they might have observed, just wasn't cricket.

On the contrary, it absolutely was cricket, through and through.

We hate cheats.

Diego Maradona thumping the ball into the net; Lance Armstrong blood doping his way to seven Tours de France; fencer Boris Onischenko wiring his épée so he could trigger the electronic scoring system with his hand and score points at will.

Boo. Hiss. Bad people.

All sports have them; all sports hate them; all sports try, to varying extents, to get rid of them, whether the cheats are trying to gain an advantage by systematic drug use, pulling the wool over the referee's eyes with various shades of skulduggery,* or, most spectacularly and shamefully, sending a basketball team to compete in the Intellectual Disability category, which contained just two players conforming to the categorisation.†

And when they're caught, as they often are, let the recriminations begin. Bans are imposed, protocols tightened, rules changed – an interminable battle against the corrupt and cynical, the trick being to stay a step ahead of people who find ever more inventive and sneaky ways to beat the odds.

Cricket, though, is different – or so we're supposed to believe. Cricket has its own ethical code, so entrenched that it's been enshrined in the Laws: the famous 'preamble' concocted by two pillars of the English cricketing establishment, Lords Cowdrey and Dexter, in the 1990s. Confirmation, surely, that cricket somehow stands apart from – some would claim above – other sports.

* Word provided by Kerry Vevers.

† This was the Spanish Paralympians, in Sydney 2000. I'm hard pushed to think of a more disgraceful and exploitative instance of cheating.

The gist of the message encapsulated in the seven bullet points of the preamble is this: 'I say, you chaps, no cheating, eh? Frightfully bad form.'

No coincidence, of course, that this edict (like the Laws themselves) was laid down from the citadel of Marylebone Cricket Club, self-appointed custodian of the game ever since its foundation in 1787. Those early years of formalised cricket are often viewed through the rosiest-tinted of spectacles – it was, after all, a social pursuit for 'gentlemen' – but you don't have to delve far to compile a dossier of dodginess to rival and even outstrip anything the modern game can offer, from relatively harmless rule-bending (batsmen wielding bats wider than the stumps) to actual deaths (a row over the eligibility of an Essex player in 1776 that descended into a fight in which one of their number was shot and killed by a Kent opponent).

It's not entirely surprising that a game founded on gambling might have had its fair share of ne'er-do-wells and rapscallions indulging in sharp practice over the years. In a way what's more notable is that the sport should at any stage have developed a sense of its own moral self-importance in the way that it did in the Victorian era. The expression 'it's not cricket' first appeared in print in 1851, but it wasn't coined in affirmation of cricket's well-established bona fides in the ethics department – far from it. The sport had suffered from a series of match-fixing scandals, and the new expression was intended to spruce up its image in the public's perception. The nebulous and subjective idea of the Spirit of Cricket could be said to have been born then – in parallel, it should be noted, with the period in history when Brits were most assiduously engaged in touring the world stealing countries and jolly well showing those bally foreigners the proper way to do things. British fair play and all that.

Anyone possessing the least familiarity with the history of the British Empire might blink in incredulity at the yoking together of the words 'British' and 'fair play', but, setting that aside for the moment, is it really true that cricket leads the way in matters of sportsmanship? Could other sports learn from the cricketing template?

Yes and no.

Make no mistake, the history of cricket is littered with examples of cheating, swindling, sharp practice and general unscrupulousness – including all the examples cited above and many more. The Australian ball-tampering scandal is the most recent,* but scroll back a few years and we find the infamous occasion when Greg Chappell ordered his brother Trevor to deliver the last ball of a One Day International against New Zealand underarm, along the ground, thus making it impossible for Brian McKechnie to score the six runs New Zealand needed to win. It was within the Laws of the game at the time, but definitely outwith† its spirit. Commentating afterwards, Richie Benaud – a man whose integrity, as both player and commentator, was unimpeachable – called it 'one of the worst things I have ever seen done on a cricket field'.

* At the time of writing – you can bet there will have been several more by the time you read this.

† Word provided by Kat Stephen. It's a fantastic word, to be read for preference in a soft Scottish accent, and I'll use it more than once in the book.

Then there's the example of Vinoo Mankad,* who in 1947 ran out Bill Brown for backing up too far.† This practice remains deeply controversial to this day. Is the batsman cheating by trying to gain a sly advantage, or is the bowler – no matter that they have the law on their side – engaging in sharp practice? Averse to confrontation, I maintain a relentlessly neutral position on the subject, seeing fault and justice on both sides.

Delving further back, the notorious Bodyline series between England and Australia in 1932–3 demonstrates perfectly the inherent difficulty of laying down guidelines about something as intangible as 'the Spirit of Cricket'. England captain Douglas Jardine's perfectly executed plan to tame the apparently unstoppable Donald Bradman – test the batsmen's courage by bowling very fast at their bodies – was, like Chappell's ploy, entirely legal. But it was cynical and dangerous, resulted in what *Wisden* described as 'probably the most unpleasant Test ever played', and led to a diplomatic incident between the two countries.

'There are two teams out there. One is trying to play cricket and the other is not.' Those words, spoken with venom by Australian captain Bill Woodfull to the England manager Pelham Warner, rang through the ages, and are still quoted as an example of the depths to which the game can sink.

Go back further, to the Victorian era, when W. G. Grace bestrode the game like a trilithon‡ on Salisbury Plain. It's

* Word provided by Tom Elwin.

† Cricket fans will already know about this; non-fans – do you really want me to explain it? Thought not.

‡ Word provided by Melinda Haunton.

difficult for us to appreciate the extent to which he *was* cricket, a superstar before superstars existed. He was the face of Colman's Mustard; grounds charged higher admission prices when he played; only Queen Victoria was more widely recognised.

But for all his fame, the great doctor was a brazen cheat, haranguing umpires into changing their decisions ('They've come to see me bat, not you umpire' is the most famous quote), once calmly replacing the bails when clean bowled and just carrying on batting, and running out an opposition batsman when he left his crease to tend to a bump in the pitch.*

Reading all this you might wonder how cricket came to regard itself as somehow morally superior to other sports. But for each example encapsulating the game's tawdry side, there's an equal and opposite example to illustrate the extraordinary fellowship and generosity it can engender.

There's that famous photograph of Andrew Flintoff and Brett Lee from the 2005 Ashes – the victor (Flintoff) somehow having the presence of mind to break off from his team's celebrations to commiserate with the vanquished (Lee) in his moment of agony; or the two captains in the first tied Test in 1961, Richie Benaud (Australia) and Frank Worrell (West Indies), leaving the field of play with arms draped wearily over each other's shoulders – united by mutual respect and the thrill of sharing an historic occasion; or Michael Atherton and Allan Donald squaring up to each other towards the end of the day's play at Trent Bridge

* This is one of the most 'not on' things you can do on a cricket field. Strange, magnificent game.

in 1998 in one of the great sporting duels, a battle between a raging animal of a fast bowler and a stoical batsman soaking up all the punishment thrown at him.

That last example epitomises the conflict at the heart of the Spirit of Cricket. The catalyst for that thrilling period of play came early in the spell, when Atherton gloved a fast, rearing delivery to the wicketkeeper. He knew he'd hit it, Donald knew, everyone except umpire Steve Dunne knew.* It was out, but according to the Laws of the game you're not out until the umpire says so, and Dunne's finger stayed resolutely down.

There are those who believe passionately in 'walking'. If you know you've hit the ball, you give yourself out without waiting for the umpire's decision – it's the honest thing to do, a mark of respect for the game. But others take the opposite view for strangely similar reasons – the umpire's decision is final, right or wrong. After all, there will be occasions when you have to accept a decision that goes against you, so take the good ones when you can.

And then there are those who don't walk simply because they want to get away with whatever they can. They accept the reprieve and thank their lucky stars. Naturally, on the occasions when the umpire gives them out incorrectly, you don't want to be in the dressing room while they 'vent their frustrations'.

Atherton was not a 'walker'. If he had been, we would have been robbed of one of the great passages of play, a duel that in its own way encapsulated the Spirit of Cricket –

* After the game, over a drink, Atherton gave Donald the offending glove, telltale red mark and all.

utmost sporting excellence, utmost mutual respect, utmost excitement.

It was golf, not cricket.

Royal Birkdale, 1969. The Ryder Cup. The final hole. All square.

Everything, in sporting terms, was at stake. Jack Nicklaus's putt rushed past the hole. He had to putt again. If he holed it, Tony Jacklin would have a shortish putt, about three feet, to tie.

Shortish, but missable.

Nicklaus holed his putt with the certainty of a champion. Then, in one of the great sporting gestures, he picked up Jacklin's ball marker, conceding the putt and ensuring that the cup was tied.

'I don't think you'd have missed it,' said Nicklaus, 'but I wasn't going to give you the chance, either.'

Golf, not cricket. But recognisable by anyone familiar with the concept as very much cricket.

No sport has a monopoly on human nature.

SIBLINGS

2,100

Subject provided by Amanda Davidson

Think of three American sisters singing in close harmony. Quickly now.

Hold their names in your head.

Is that your final answer?

Are you absolutely sure?

If you're thinking of the Andrews Sisters, award yourself one point for trying.

If, on the other hand, you're thinking of the Boswell Sisters, award yourself all the points and a little victory dance around the room, but careful not to trip over the cat – oh darn it, too late. I hope it doesn't hurt too much; maybe put some arnica on it?

I can't blame you for thinking of the Andrews Sisters. I would have. They were, and are, more famous, renowned especially during the war years for their peppy renditions of songs like 'Bei Mir Bist Du Schön', 'Beat Me Daddy, Eight to the Bar', 'Rum and Coca-Cola', and the one I particularly associate them with, 'Boogie Woogie Bugle Boy'. They sold 75 million records, were among the most successful and recognisable musical groups of the first half of the twentieth century, and were very very good. I'm not here to bash the Andrews Sisters.

But spare a thought for the Boswells, their immediate predecessors, inspirations and (OPINION KLAXON) superiors.

There is no objectivity in that statement. I merely prefer listening to the Boswells to the Andrews. That's all.

But I'm getting ahead of myself. You probably don't even know who the Boswell Sisters were.

A little history.

New Orleans in the early 1920s. To be specific, 3937 Camp Street, the home of Clyde and Meldania Boswell and their children: Clyde Jr ('Clydie'), Martha, Connie and Helvetia ('Vet'). A solid, white, middle-class family. Clyde Sr is an ex-vaudevillian, Meldania a music lover; between them they introduce their daughters to music, signing them up to lessons with Professor Otto Finck. Martha plays piano, Connie cello* and Vet violin. A nice classical piano trio. Talented and hard-working, with ambitious parents, they are being primed for a concert career.

But parental plans rarely work out, and you don't live in New Orleans in the 1920s without exposure to African-American music. Blues and rag and gospel and jazz. Influences come at them from all parts: the black household staff introduce them to gospel; their parents and aunt and uncle sing quartets; Meldania takes them to the Lyric Theatre, where Connie is in thrall to the big and bold blues style of Mamie Smith; and older brother Clydie, the first of the siblings to break ranks from classical to jazz, introduces

* Word provided by Jonathan Ayling, who plays a pretty mean cello himself.

them to the young New Orleans jazz set. Almost immediately, piano, violin and cello become piano, banjo and saxophone – I suspect if you'd thrown them an alphorn or a didgeridoo* they would have learned how to make music in twenty minutes flat – and the house on Camp Street becomes a sort of salon for the cream of New Orleans jazz.

Of all the musicians thronging to their door – names like Leon Roppolo, Nappy Lamare, Wingy Manone, Al Gallodoro and the Prima brothers† – the biggest influence on the sisters is a cornet player called Emmett Louis Hardy, whose death from tuberculosis at just twenty-two robs the jazz world of a potentially great (and sadly unrecorded) musical voice. An even bigger blow is the death of older brother Clydie at just eighteen.

The sisters, tough and determined (they tour, unchaperoned, when Vet is still only fourteen), launch themselves on the world, first in regular gigs around New Orleans, then in recordings and radio broadcasts. And it's during a broadcast that, almost by accident, they experience a defining musical moment.

Connie has a cold – she can't hit the high notes, and has to sing with reduced volume and energy. Martha muffles the piano with burlap, they rearrange the song to suit the new, enforced range of Connie's voice, and crowd close around the microphone, singing soft and low. The moment they hear the playback the following week they know they're on to something, a new and unique style that will set

* Words provided by Andrew Osborne. He used to play the horn, but I've never heard him on the didgeridoo.

† If you've seen *The Jungle Book*, you know the voice of the younger Prima brother, Louis – he voiced Louie, King of the Jungle ('I wanna be like you').

them apart. There's an intimacy to it, the voices drawing you in rather than reaching out and trying to grab you.

A breakthrough comes in 1930, their first coast-to-coast broadcasts catching the nation's ear. They head to New York, recording for Brunswick Records under the guidance of record executive Jack Kapp. Between 1931 and 1935 they release a series of recordings that come to be seen as milestones in the history of vocal jazz. With radio and the phonograph bringing music directly into people's homes, that intimacy counts for a lot, but their defining feature is the 'Boswell sound' – they play fast and loose with the accepted way of things, throwing in instrumental imitations, speed singing, scat, and a nonsense language of their own devising that they call 'Boswellese'. Their arrangements are exuberant, eccentric and subversive. Songs in major keys are sung in the minor, and vice versa; they change speed several times in the course of a song; they throw in odd phrasings, articulations and syncopations; their exceptionally close harmonies enable them to hide the melody or pass it from one voice to the other, so the song is recognisable but distorted. As Connie says many years later, 'At that time I'm sure that to the average ear we must have sounded like little green people from outer space.'

These arrangements are often attributed to Connie, but according to her the process was subtler, more convoluted than that: 'We put the cart before the horse; that is, we start at the end of a number and begin arranging forward. We couldn't think of beginning at the beginning as most mortals do. We never put our arrangements in black and white, as we learn them by ear, and once learned, they always stay in our minds.'

If the eccentricity of the arrangements catches the ear, the Boswells' singing style holds it. In the slower passages the authentic New Orleans drawl and flexibility of their voices comes to the fore – expressive and soulful; in the fast sections there's an irrepressible energy, underpinned by an unshakeable sense of pitch, rhythm and ensemble. They breathe together, phrase together, articulate together. Their rhythm has that looseness that comes with absolute security – you have to know the rules before breaking them – and at times their unanimity of phrasing borders on the freakish.

Their voices blend to perfection, thanks to the telepathy of sorority* – bewildering to the outsider, as natural as breathing to the siblings. According to Vet, 'I'd be in the bedroom, Martha would be in the kitchen and Connie in the living room, and we'd start singing the same song at the same time and in the same key. That's how in tune we were to each other.'

If their aural style is full of energy, visually they're forced to be static. Connie – whether because of a bout of polio when she was three, or, according to her, a nasty soapbox-on-wheels accident around the same time – is confined to a wheelchair, so their standard seating arrangement is with Connie and Martha sitting on the piano bench and Vet standing behind them, bending over so their heads form a close triangle, the physical connection enhancing the uncanny synchronisation of their ensemble. Breathe together, move together, sing together.

Crucially, they sound black. This isn't an affectation – it's a natural part of their sound, the result of their upbringing, their immersion in black music from an early age. There's

* Word provided by Philip Sheppard.

no hint of their attempting to co-opt black culture, but there's equally no denying that their appearance – demure Southern Belles – is at odds with their sound, to the extent that listeners in those early years are confused. One writes to their radio station: 'I should like to know if the Boswell Sisters are white or colored. I am asking you to settle a long argument to the above question.'

It's almost as if the colour of the performer makes a difference to their popularity with the general public.

Jack Kapp, meanwhile, has found his marketing ideal. The sisters are white, singing white 'Tin Pan Alley' music, but in the black style. They appeal to conservative and liberal audiences alike, and his astute commercial instincts impel him to exploit this to the full. He has them working with some of the finest musicians of the time – naturally this, in his eyes, means 'the finest *white* musicians of the time'. On the recording sessions are violinist Joe Venuti, Jimmy and Tommy Dorsey on alto sax and trombone, guitarist Eddie Lang, and future clarinet legend Benny Goodman. It would be easy to assume that those men, pre-eminent in an almost entirely male-dominated world, provide the musical impetus, but don't be fooled: the sisters call the shots. Glenn Miller is listed as 'arranger' on some of the 1932 recording sessions – in reality, to save time, he's taking dictation from Connie.

For five years their success grows. They appear thirteen times on the radio show *Bing Crosby Entertains*, undertake two tours of Europe, appear in films and on the new medium of television, advertise beauty and household products in magazines.

With success, naturally, comes criticism. Their musical sophistication and individuality aren't universally popular.

A Californian radio station receives a letter: 'Please get rid of those awful Boswell sisters. They're always changing the melody, and my friends and I always turn them off. We call them "the savage chanters".'

It's tough to take criticism, especially when delivered with such brutality. On hearing these words, Martha starts to cry. But Connie is delighted. She snatches the letter with a laugh.

'You see, girls? I told you we were on the right track!'

Ultimately, though, the eccentricity of their renditions puts them at odds with Kapp. He has become famous for demanding his artists 'stick to the melody', and his determination to keep the sister act in the mainstream causes tensions and conflict. In 1936 he breaks away from Brunswick Records and forms a new company, Decca. The sisters make three discs for the fledgling label, but their lives are changing rapidly. All three of them get married at around the same time, and the group disbands in early 1936. Vet and Martha retire for good to devote themselves to marriage and family. Connie – changing her name to Connee a few years later, allegedly because her polio-stricken hand gets tired from dotting all the 'i's in her name when signing autographs – continues as a solo artist, softening her image and working for another thirty years, but without the success of the sisters' all-too-brief moment in the limelight.

The year after they disband, another sister act forms, setting themselves up as imitators of the great Boswells. Seventy-five million record sales later, their flame still burns bright, while their immediate predecessors, inspirations and (OPINION KLAXON) superiors languish in relative obscurity.

Sibling acts have an appeal all their own. There's a ready-made story there, a marketer's dream. The Jackson Five, the Osmonds, Sister Sledge, the Pointer Sisters, the Bee Gees. Yes, even the Nolans. We have an image of them, unlike other 'normal' families, united in purpose, devoting their time together to honing their act, their individual ambitions subsumed in pursuit of the common goal.

That's the idea, anyway.

The Boswells were among the first and finest. Musically, they're as good as it gets – tight, inventive, exuberant and heartfelt. Listening to their signature tune, 'Heebie Jeebies' – no more than a novelty number in other hands – you realise you're in silk purse/sow's ear territory. From the opening, with synchronised voiceless slidings – like a trombone trio – through an understated, half-crooned bluesy verse, in and out of several speed changes, and through the playout before a delicious swell* and slide up to a final hummed chord, it's three minutes of musical irresistibility.

You get the impression that they would have done it anyway, that even without the success they would have made music together, perhaps entertaining family and friends in the front room at Camp Street.

Lucky family, lucky friends.

And you can never dispel the feeling, whatever their individual talents, that they make up a whole that is larger than the sum of the parts. As Vet once said, with admirable humility, 'The three of us made one good person.'

---

* Word provided by Deb Conner.

THE FOUR TEMPERAMENTS

2,000

Subject provided by Alastair Hume

Be warned: this could get maths-y. And music-y.

Maths-y types will roll their eyes at my definition of maths-y; likewise, no doubt, music-y types.

People who are both or neither might already have moved on.

I'll try to ease you in with some comedy.

There is a sketch by John Finnemore about Pythagoras. Here's the conceit: Pythagoras is pitching his second theorem to a Hollywood-mogul type.

'Look, Pyth, you're gonna hate this, but it has to be said. Pyth, is there a place in this one for the hypotenuse?'

You get the idea. Or, in fact, you don't, because there's always more to a John Finnemore sketch than meets the eye. His producer Ed Morrish described him as 'like Jimmy Anderson – you never know which way the ball's going to swing'.

Translation: John Finnemore is very good at writing comedy. Have a listen, if you don't know him. You'll be rewarded.

When I think about that sketch, I think 'Go on, John. Now do one about Pythagorean Temperament. It's Radio 4 – they'll understand. Or at least they'll pretend to.'

Because when we think of Pythagoras of Samos (c. 585–500 BCE) we inevitably think of the square on the hypotenuse, which, as any on-the-ball thirteen-year-old can confirm, is equal to the sum of the squares on the other two sides.

As a musician, I wish everyone was equally familiar with Pyth's interest in music, and his resulting influence on tuning systems through the ages. I suspect, though, it's a forlorn hope. But let's start with him, because he came first.

According to legend, it was a blacksmith who piqued Pyth's interest. He noticed the resonances of the hammerings coming from the smithy, and observed the difference in pitch between the various kinds of metal sheet being hammered: larger, heavier sheets produced lower sounds than smaller ones. From there to experimentation with pipes, bells and glasses filled with various levels of water was a short step; and from there to a rudimentary stringed instrument called a monochord was a shorter step still.

He noticed this: if he placed his finger exactly halfway along the string and plucked the string with the other hand, the note produced was exactly one octave* higher than when he plucked the open string. So the ratio of length – 1:2 – had its equivalent in the sounds produced.

He experimented further, observing that all the following ratios produced intervals† pleasing to the ear: 1:2, 2:3,

* What we now call an octave, at any rate. Pyth didn't have that word, for the obvious reason that it didn't exist yet. Also, he was Greek.

† The difference between two notes.

3:4 (what we now know as the octave, fifth and fourth respectively).

This all tallied with the view he was building of a universe governed by simple numerical ratios. He was wrong, of course, but let's give him credit for the tidiness of his argument.

How was he wrong – in musical terms, at least?

Let's turn theory into practice. You'll need a long piece of string, several pieces of wood and a piano.

Or some imagination will probably do.

Imagine your piece of string is of a suitable length and thickness, and is stretched tautly enough to vibrate at 25 Hz – twenty-five vibrations a second. This is quite low in the human hearing range – very roughly equivalent to the lowest A on a piano (which is in fact 27.5, but I've rounded down to make the arithmetic easier, so back off, musicians). If you halve the length while maintaining the same tension, it will vibrate at 50 Hz (which produces the same note, A, an octave higher). Halve again, and it'll be 100. And so on. Do this seven times, and the string will vibrate at 3,200 Hz. Also an A,* seven octaves higher than the first one.

Now go back to the beginning, with the string vibrating at 25 Hz. What we're going to do is go with Pythagoras's second ratio: 2:3, shortening the string not by half, but by a third each time. This will mean jumps of not an octave, but a fifth.† If we do this leap twelve times, we will, in theory, reach the same A we reached with seven octave leaps. Like this: A – E – B – F# – C# – G# – D# – A# – F – C – G – D – A.

* Yes, I KNOW.

† Non-musicians: a fifth is five steps above (or below) your starting note, counting the starting note as one.

Stay with me. You're doing fine.

Here's the arithmetic.

25 x 3 = 75

75 ÷ 2 = 37.5

A frequency of 37.5 Hz gives you the E in the sequence above.*

I'll spare you my workings. But trust me, if you do that sum twelve times, hopping in fifths through the list of notes above, you get 3,243.658447265625.

That's Numberwang!

You'll have noticed that 3,243.658447265625 and 3,200 are not the same number. And those two frequencies, naturally, don't produce the same note. One (obtained by going up in twelve leaps of a fifth) is higher than the other (obtained by going up in octaves). The difference is so marked that even someone deeply unmusical would wince and say, 'Hang on, something wrong there, surely?'

But according to Pythagoras's theory, they're the same note.†

And there's your problem, right there in that 43.658447265625 Hz. Pyth's pure mathematics were out of step with acoustic reality. Turn *that* into a Hollywood theorem.

It's a bit like tiling a floor in a room with a slightly irregular shape‡ – tiny discrepancies, not visible at first, add up, until you're left with an irritating space by the fridge that

---

* Musicians: again, I KNOW. It's just an example. Imagine it's a very flat E, OK?

† This difference, incidentally, is known as the 'Pythagorean comma', a phrase I'm sure you'll now be dropping casually into conversation in whatever context you choose.

‡ All rooms have slightly irregular shapes, as anyone who has ever tiled a floor or hung wallpaper will know.

you have to fill with offcuts and it all gets a bit fiddly and bothers you every time you see it.

It was fine, for a while. Centuries, in fact. Music remained simple, using only a few notes for melodies, without accompanying harmony. Musicians created tunes with the notes that were deemed acceptable, avoiding anything dissonant.

But then the sixteenth and seventeenth centuries came along, and musicians began to vary that simple scale: thirds and sixths, both major and minor, with their mathematically awkward frequency ratios of 4:5, 5:6, 3:5 and 5:8. And they started to want to modulate – to move from one key to another. Not a problem with keys that were closely related, like C major and G major. But say you wanted to go from playing in C major to B major?* Instruments of variable pitch, where tuning is done by adjustments of the finger (violin, say) or tuning slide (trombone or sackbut,† for example) or other methods, have no problem with this. But a keyboard instrument, with fixed tuning, can't do it using Pythagorean tuning. You're OK in C major, but shift to something even slightly remote, and the whole thing goes out of whack and sounds terrible, because maths.

At this point, if you were reading a textbook on acoustics or temperament, you'd be presented with a vortex of horrific equations and brain-frazzling jargon. Here's just one example from a book I've been reading on the subject: 'If we

* Even though C and B are next to each other on the keyboard, they're harmonically remote – like when you lived next door to that ghastly neighbour who played terrible music at all hours, threw his cigarette butts into your garden and complained when you put up a bird box because 'they crap everywhere'.

† Word provided by Josh Hillman.

consider the syntonic comma to be 21.5 cents, a fifth diminished by ¼ comma will be 702.0 – 5.4 = 696.6 cents.'

My eyes glaze over, my chin slumps to my chest, and I wake up an hour later with drool dribbling onto my shirt.

Maybe you've reached that point already.

So I will, if you'll permit me, cut to the chase.

It boils down to this: Pythagoras recognised the existence of the octave, and as music developed, there grew an ever-expanding number of ways to divide that octave, each with its own inconsistencies and frustrations and unsquared circles. Which you chose to use was, for a while, a matter of taste – a conscious decision to prioritise the importance of certain intervals over others. There was just intonation, which favours bright, resonant perfect thirds, but whose maths mean the fifth is pushed out of tune; with meantone temperament, in all its varied manifestations, there is a bit more of a compromise made by evening out discrepancies over a larger area.

The differences between all these tuning systems aren't necessarily obvious to the average listener. They just seem slightly off. This is partly because people have different levels of musical acuity, but mostly because of equal temperament.

Equal temperament, the compromise of all compromises, divides Pythagoras's octave into twelve exactly equal steps.* It's a homogenised, pragmatic division designed to enable a

* There are other equal temperament systems, dividing the scale into many smaller parts – twenty-three-tone, for example, or ninety-six-tone (this would require a huge keyboard, assuming one key per note). But twelve-tone equal temperament is what your piano keyboard is based on, and is as good as universal.

jump from C major to B major to E-flat minor to A major without everything sounding excruciating.

It's great. But it's also awful.

Think of musical notes as a sound spectrum. A single note isn't just a note – it carries inside it a wealth of overtones, in the same way that green isn't just green but a combination of other colours, their proportions adjustable to produce many greens.

A greeny green is one thing, but a bluey green can still be green while also thinking about changing to blue, and a greeny blue is different again. Equal temperament, pragmatically enough, does away with many of those nuances and presents you with a default colour palette, like the standard selection offered by your computer.

'This is what "in tune" is,' it says, 'and "in tune" sounds the same, regardless of what key you're playing in. That F sharp on your piano? Before I came along you'd tune it differently depending on context, but we're doing away with that. That F sharp will now always be an F sharp, whether it's the first note in the F-sharp minor scale or the penultimate one in G major.'

We have got so used to this idea in the last few centuries that performances of music using other systems (vocal groups specialising in early music, for example, might perform using just intonation) can at first sound out of tune to our anaesthetised ears, in the same way as music from cultures outside the Western canon sounds different. It makes us uncomfortable. But if we listen enough to other tuning systems, we recalibrate and they begin to sound normal.

Lou Harrison, an experimental twentieth-century American composer, had this to say on the subject: 'Equal temperament destroys everything and is not for the human ear.'

Considering that pretty much all of modern Western music,* from Beethoven to Beyoncé, Sibelius to Shakira, is based on equal temperament, this is provocative stuff.

His point is that while equal temperament enabled vast flexibility in harmonic development, its homogeneity destroyed the nuance of musical colour based on infinite minute variations of tuning. Yes, you can play in all keys as if they're the same, but when they all *sound* the same, what's the point?

What indeed?

So those are the four temperaments: Pythagorean, just, mean and equal. Not to be confused with blood, phlegm, yellow bile and black bile – the four temperaments central to Hippocrates's medical theory of humorism.

But that's another story.

* Let's not forget that many other kinds of music exist: Chinese, Indian, African and so on.

DEREK BROCKWAY

1,900

Subject provided by Lauren Hamer

Hello, reader.

It's entirely possible, what with one thing and another, that you need a break from the intellectual rigours of some of the pieces presented so far in this book.

Pythagoras, Sibelius, Stradivarius.

The Wombles.

That last piece, for example. Easy enough to follow for musicians, I would hope, and just about manageable for a mathematician with some musical knowledge. But just possibly a bit music-and-maths-y for the layperson if you're having to read every sentence twice in an effort to keep up.

Relax.

Don't worry.

Spend some time in safe, reassuring hands. Sit back in the armchair, reach for the remote control. Got your cup of tea? Chocolate digestive? OK then.

Meet Derek Brockway.

Full disclosure: I hadn't heard of Derek Brockway[*] before Lauren suggested I write about him. So when I got her message, I had one of those sudden panics familiar to anyone who has let their grip of everything current slip. Had Derek Brockway manoeuvred his way to global notoriety while I wasn't watching? Was he the latest hip-hop superstar? A footballer? The new custodian of the fungarium[†] at Kew Gardens?

Was hip-hop, now I came to think of it, even a thing any more?

There's nothing like ageing for making you feel mired in confusion[‡] and utterly out of your depth.

Praise the Lord for (non-specific, unbranded) search engines.

Derek Brockway, it turns out, is a Welsh TV weatherman. On learning this, I feel slightly better about myself. A side effect of my largely avoiding the television news these last few years has been that I've also unconsciously avoided the weather reports. And while there might be those who can reel off the names of present-day meteorologists the way I could once blithely have reeled off Bill Giles, Michael Fish, Ian McCaskill and . . . umm, the other one[§] . . . I am no longer among their number. And if I can't name any forecasters for London, where I live, there's no earthly reason why I should be expected to know the Welsh ones.

As I delve into Derek Brockway's online presence, he's

---

* Derek, if you happen to be reading this, I'm sorry. But now I have heard of you, count me among your loyal fans.

† Word provided by Eileen McManus.

‡ Word provided by Calum Macaulay.

§ John Kettley! I knew I knew it.

revealed to be a genial, engaged, personable man. This is just as well. The last thing you want is a weather presenter who thinks it's all about them, treating each bulletin like a showreel for their stand-up routine. But nor do you want the droney type, the kind of person who sends you nodding off with a single mention of a band of steady drizzle sweeping down from the north.

Derek has the balance just right. The smile is in place – winning, but not too winning; he's jovial but not irritatingly jokey; he has good weatherman hand technique, the gestures subtly matching the projected display behind him – when Derek talks of a low front pushing in from the Atlantic, the graphic appears on cue and bends to his will; and when Derek talks, serious but not solemn, about a 'red' warning of snow, you sit up, take notice, and prepare for a day of not going out unless your journey is absolutely necessary.

As well as the video clips, I pick up some biographical details: his birth in Barry in 1968; the sparking of a fascination with the weather during the hot summer of 1976; the A levels in maths, physics and geology in anticipation of a life immersed in meteorology; an early stint as a weather observer at the Met Office, which took him to the Falkland Islands for eight months; his qualification as a forecaster, leading to his first presenting job at Birmingham Weather Centre; the move to London in 1995, where he worked for ITV and Channel 4 and presented the weather on GMTV's *The Sunday Programme*; the return to Wales a year later, where he has become, as far as I can tell, a universally loved and respected institution of Welsh television.

Among Derek's many TV credits – he appeared in *The Big Welsh Challenge*, in which Welsh personalities are challenged to learn Welsh, and he also appeared in series three, episode one of *Gavin & Stacey* as himself – is the long-running programme *Weatherman Walking*, now into its twelfth series. Pleasingly, *Weatherman Walking* does exactly what the title suggests. Derek goes for a walk somewhere in Wales and talks to people about the points of interest along the way. It's a simple format, almost entirely dependent on the likeability of the presenter.

I watch an episode. Then I watch another. Soon I have watched a whole series.

It is good.

Actually, to say 'it is good' merely damns *Weatherman Walking* with faint praise. It is very good, the kind of programme that steals beneath your radar and leaves you craving more without your quite realising why. It's not as if there's a shortage of generally relaxing content on our screens these days, but there's something about Derek's presentational style that ticks all the necessary boxes. It's entirely unforced, not trying too hard. I realise after a couple of episodes that this is because Derek's not a Good Bloke, donning the persona for the cameras; he's just a good bloke. And in a world of taut thrillers, edgy comedies and relentless breaking news, there's a lot to be said for spending half an hour watching a good bloke walking round the countryside, engaging with people in a natural way and being genially informative about castles and guillemots and noctilucent clouds.

I come away from watching the programme thinking that it's too good to be true. There must be something wrong with Derek Brockway.

I delve further, reaching page three of the search results.

Derek's hobbies are walking, travel, learning Welsh, yoga, tennis and squash.

He was photographed naked for a calendar in aid of Autism Cymru.

He lost control of an umbrella in high winds while broadcasting during the Rugby World Cup in 1999. Nobody was hurt.

According to famousbirthdays.com he's the tenth most popular Scorpio named Derek, the twenty-sixth most popular fifty-one-year-old TV show host and the eighth most popular TV host born in Wales. These are good, solid numbers. You can't argue with them. You also can't resent them for their flamboyance or overweening excellence.

I find a clip in which Derek learns how to rap – neither well nor appallingly. It's the kind of thing that could taint one's view of someone, a piece of nonsense with no real reason for existing. But Derek does it in a library to encourage youth literacy. How can you object to that? At the very worst you're just going to think it's a bit naff.

He even – and this is quite a feat – manages to deliver the weather forecast in appalling rhyming couplets without making me reach for the sick bucket.

I'm beginning to flag. There's not a whiff of anything remotely controversial or disagreeable about Derek. It's a stream of relentless affability. There's nothing to dislike about him. He's professional but not overtly driven, warm without the cloying charm of a Wogan, approachable without making a song and dance about it. He does good works, but not ostentatiously. And you can't fake the genuine pleasure with which he is greeted by members of the public as he walks his way round Wales on *Weatherman Walking*.

I delve deeper.

'BBC Wales weatherman Derek Brockway visits Porthcawl RNLI.' 'Jade Jones and Derek Brockway promote the value of reading.' 'Weatherman Derek Brockway joins 3rd Prestatyn Scouts as they work to secure habitats for sand lizards on Gronant Dunes.'

Nothing to see here. Move on.

And there's the problem. In order to research this piece, I've watched Derek Brockway on the television, I've read one of his books, I've gone through search results, found YouTube footage. I have, in short, mined the Brockway information dump fairly dry. And all I've found is the story of a hard-working, likeable, modest and decent man who seems to enjoy life and has a passion for weather, an aptitude for communication and an ability to get on with people from all walks of life.

It's not that he's dull. If he were dull that would at least give me something to work with, even though I'd have to wrangle with myself about the ethics of poking fun at the innocent.

In a weird kind of way, it would be better if he were awful, if he plumbed Partridge-esque depths of vainglory, incompetence and hubristic vulgarity. I could go to town, safe in the knowledge that any excess of cruelty would be mitigated by the knowledge that the subject of my mockery was a thoroughly deserving recipient of it.

But he's neither dull nor awful. That's the terrible thing. He's just very good at being himself on television, something we take for granted but which is in fact a fine art. First you have to have a 'self' to be, as it were. No use being shy, no use being drab. But try too hard and you're scuppered. The desperation shines through. And if you have certain tics or quirks or annoying habits, you can put people's backs up for no particularly good reason. I'd be surprised and disappointed if anyone's back were put up by Derek Brockway.

Then, at last, on page six of the search results, I find it. 'Derek Brockway being interrupted presenting the weather on BBC Wales Today.'

Click click click. I can't wait to watch this. Some controversy at last. Perhaps someone comes onto the set and Derek bundles them to the floor, always remembering his yoga techniques and keeping a strong core to avoid injury; perhaps it's a protester brandishing a placard – Derek firmly but politely ushers them to the door, mindful of the need to preserve the continuity of the broadcast while respecting the protester's right to freedom of speech. Perhaps it's an incident that has gone into the folklore of local television. The time that Derek Brockway finally cracked. Derek's demise. Brockway in Foul-Mouthed Breakfast Tirade!

But no. Alas and alack and all things disappointing.

Derek is giving the forecast, as normal. A voice is heard off-camera. Derek's professional demeanour is undisturbed. The voice is heard again. For an instant a cloud descends over his eyes, and they dart for the briefest second towards the source of the sound. If I were to describe the expression on his face, it would be with the words 'the mildest of irritation, as if a fly had just landed on the rim of his beer glass'. And then he's back, flow undisturbed, communicating the prospects of rain over the Gower Peninsula in the next twenty-four-hour period.

Colour me disappointed.

A decent rule of thumb for life is that you should never commit anything to print about a person that you wouldn't be prepared to say to their face.

Here goes.

Derek, you're a thoroughly likeable and professional screen presence and you have made my life better in small and intangible ways. My discovery of your work has added to the undertow of Good and Worthwhile Things in which I find solace in times of perturbation and despair.

Damn you to Prestatyn and back, you shining exemplar of quiet and undemonstrative geniality. I think I hate you.

MUSIC TO EAT CAKE BY

1,800

Subject provided by John Holland

Cake.

Cake cake cake.

Cake cake cake cake, lovely magnificent cake.

Sorry, got distracted for a moment. Because a good cake is a thing of joy and wonder, and worth dwelling on for a few seconds. From the humble simplicity of a pound cake* to the excess of a towering croquembouche† and every stop between, there are few things as enticing as cake.

And rare is the cake that doesn't benefit from some extra attention, a hint of formality and ceremony. The plate, the fork, the tea or coffee (depending on geography and culture), the napkin.

The doily.

You could eat your cake in silence, unbroken save the occasional clink of fork on china and the low murmur of appreciative noises. That would be fine. It would still be cake.

* Traditionally made with a pound each of flour, eggs, butter and sugar.

† Make a load of profiteroles, pile them up, embellish with threads of caramel.

But let's say you want to add some ritual to your cake experience, to pay it the respect it deserves and imbue the occasion with a sense of ceremony, whether you're sitting alone in the kitchen or entertaining guests; let's say that without the accompaniment of some sort of soundtrack, the cake will somehow be indefinably lacking; let's say* you love both cake and music, and want to take any opportunity to combine your passions.

This is only natural.

But tread carefully. A mismatch could cause perturbation and despair. Pick the wrong music and your cake will turn to ashes in the mouth, and your listening experience will curdle as surely as a badly blended batter. What we're after is the perfect balance, a cake-to-music compatibility rating of 100 per cent.

And if you doubt the importance of careful pairing, imagine eating a rock cake while listening to Vivaldi, pairing the delicacy of a selection of *petits fours* with the bombast of Bruckner, or washing down a dainty fairy cake with the splenetic excess of the Beastie Boys, and you'll get an idea of the importance of these decisions.

The good news is it's all a matter of taste. There's no objective truth here. So I can go ahead and make my recommendations safe in the knowledge that any objections can be dismissed with a blithe 'Well, I like it, so *nur*.' And objections, human nature being what it is, there will be.

The first cake that springs to mind, simply because it's fresh in my memory as I write, and my birthday isn't for

* This is just one of several examples in this book of anaphora, a rhetorical device that involves starting a series of sentences with the same word or words. Word provided by Bernard Hughes.

three months, is Christmas cake. Here the emphasis won't be on the qualities of the cake itself (solid fruit cake, marzipAAAGGGHHHYUCK, icingYUMMMMM) as on the festival it commemorates. So the first thing on your playlist will be Leroy Anderson's 'Sleigh Ride'.* From there you can pick and choose according to taste. Perhaps the Rat Pack's Christmas album is your style; maybe even Michael Bublé, because honestly you might as well go the whole hog. Cakers of a more traditional bent might prefer Bach's *Christmas Oratorio* or even *Classic Christmas Carols* by the Choir of King's College, Cambridge – fading out, obviously, before you get to the dirgy obscure ones. You'll have finished the cake by then anyway.

By the same token, when presented with a Schwarzwälder Kirschtorte (Black Forest gâteau, if you prefer – and what wonderful images of the 1970s those three words conjure up), it doesn't take a monumental leap of imagination to pair it with a gorgeous† selection of polkas and waltzes by the Strauss family. Objections that this is geographically inaccurate, the Black Forest being some 430 miles from Vienna, where the Strausses hung out, can be met with a pert rejoinder: the cake is named not after the forest but the cherry liqueur of the same name. So, well, *nur*.

While we're in Vienna, we can be even more specific about an aural companion for a slice of Sachertorte. This borderline indecent combination of dense chocolate sponge, apricot jam and chocolate icing was invented in 1832 by the sixteen-year-old Franz Sacher, who, as an

* Purists will argue that as this enduringly popular lollipop was composed during an August heatwave, it should be disqualified. Pish.
† Word provided by Stef S.

apprentice to the kitchen of Prince Klemens von Metternich, was ordered to step in at short notice to replace the ailing head chef, and to create a special dessert for the guests. Also in Vienna that year, Johann Strauss I composed his waltz *Die vier Temperamente (The Four Temperaments)*. Even though the waltz lacks the oomph of some of his better work, the chronology and mood are perfect, so we need look no further.

In those examples it feels natural to match cake with music according to nationality or historical associations, but this apparently foolproof approach is fraught with danger. Classical music fans with a smattering of background knowledge and access to Wikipedia might instinctively think, on seeing the words Esterházy torta, 'Aha! Esterházy! Would that be the selfsame Esterházy family into whose employ the great Austrian composer Franz Joseph Haydn entered in 1761, and whose scion Nikolaus remained the musician's patron for nearly thirty years? In which case, why not listen to some Haydn while tucking into the delightful confection, which as everyone knows comprises cognac-custard buttercream layered with almond meringue sponge and decorated with chocolate stripes? We do, after all, have a lot of music to choose from, what with Haydn having composed over a hundred symphonies, sixty-eight string quartets, a veritable smörgåsbord* of concertos, masses and operas, and copious amounts of keyboard and chamber music. Who knows, I might even hire a string quartet for the occasion.'

* Smörgåsbords are always 'veritable'. It's the rules.

Rookie error. Understandable, but naive. Because while all the above is indeed true, this cake wasn't invented until the late nineteenth century, by which time Haydn had been dead for at least seventy-five years. This blatant anachronism would be enough to lend the torta, usually so delicious, an unpleasantly cloying taste, perhaps even a slight and unwelcome bitterness.

Much safer to opt for a piece like Zoltán Kodály's *Dances of Galánta* or even Béla Bartók's delightful *Hungarian Sketches*, either of which, wearing their patriotic charms lightly, would make an ideal partner for the uniquely Hungarian character of the cake, while also bearing the hallmark of chronological authenticity. The later works of Franz Liszt might also fulfil that brief, but their lugubrious outlook would overpower the cake, as well as sending the listeneater into the proverbial slough of despond, possibly never to emerge.

Staying in Eastern Europe, the Kiev cake, combining the crunchy lightness of a nutty meringue – ideally as crusty as caliche,* but without the salty afterburn – with the richness of Russian buttercream, would be complemented by Stravinsky's *Feu d'Artifice*, a sparkling three-minute offering for those in the mood for something short and snappy. Or, for the longer haul, his 1910 ballet *The Firebird* would suit – something with a bit of fizz to match the old-school Russian tradition from which it sprang.

'That's all very well,' I hear you cry, 'but what about

* Word provided by Lissa Evans. It is, I learn, the crust of calcium carbonate that forms on the surface of soil in arid regions. Head to the Atacama Desert in Chile or the Makgadikgadi Pans in Botswana to get your fill of it.

good old stiff-upper-lip-Mary-Berry-Delia-Smith-ooh-creamy-England-how-I-love-you-we-invented-the-bake-off-dontcha-know British cake? What'll you do there, eh?'

What indeed?

To start with the basics, at the very heart of the music-caker's craft, let's examine the Victoria sponge. Nothing could be simpler or, when executed correctly, more satisfying – the very stuff of Major Balderdash of Tunbridge Wells's headiest fantasies. Light but not insubstantial, buttery but not cloying, representative of those great British values that we so selflessly spread around the rest of the world while nicking other people's countries.

This is a job for Gilbert and Sullivan.

For the richer pleasures of a solid fruit cake you want something with a bit more heft. Bushy-moustache-and-weskit music. Again there is a ready candidate in the patriotic stirrings of Sir Edward Elgar – any of the *Pomp and Circumstance* marches will do. Or, for those who favour something even more lip-trembling, might I suggest the same composer's *Enigma Variations*?

Taking it northwards, how about a double dose of Orcadian* delight in the form of a slice of Orkney fudge cheesecake to the dulcet strains of Sir Peter Maxwell Davies's *An Orkney Wedding, With Sunrise*?

A lighter offering is the brightly coloured Battenberg. Despite the Germanic implications of its name, this is a quintessentially British cake, staple of cricket teas throughout the land, so Holst, with his similarly confusing name, looks to be your go-to Gustav. As it turns out, he was a talented

* Word provided by Ian Noonan.

cricketer in his youth, so the association is doubled. Even more appropriate would be the cricket-themed pop croonings of Irish duo The Duckworth Lewis Method.

This departure from the strict confines of classical* music leads us across the pond, where we have a number of cakes to choose from. Pairing your creamy, chocolatey, ooh-everythingy Boston Cream Pie with the band Boston's timeless classic 'More Than A Feeling' might seem trite, but consider the possibility that no no, you're right, it's a terrible song and a disastrous combination – much better to go with Bostonian Donna Summer's creamy, chocolatey, ooh-everythingy 1970s disco classic 'I Feel Love', no?

Yes.

And when it comes to the lush gooeyness of possibly the greatest foodstuff to emerge from the United States,† the chocolate brownie, sample the output of Duke Ellington or Count Basie while savouring chocolatey paradise. For those with a yen for the edgy, the addition of marijuana to the brownie can be matched by the avant-garde noodlings of Lester Bowie's Art Ensemble of Chicago.

I could go on: panettone and Puccini, lemon polenta cake and Verdi, etc. and so forth. But the above examples should give you some guidelines on which to base your cake/music pairings – armed with these precepts, you can feel emboldened, taking into your musical cake adventure a sense of enterprise, but also a basic understanding of the ground rules governing this deceptively complex area.

---

* Such a bad name for a range of music covering everything from the Renaissance stylings of Josquin des Prez to Brian Ferneyhough's demanding New Complexity – but we kind of know what it means, so I stick with it.

† Please don't write in.

Most of all, never let anyone shame you into refusing either another slice of cake or the luxury of sitting back and letting your favourite music invigorate your soul.

TASHKENT CRICKET

1,700

Subject provided by Quentin Maxwell-Jackson

The nights draw in, summer's heat is a distant memory, darkness descends ten minutes after breakfast. Weather forecasters start to use words like 'winter woollies', 'wrap up warm', 'brace yourselves' and 'quite chilly, even in the southern regions'.

Winter is here.

There are pleasures to be had in winter. Long, hearty walks. Comforting red-winey stews. Buttered crumpets. Heating on, woolly socks, a duvet and series two of *Detectorists*. Maybe a dog at your feet – a proper dog, mind, not the sort Billy Connolly described as 'growing out of rich ladies' armpits'. A Labrador, maybe. The kind of dog that greets you with the eagerness of one who has been waiting ever such a long time for you to get home, where on earth have you been, now can we play? Come on, PLAY WITH ME.

But for the cricket fan the greatest of these wintry pleasures is *Wisden*. Small, chunky and stuffed to the gunwales with crickety information, this institution, published annually since its inception in 1864, is known to aficionados simply as 'the cricketing bible'. Which, when you come to think of it, doesn't make sense, because it's much quicker just to say 'Wisden'. It's customary for a cricket fan to have a bookshelf devoted to these stocky volumes – maybe even two, or perhaps, in extreme examples, an entire wall. Its reassuring yellow presence on my own shelves gives solace, a sense of tradition and continuity in a world of Monster Biff T10 competitions. It's also an invitation to dip in and out of those many pages in search of entertainment, enlightenment or arcane titbits such as the delicious fact that, at the end of his career, Derek Pringle's batting and bowling averages were identical.

The first edition of *Wisden*, just 112 pages long, wasn't limited to cricket news alone. It included (in an apparently random decision) dates of battles of the English Civil War, winners of classic horse race the Oaks, and the rules of quoits. As years passed, some much-needed discipline was imposed on the contents, and now it's safe to say that in cricketing terms, if it doesn't appear in *Wisden*, it didn't happen.*

A modern *Wisden* typically runs to 1,500 pages or so. While nearly a hundred of those are devoted to the register of every single person who has played Test cricket, and other wodges are filled with reams of statistics, there are illuminating articles throughout, the writing is of a uniformly high standard, and it remains the cricket aficionado's primary annual purchase, the way we keep up with

---

* This would be disputed by plenty of people on the subcontinent. *Wisden* is based on the English season, much to the chagrin of legions of Indian fans, who habitually berate the long-suffering editor on Twitter for his wilful snub of their heroes. The establishment in 2013 of a separate *Wisden India* volume should have gone some way towards appeasing them. It didn't.

everything that's happened in the cricketing world. If a complete collection of *Wisden* was the only thing left of cricket, you would need nothing else to gain an in-depth knowledge of the game.

I get it every year for my birthday* – birthday Santa knows what I like – and I've developed a routine: invariably, I read the introduction, the main essays, the reports on the action of the previous season, the assessment of the five Cricketers of the Year; invariably, I check some statistics, the records section, world rankings; invariably I then forget about it. Until winter. Because summer is for cricket itself: playing it, watching it, listening to it, savouring every last maiden, googly and cover drive while I can. Winter is for *Wisden*. The winters of my childhood were cricketing wastelands, but nowadays, with the preponderance of overseas tours and domestic T20 competitions, I could, if I wanted, watch cricket almost constantly, especially if I were prepared to stay up through the night. But there's a limit to my dedication† and *Wisden* is a long and rich read. And so begins the deep perusal, the trawl through the darker, less explored end of the almanac.

It's in December that I turn to page 736 to read about the Watsons Village Cup, or to page 172 to read an essay on cricket and gardening that somehow escaped my attention first time round, or to page 1085 to read about cricket round the world. These arcane delights provide moments of light in the all-pervading gloom of those dark and apparently endless months.

---

* 27 April, since you didn't ask.

† Some might call it an obsession. I could not possibly comment.

It's somehow uplifting to read the 'Cricket Round the World' section – the game is played in surprising places. Here you can read about how cricket in the British Virgin Islands recovered from two hurricanes; the travails of expatriate cricketers in Italy; what happened when a team of authors visited Iceland. The stories, for all their textual variations, tend to follow a similar pattern: cricket's introduction and survival in these unlikely places often depends on the efforts of expatriates keen to keep the home fires burning and imbued with evangelical zeal to convert the natives. The 2014 edition of *Wisden* contains short articles on cricket in Ethiopia, Colombia, Hungary, Japan, Myanmar, Poland and Vatican City.

And, glory be, Uzbekistan.

The words 'Tashkent cricket' are an unlikely juxtaposition, like 'canine bassoonist' or 'skateboarding badgers'.* Much as I love cricket, nobody could ever accuse it of being a truly global game. And while the International Cricket Council now boasts 104 members (compared to FIFA's 211 and the International Handball Federation's 209), the game's expansion is hindered by many factors – not least among them the undeniable truth that it's regarded by much of the world as inexplicable, interminable and pointless. So it's hardly surprising that it doesn't play a pivotal role in Uzbek culture. While its neighbour Afghanistan has enjoyed the most extraordinary success – largely a consequence of Afghan refugees in Pakistan becoming enthused by cricket during the 1990s – Uzbekistan's cricketing history is as thin as graphene dental floss. They are not a member of the

* The word 'badgers' was provided by Julia Croyden.

International Cricket Council, there is no national team and, frankly, there's scant evidence of any cricket ever having been played there.

But scant evidence is better than no evidence at all.

In 1997 Bharat Shah, president of an Indo-Uzbeki healthcare company, arrived in Tashkent. Like the vast majority of Indians, he had a keen interest in cricket, and had soon established a weekly game among his employees. They played two innings of ten overs each on a matting wicket laid down in the middle of a football stadium, and the winner of the Man of the Match award each week was treated to dinner for two at a local Indian restaurant. Social cricket, the kind I'm most familiar with – friendly but with an undercurrent of competition and occasionally the added frisson of a really tight finish, to be recounted in post-match pub visits down the ages.

The following year a game between a 'Commonwealth XI' (put together by Shah and comprising players from India, Pakistan, Bangladesh and Malaysia) and the British Embassy was also played. The inaugural match in 1998 was a close-run thing, the British Embassy prevailing with just nine deliveries to spare. It would seem that the bitterness of defeat spurred Shah to up his game, fielding an 'Indian XI' the following year – were the Pakistani, Bangladeshi and Malaysian players not up to scratch, or had key officials left the British Embassy in the intervening period? Whatever the reasons, it was a mismatch, the Embassy subsiding to a comical 17 for 8 before Shah's men took their foot off the gas and allowed a slight recovery. There is something endearingly humane about this practice, common in the friendly style of cricket that has been my stamping ground for the last thirty-five years – 'We're going to thrash you, obviously, but we'll back off near the end, just enough that it's clear we meant to do it. That way you'll be able to pretend to yourselves that you weren't hopelessly outclassed, and take at least a modicum of pleasure from the day. But we'll all know that you were several levels below us, and only the most joyless and hard-nosed of our number will take any satisfaction from the experience.'

The rematch in 2000 was an equally one-sided affair – it was also the last for which I can find any record. Tashkent cricket disappeared – mourned, one suspects, by few.

Cut to 2013, and the Ulugbek International School in the centre of Tashkent. Two Pakistani brothers, Zeeshan and Irfan Karimi, then thirteen and eleven, took it upon themselves to organise Uzbekistan's first cricket league, an after-school affair with four competing teams. Local rules, a concept familiar to anyone who has ever played a sport on a pitch not designed for it, prevailed. Hit the ball onto the school roof and you would pay with your wicket; lose it and the penalty was a small fine, enough to pay for the cost of a new one. The matches were dominated, as you'd expect, by non-Uzbeks – any sport is easier if you've grown up playing it, and cricket's arcane techniques and rituals take a bit of getting used to for a newcomer – but the locals, familiar with the sport from Bollywood movies, were keen to take part.

There was hope that Tashkent cricket would expand – an Australian teacher at the school, Jarrod Dale, planned to teach the game to his pupils, but he moved on, and it remains to be seen whether the flickering flame can take hold.

And now, as I read more about Uzbekistan, I discover a delightful piece of trivia: it is one of only two double-landlocked countries (surrounded, that is, entirely by other landlocked countries) in the world. And I am now consumed with a desire to broker a cricket match between Uzbekistan and its European double-landlocked counterpart Liechtenstein, for no other reason than that it would be a suitably bizarre thing to do, and would therefore be entirely in keeping with the noble history of eccentricity associated with this most ridiculous of sports.

ELEPHANTS

1,600

Subject provided by Jeannie Borsch

The piano is out of tune – not badly, not quite enough to make you stop listening, just the odd note gone noticeably twangy. It's a black upright, of the kind you might find in a church hall. But we are not in a church hall – we are on a hill in, it turns out, Thailand. There is extensive vegetation, there is a bespectacled Yorkshireman called Paul, and there is an eighty-year-old blind elephant. Paul explains to the camera that he's going to play some Bach to the elephant, whose name is Lam Duan, and then, clearly a man of his word, he sits down and plays some Bach to the elephant. The C-major prelude from *The Well-Tempered Clavier*, if you're interested.*

It's a scene both slightly surreal and peculiarly touching. As Paul plays, Lam Duan stands beside the piano and listens. At least, we assume she's listening because we like to anthropomorphise. She might just be standing there because she likes hanging around Paul and can't be bothered to wander off. She is eighty, after all.

---

* A piece I, and many others like me, have murdered at one point or another.

But there is something about her demeanour, a stillness, that we take as a sign of attentiveness. She flaps her ears occasionally – that's nothing to do with listening, just the elephant's natural air-conditioning system at work – or sways from side to side for a few seconds. And her trunk is never entirely still – I'd imagine keeping something that contains up to 150,000 muscles* entirely motionless is such hard work it's barely worth the candle, so the trunk flexes and coils continuously. At one point she shakes her head gently, almost with indulgent dismay. Was Paul's phrasing not to her taste? Maybe he was overusing the sustain pedal? Or was she just trying to shoo away a fly?

What's most striking, apart from the idiosyncratic strangeness of the whole shebang, is the touching intimacy of the scene.† A man, a piano and an elephant. And Bach.

It might be that Lam Duan has merely grown attached to Paul, and follows him wherever he goes. Whatever the truth of the matter, watching and listening to this is a pleasant and quietly moving way to spend five minutes; and it strikes me that Paul's time, attempting to musicate‡ a creature for which humans have an understandable fondness, isn't exactly wasted, either. If people in general played more

* Just so nobody writes in: estimates vary about how many muscles there are in an elephant's trunk, and strictly speaking they're muscle fascicles – tightly packed bundles of muscle fibres held together by connective tissue – rather than the kind of muscles we have (of which the human body contains 639).

† We leave aside for the moment the fact that Paul has chosen to film this and upload it to YouTube.

‡ Word provided by Wendalynn Donnan. I confess it's not a word I knew – a shameful omission on my part. It just shows how language sneaks up on you. It means 'to educate about music'.

Bach to elephants, either literally or figuratively, the world would be significantly improved.

Lam Duan is, of course, an Asian elephant. You won't, if you know your elephants, need me to tell you that three species of elephant are currently recognised: the African bush (*Loxodonta africana*), the African forest (*Loxodonta cyclotis*) and the Asian (*Elephas maximus*). Nor will you need telling that the Asian species divides into four subspecies: Sri Lankan, Indian, Sumatran and Bornean. And if you really know your stuff, you'll be aware that Thai elephants, while classed as belonging to the Indian subspecies, are generally slightly smaller than their Indian counterparts, with shorter front legs.

These are small details, irrelevant to many people. Whether your reference point is Dumbo or Ganesh, white or pink, Nellie or Babar, Saint-Saëns' lumbering double bass or Stravinsky's comedy polka troupe, Kipling's curious Elephant Child or one of Pratchett's four mighty World Elephants,* carrying the Discworld while standing on the shell of the turtle Great A'Tuin, elephants are elephants, and mighty lovable they are too.

Lovable? Perhaps not to anyone who has ever seen an elephant in 'musth', that state of hormonal imbalance in the throes of which a male elephant will be a violent danger to anything around them. And perhaps not to those who live in fear of elephants rampaging through their village causing death and destruction, as has happened in several areas of India in recent years.

But while there are those who fear them (and another ugly subsection of society who treat them with horrific

* Tubul, Jerakeen, Berilia and Great T'Phon.

cruelty), they are revered and regarded as sacred in many cultures; and in the West, where we don't generally come across them on a daily basis, our image of them is overwhelmingly positive. For all their massiveness, strength and potential for rampaging destruction, we see them as gentle, intelligent and capable of empathy and emotion. Young elephants are almost insufferably cute, old ones wise and thoughtful. Obviously associating them with desirable characteristics, organisations ranging from sports teams to political parties* have appropriated them as their emblem. We know they have excellent cognition, up there with our other favourites, dolphins, and our close relatives the chimpanzees. They live in close-knit, matriarchal communities, grieve for their dead, are able to recognise themselves in a mirror, and display strong signs of altruism – stories of their helping or protecting humans and other animals abound. All these qualities tie in with the way we'd like to see ourselves, so only serve to enhance that interspecies empathy.

Whenever we think of non-human animals, we empathise with the traits we have in common – elephants' capacity for emotions, grief and self-recognition all help to endear them to us even more. But we also thrill to the things animals can do that we can't – the navigation skills of pigeons, the speed of the cheetah, echolocation in bats, the owliness of owls, the everything of hummingbirds. But where elephants are concerned, high on the list of unfathomable mysteries is the phenomenon of infrasound.†

* Basketball team Alabama Crimson Tide, for one, and the Republican Party for another.

† The '150,000 muscles in the trunk' thing is pretty darn cool, too.

Human hearing is fairly good, as it goes. We have a wide range, from 20 Hz to 20 kHz, more or less, and our acuity is decent. It all goes to pot as we get older, naturally, but that's only to be expected. And even when our range does contract in our later years, the top end only comes down to about 12 kHz, which is where elephants' hearing tops out anyway. But where they have it over us is at the lower end. Twenty Hz is low, by any standards (the lowest note on a piano is 27.5 Hz), but take it down just 3 or 4 Hz and you get into the realms of infrasound, detection of which is outwith* our capabilities. Not only can elephants hear sounds at those frequencies, they can produce them as well, enabling long-distance communication through what I can only call Amazing Miracle Magic Elephant Rumbling – if it has a more scientific name, I don't want to know it – the high volume of which (up to 117 dB) enables a range of up to six miles. Add to this their ability to produce and receive infrasound waves through solid ground, to be sensed by herds hundreds of miles away, and we're firmly in 'Oh crikey, isn't nature amazing, did you see that programme about the lizards?' territory.

Armed with this knowledge, I watch the video again. The apparent simplicity of Bach's music is deceptive. A trained human ear detects patterns: each eight-note phrase is repeated, the harmony changing slightly, the whole connected by a coherent harmonic sequence and leading to a satisfying conclusion. But what does the elephant hear? Does Lam Duan respond to the gentle undulations of the music? Would she be disturbed by the contrasting mood of

* There's that word again. I hope you're satisfied, Kat.

the next prelude in the book, an agitated cascade of semiquavers in C minor? Would she appreciate the intricacy of the accompanying C-major fugue, its simple lines intertwining in a way that would surely meet with the approval of Spinal Tap's Nigel Tufnel? Does she quietly yearn for some lower sounds – the prelude has a range of three and a half octaves, but barely exploits the lower reaches of the keyboard until near the end.

These are pointless questions. All is conjecture. We can't know what's going on in an elephant's head. All we can do is observe, hypothesise and learn, adding each observation to the sum of human knowledge. Perhaps Lam Duan's reaction to Bach will reveal some hitherto unsuspected understanding of elephant behaviour. Or perhaps the exercise merely serves to help pass the time of day in a gentle and benevolent way.

YouTube automatically gives me another video. Same pianist, different elephant,* different music. Debussy's 'Clair de lune'. Paul adjusts the seat, allows a short silence to establish itself, setting the tone and mood, then, gently, starts to play. The chords ring out, soft and bell-like, deliquescent† in the mountain air, and Ampan stops and listens. A small bird flits briefly past, there's a gentle buzz of insects, another bird calls, the music comes to a gentle close. The world turns . . . tangibly enhanced by a man, his piano and an elephant.

---

* This one is called Ampan, and is only blind in one eye.

† Word provided by Susan Metcalfe. Its general meaning is 'melting away'.

HAVING AN ALLOTMENT

1,500

Subject provided by Andrew Osborne

It's an incomparable feeling. A sense of satisfaction and achievement born only of my own hard work and dedication. When I think about the state of the place when I took it over, it's hardly possible to believe the transformation. And I did it. All by myself. Nobody else. Definitely not. Well done me.

Ahem.

There have been myriad difficulties along the way. The incalculable* amounts of digging, for starters – anyone who's had to deal with claggy London clay will be able to tell you what back-breaking work that is. And when you take over a neglected plot, you inherit all manner of other things to deal with. There's the weeding. The constant weeding. Turn my back for a second and there they are, taking hard-won nutrients from deserving recipients. The previous incumbent was less than rigorous in their weed control, despite the Association's immutable rule about 75 per cent cultivation, so there were some well-established

* Word provided by Lesley Cookman.

nuisances to deal with: mare's tail and couch grass and creeping shiteweed,* all painstakingly dug out, as far as was practical. Pernicious, that's the word. Botanical vermin.

AHEM.

Then there were the stones. Soil riddled with stones and pebbles of all sizes. Not to mention bits of pottery, glass, plastic, nuts and bolts and much more – all of it has to be removed to improve the soil, to make it suitable for cultivating crops. What you're after is what is known as 'fine tilth'† – with some soil you're never really going to get there, and at best it feels like two paces forward and one pace back, but you have to keep doing it, constantly maintaining and monitor—

OI! ARSEHOLE!

I recognise that voice. Yet somehow I don't recognise it. You're not my Inner Pedant any more, are you?

Far, far from it.

Then who are you?

I'm your Inner Ethics Monitor.

You sound like fun.

Depends on what you mean by fun.

What can I do for you?

Stop lying.

Hmm?

'MY own hard work?'

Shush.

You haven't been up there in six months, and that was to pick some raspberries because Tessa was ill.

---

* Not an actual weed.

† What a magnificent word 'tilth' is. I only recently discovered the obvious fact that it's derived from 'till', as in 'tilling the soil'.

Look, nobody said this was going to be a work of pure fact. We have to allow for some writerly invention.

When you say 'invention', you mean 'lies'.

Oh, well, if you're going to quibble . . .

You going to give her credit at any stage?

Look, you're ruining this, you know.

How so?

I was building up to a big reveal.

What do you mean?

I was going to do a whole thing about what hard work *my* allotment has been, and how rewarding it's been to see the fruit of *my* endeavours, and to see all that produce coming up from the ground and knowing it's a result of what I did. I had a big spiel about how much I've learned about gardening and horticulture, and how it goes to prove that you can take things up at any time of life and learn about them and how jolly it all is, and then, right at the end, I was going to do the big reveal – TA-DAAAA! – it wasn't me, it was my wonderful wife who haz all da grdnng skillz.

'Haz'? 'Grdnng'? 'SKILLZ'?

I might have edited it.

I am not impressed. This is my 'not impressed' face.

OK then. May I continue?

If you insist.

I've lost my flow now. Might have to start over.

My sympathy, frankly, is limited.

Pfft.

There's a little shed on one corner. It's just about big enough, in theory, for one person to shelter from the rain, although you'd have to ask the hoes, rakes and spades to budge up a bit. Running along one of the outside walls is a bench, sheltered by a small overhang, so you can sit and pour a cup of tea from the thermos and maybe put your feet up on the lid of the compost box and listen to the robin singing behind you and look at the signs of growth all around. One last crop of winter vegetables – leeks, parsnips, fennel – ready for harvesting; broad beans, garlic and purple sprouting broccoli nudging their way gradually through; apple blossom beginning to show on the gnarly, stunted branches, although what fruit it might yield later in the year will be best left for the birds. A few more weeks yet.

The view alone would be worth it. The plot is on a hill, affording (as an estate agent might say) a delightful and unimpeded view of London. It might be an illusion, but the air feels clearer here, an impression only enhanced by the exercise. You could almost believe you weren't in a city, were it not for the low background hum.

A green woodpecker gives its laughing call from the trees off to the left. A blackbird hops along the fringes of the neighbouring plot, then, spooked by agent unknown, lifts its skirts and quickens its stride before taking to the air in a flurry of alarm, *sk-skli-skli-pli-pli-pleee*. It'll know where the apples are when the time comes. It'll be welcome to them.

It's blustery today, the low clouds scudding across the sky, the possibility of a light shower in the air. And there's a chill, too, early spring still very much wearing its winter undershirt. Best not to sit around; best to keep active.

I tidy, I weed, I pick some stones from the asparagus bed, unload a bag of compost onto an empty section of the plot and nudge it around until it's evenly spread and satisfyingly neat-looking, ready for whatever Tessa decides will be planted there.

All my own work? Nothing like. I can barely even say I lend a hand. This visit is a rarity, the latest in a series of aborted attempts to incorporate the allotment into my life. Perhaps, if I weren't married to a proper gardener, I'd find the will to do all this myself.

No. Stop kidding yourself.

The division of labour works well, a Mr-and-Mrs-Sprat-like arrangement of growing and cooking, fork to table. Tessa – patient, outdoorsy, a garden professional – digs and hoes and plants and sows and brings back produce by the bucketload. A cornucopia* of potatoes and carrots and parsnips and fennel and tomatoes and lettuce and beans and peas and leeks and radishes and spinach and chard and courgettes and broccoli and garlic and onions and asparagus – ah, asparagus! – and plenty more besides.

Meanwhile I, much more comfortable in the kitchen than with soil under my fingers, use the seasonal gluts as opportunities to experiment. This grilled with that, and that roasted with the other, and still a fridge-load left over for soup.

And sometimes, just sometimes, I make my way down the hill and along the high street and across the South Circular and up the hill to see if I can be of use. It does me good; I should do it more often. Just to be in a place devoted to growth is cheering enough, but there's an extra fascination with allotments that you wouldn't get on a farm† – the

---

* Word provided, as was the subject, by Andrew Osborne.
† In the interest of balance, I also like a good farm.

patchwork nature of these places, each little area personalised, bearing the imprint of those who work on it. Plots organised to within an inch of their lives, everything regimented and labelled and ushered into life with meticulous care; plots devoted to just one or two crops, mixed willy-nilly and left to their own devices; plots with trees; plots with flowers; plots running wild, the upkeep too much for the leasers to whom it seemed such a good idea at the time; plots that look as if nothing nourishing could ever be grown on them, yet somehow yield multitudes year upon year.

Next to ours, a messy one, for a long time looked after by Jocelyn. He was old, slowing down, his feet causing him gyp. His lease of the plot pre-dated the middle-class resurgence in interest in allotments by several decades. Every day he came on the bus from Brixton and did what his ageing body allowed, kept going by his contribution to the cycle of life, by the routine, by force of habit.

Not for Jocelyn the neat division of his plot into identical and symmetrical rectangles. He grew potatoes, corn, cabbages, strewn every which way. And the vegetables loved him, coming up in throngs, fending off the competition to grow big and full and copious.

And then one day he walked across the path and held his hand out and said this would be his last day because his feet couldn't do it any more and then he put on his cap and said goodbye and shuffled down the hill to the gate and went.

CRICKET CLOTHING THROUGH THE AGES

1,400

Subject provided by George Carbutt

'Tradition ist Schlamperei!'

The words, allegedly, of Gustav Mahler. I say 'allegedly' because I doubt whether that legendary purveyor of the lengthy* was capable of such brevity and pith, but there is plentiful evidence that he at least said something like it.

It means, incidentally, 'Tradition is sloppiness!', and while it was aimed at nineteenth-century Austrian opera houses, and not the global cricket community, I'm nonetheless going to use it as a starting point for this piece. Because he was right. Blind adherence to tradition 'just because' is lazy. 'It's always been done this way' is the argument you offer when you have no others. It also ignores the possibility that the tradition was started by someone making it up as they went along, who might have done it differently if given another chance.

In Mahler's case, he was railing against the lackadaisical habit of trotting out the same tired old opera productions

* You can play Sibelius's last three symphonies in the time it takes to play Mahler's third and still have time left over for a Dvořák tone poem.

year after year, each version more moribund and barnacle-encrusted than the last. The audiences might have enjoyed them – this is often the way when you serve up something comfortably familiar and unchallenging – but nobody could ever have accused them of pointing the way towards new and exciting musical directions; unlike Mahler, whose music took the symphonic form into new realms of sophistication and harmonic advancement.*

I don't know if Kerry Packer was a Mahler fan. Doubtful, somehow. The Australian business tycoon strikes me as more of a Schoenberg kind of guy.† But he might have agreed with the gaunt Austro-Bohemian symphonist‡ about tradition. Packer, in the world of cricket at least, was a disrupter, and in the 1970s he released a lean and hungry cat into a straggling flock of hitherto happily foraging pigeons. In this analogy, the pigeons are played by the international cricketing establishment, while the cat is represented by Packer's brainchild and bane of traditionalists everywhere, World Series Cricket.

There were many things about World Series Cricket that had retired majors in Tunbridge Wells snorting into their pink gins: it subverted the established hierarchy; the players, lured from their national contracts with what back then seemed like obscenely large amounts of money, were for the

* And, but do stop me if I've said this before, length.

† I've just had a blinding vision: Kerry Packer expounding to a bewildered audience on the virtues of Schoenberg's twelve-tone masterpiece, *Variations for Orchestra*. It's compelling, and will leave my cerebral cortex unwillingly, if at all.

‡ Another image has sprung up: Gustav Mahler looking on, nonplussed, as a medallioned and moustachioed Dennis Lillee sprints in to bowl to an implacable gum-chewing Viv Richards. No more coffee for me today.

first time paid decently; and – gasp! stagger! reel! – they wore coloured clothing.

It went against everything cricket stood for. The vulgarity of it, expecting to be paid a wage concomitant with the international status of the sport – good Lord, wasn't the privilege of being chosen to represent your country enough? Dammit, man, if I'd been selected for England I'd have forked out double the match fee and laid on the teas meself, dontcha know, wot?*

And as for the clothing – cricket is traditionally played in whites, always has been. Everyone knows that.

Absolutely. Except it isn't, it hasn't, and they don't. Apart from that you're spot on.

Go all the way back to the 1760s. Cricket has been around for a while, the players' attire varying according to personal whim. Some precepts, though, seem to have been established. A portrait, *The Young Cricketer*, by Francis Cotes, dating from 1768, shows a dashing young blade in confident pose, one hand on hip, the other holding a cricket bat to the ground at an angle somewhere between jaunty and rakish. His frilled shirt is open to the chest, billowing sleeves bunched at the wrist, the left leg of his breeches casually unbuttoned and turned up to expose a few arrogant inches of upper-class knee. Both breeches and waistcoat are of a resplendent emerald satin. Black shoes with a gold buckle complete the ensemble, the whole embellished with an entitled gaze into the middle distance. He looks to me like the kind of player who would irritate teammates and opposition alike – he would swipe a studiedly careless

* A Tunbridge-Wellsian writes.

30-odd, run his partner out and then refuse to do umpiring duty, all the while treating those around him with cynical disdain. Then at tea he would take all the egg mayonnaise sandwiches and four Mini Rolls, leaving everyone else to scavenge for fish paste and Rich Tea.

But maybe I'm judging him on scant evidence. What we do see from this and other contemporary artworks is that there was no fixed cricketing dress code – prevailing fashion, certainly, but no rules.

So how did cricket get from 'wear what you like' to 'all-white clothing only, please'?

Gradually.

There was no sudden edict, no laying down of the law from on high. Over the next century each element of the cricketer's garb was subject to incremental change: the tricornes worn by many (but not our privileged young friend) gave way to top hats, and then to softer, fuller, flannel caps; breeches yielded to long trousers; shirts became less frilly and more high-collared; short white jackets began to appear; spreading bow ties were worn, and belts with metal clasps; wide braces were popular among the burgeoning population of professional cricketers; black Oxford shoes were the norm.

Fashion, in short, held as much sway on the cricket field as off it. But still there was no uniformity.

It was only with the continued growth of the game into the Victorian era that there was some attempt to imprint corporate identities on the many emerging clubs of that age.

Hambledon, the great Hampshire club of the late eighteenth century, were the first, the buttons of their sky-blue coats engraved with the letters 'CC'. Marylebone Cricket

Club, self-appointed arbiters of the game to this day, opted for coats of a darker blue. I Zingari, one of the first nomadic clubs, took it a stage further in the 1850s, establishing their own club colours of black, red and yellow – these were worn as ribbons round the white bowler hats that were coming into fashion as the headgear of choice. From there, coloured caps became standard, while some clubs chose the shirt as their identifying feature, like the All-England XI and their white shirts with pink spots.

It wasn't until the very end of the Victorian era, with the spread of the professional game, that white clothes became universal. And so it stayed until Mr Packer's brave new tradition-busting world of razzmatazz, with its dangerous innovations, a lot of which have remained central to the game to this day. Coloured clothing wasn't necessary to differentiate the sides in the field – the fielding side are the ones without the bats – but just an effort to rid the game of some of the fustiness in which it had become shrouded. *Tradition ist Schlamperei*, after all, and Packer wanted young people and women to be drawn to the game. He also liked tweaking the tail of the establishment. Cricket is, by and large, a conservative game.* Traditionalists hold sway, eyeing novelty with suspicion. To be fair to them, some of the outfits in those early years of 'pyjama cricket' – the new brand of one-day cricket spawned by Packer's brave new world – were utterly egregious. It was, after all, the 1970s. Google 'New Zealand ODI kit' if you don't believe me – a monstrosity of beige and taupe to test the hardiest stomach.

* The aforementioned MCC finally allowed women to join their number in 1998. 1998. Ye gods.

What the traditionalists fail to appreciate is that, contrary to what they believe, cricket has never been set in stone. From its origins as a betting game to the present day, it's undergone change: from two stumps to three; curved bats to straight; underarm bowling to overarm;* constant tweaking of Laws and playing conditions; coloured clothes to whites and back again – flexibility has always been at the game's heart, allowing it to adapt and survive.

Just don't tell Major Tunbridge-Wells – it might finish him off.

* All these expressions, and more, will be utterly incomprehensible to the uninitiated. Sorry about that.

CHINESE WHISPERS

1,300

Subject provided by Stuart Hancock

Let's play a game of Chinese Whispers.

Stop right there.

What?

Racist.

Sorry, what?

Chinese Whispers is a racist term. Don't use it – you'll offend people.

Umm . . .

No, it's true: the internet said so.

Ah.

What do you mean ah?

Well . . . the thing is . . . it isn't racist.

Yes it is. What are you, some kind of fasc—

Please don't.

Well, anyway.

Right. Let's walk this back, shall we?

There's a game, often played at children's parties. It's based on the premise that messages get gradually garbled in multiple repeatings, so the final version is some way from the original. An example is: 'We're going to advance – send reinforcements,' which hilariously turns into: 'We're going to a dance – send three and fourpence.'

That's funny!

Yes. Now then. Depending on where and when you grew up, you might know this game as Telephone, Broken Telephone, Operator, Grapevine, Gossip, Secret Message, Don't Drink the Milk, Whisper Down the Lane, Russian Scandal or Chinese Whispers. North Americans seem to have favoured one of the telephone ones; if, like me, your early years were spent in Britain in the 1970s, it will have been Chinese Whispers.

With you so far.

Good. Now here's where it gets a bit tricky, because whether the term is deemed racist or not must surely depend partly on its provenance. Nobody reasonable will be offended if you ask them to dance an American Smooth or eat a Greek salad, or tell them you play the French horn.

I don't know about that. The French horn can sound pretty ropey.

Don't be mean. It's commonly thought to be among the most difficult instruments to master. Have you ever tried blowing through a tightly wound twenty-foot-long brass tube? No you have not, so shush.

Anyway, back to racism. You've heard the term 'to have a paddy', yes?

Yes.

Well, maybe think before you use it. Underlying this apparently harmless phrase is the inherent assumption that Irish people are prone to fits of violent temper. So yes, it's pretty racist, especially as it came into common parlance in England, whose record vis-à-vis relations with their

Hibernian neighbours has historically been more than somewhat . . . ahem.

Ahem?

Ahem. Meaning 'let's not go there'.

To Ireland?

Stop it. Similarly, look at a term like 'welshing* on a bet'. Pretty derogatory, right? The English considered Welsh people so untrustworthy, so likely to renege on deals, that they gave them their very own verb.

Really?

No.

Damn you.

Quite. It's often assumed that the expression is offensive to the Welsh, but an alternative derivation is that it refers to the practice of English bookmakers who, when England and Wales had separate legal systems, would hop over the border to avoid paying out on losing bets.

So it's rude about the English?

It depends which derivation you choose to believe, but there is certainly uncertainty.

How confusing.

Indeed.

Ooh what about 'to scotch a rumour?' I bet that originates from something rude about Scottish people.

No such luck. It comes from a Middle English word, *scocchen*, meaning to score, gash, or make an incision.

Oh.

Sorry.

---

* Or 'welching' – both spellings pertain.

Nevertheless, none of this is painting the English in a good light, is it?

The English part of me is dismayed to admit it; the Armenian part, on the other hand, is perfectly happy to do so.

Armenian? Aren't they supposed to be a bit—

I'd definitely stop there if I were you.

Good idea.

So, what about Chinese Whispers?

I don't know. I'm just desperately tiptoeing on the eggshells of intercultural sensitivity and trying to stop myself from falling into the foetid cesspit below, to be devoured by the self-appointed everything-ist police. Cut me some slack.

As you wish. The expression 'Chinese Whispers' is said to derive from the first encounters between Europeans and the Chinese in the seventeenth century, an occasion that might reasonably be assumed to have been fraught with mutual incomprehension.

Eh?

They didn't understand each other.

Ah.

Now, it's quite a leap from 'we don't understand what they're saying' (really not racist) to 'we don't understand what they're saying, *therefore they're stupid*' (really quite obviously racist), but that's what some people understand as the underlying implication of the term. And, given the long history of the English denigrating pretty much everyone who didn't have the luck to be born among their number, those people might have a point.

But at the most basic level, is it really denigrating the

Chinese to suggest that their language* is incomprehensible to the English? And, I might add, vice versa?

At this stage I feel like crawling into a corner and never saying anything to anyone ever again. It's a can of worms. Is that vermiphobic? Oh God.

Calm down.

Don't think I can.

Would it help if I said that in a rigorously scientific poll† with a large sample size,‡ the general feeling was 'No, it's not racist, but I'm not going to say it just in case', which only goes to show how careful we have to be not to be too readily offended on other people's behalf. It's that desperate tiptoeing thing you said earlier.

What did the Chinese people say?

Interestingly, neither of them was at all offended, possibly because they've been on the receiving end of much worse. Mind you, I'll be the first to admit it wasn't a representative sample.

So what's your point?

Only that things are more complex and nuanced than the binary and combative nature of modern public discourse would lead you to believe. Also that there's a danger we'll use up our outrage on small things, and so have none left for the truly venal.

I mean, yes of course we should consider the feelings of others, and yes of course we should listen when people say

---

* OK, languages. The slightly inconvenient truth that China has two official languages, plus a host of other indigenous ones, might undermine my point a tidge.

† On Facebook, yes I know.

‡ OK, forty people, but two of them are of Chinese descent (even though one of them's never been to China. Leave me alone).

they're hurt by our words and deeds, and yes of course we should apologise if necessary and make a conscious decision to do better in future, and yes of course – and especially those of us from countries with a history of wholesale insensitivity towards people they considered inferior or worthless – we should examine our behaviour and attitude towards other cultures, and better understand our place in an ever-changing society and how we're seen by the many millions whose world view might differ either slightly or radically from our own.

Yes, of course.

But what?

I forget.

Oh dear.

No, hang on, it's this. It is, quite literally, the thought that counts. If we think, after careful consideration, that the term 'Chinese Whispers' isn't racist, that doesn't turn us into a rug-chewing, mouth-foaming EDL-supporter. Just as if we decide after extensive thought that it *is* racist, or at least it could be considered by a reasonable person to be so, and we'll therefore choose not to use it in future, that doesn't make us a lily-livered tree-hugging lefty snowflake.

Wow. You got on one there.

I did.

Anyway, to summarise: has there been a history of casual racism towards Chinese people? You betcha. Is this an example of it? Debatable. Is it, in light of some of the very real, terrifying and virulent racism knocking about the place these days, terribly offensive and to be avoided at all costs? Not in my book.

Now, legs splayed again – try these wee spurs.

Sorry what?

Lev's flayed a gay, knob-shy knee wrist burrs.

Fuxake speak up, will you?

Listen up, cloth-ears. I said, 'Let's play a game of Chinese Whispers.'

POOPS

1,200

Subject provided by Susie and Mei Harries

We all remember our childhood pets. Cats, dogs, guinea pigs, bunny* rabbits, goldfish, stick insects, cobras, whatever. They were our constant friends and companions, offering solace in hard times, even if all they contributed to proceedings was to swim around their bowl forgetting things.

You wouldn't necessarily call the series of goldfish I won at Thame Fair over a few years in the early 1970s 'constant companions', though. They rarely lasted long enough for that. The only one I remember with any specificity was called Harpo. Harpo had big, bulgy eyes that seemed to go in different directions. I immediately loved him† and took him home in the plastic bag provided and decanted him into the fish tank where I fed him from the little pot of fish food and watched in fascination as long ribbons of poo came out of him and floated in the water, and then just a

---

* Word provided by Seta White.

† I assumed it was a 'him' because he reminded me of Harpo Marx and Harpo Marx was a 'him', but obviously he might equally have been a 'her' for all I know, which is barely anything.

few days later I came home and it was Harpo who was floating, and that was that for Harpo, and I learned a bit more about life and death.

I assume I formed a closer attachment to Tig, the little tiger cat brought with us from London to the new house in the country. But I was very young, and Tig was very old, and the only thing that really lives on in my memory is a photo of him lying on a chair in the sunshine looking Tiggish. Of the physical reality of him, no memories endure.

But most of all there was Poops.

Poops was a most excellent dog: glorious and stupid and loyal. He was the same age as me, so we grew up together, and had, so I liked to think, a special bond. I have, in an album, a photo of us together. We're on the lawn. I'm sitting – at that age, about nine months, it was all I could do except roll around on my back – and he's nuzzling my chin. At least that's what it looks like. He might have been slobbering all over my face or about to mount a full-on attack. In any case, on my face is an expression of pure babyish pleasure, mixed with a tinge of 'not sure this fur tastes very nice actually, now I come to think of it'.

Opinions vary about the right size for a dog. Some go for galumphing Great Danes, while others prefer what Eddie Izzard calls 'small yappy-type dogs'. Poops, I maintain, was the perfect size, especially for a child. Big enough to grab hold of and give a proper schnuzzle, but not intimidating. And, well-behaved dog that he was,* he endured my regular hugs and cuddles with forbearance.

---

* All dog owners – ALL of them – think their dog is well behaved, just as all parents think their child is 'just above average'. But Poops really was.

He was the kind of dog that makes you say, 'Oh yes, you'll do,' and, 'Now THAT'S a dog,' and, 'Get down, there's a good chap. I said GET DOWN.' The kind of dog, in short, who makes you realise how good dogs can be. Like all proper dogs he had the ability to eat all the table scraps and then look at you with the 'Oh no, I haven't eaten anything, please give me some scraps – why haven't I had any food in, like, for ever?' eyes that are the stock-in-trade of any great dog.

A cross between a Norwegian elkhound and a Border collie, he retained vestigial instincts of both those fine breeds, occasionally embarking on long trots round the garden while intuitively looking out for sheep. Had he ever encountered a flock of them, I suspect they would have treated him with all the disdain they could muster.

Poops wasn't a dog to do things by halves. He didn't go in much for chasing rabbits, but when he did, the rabbit stayed well and truly chased. Never caught, just chased. In moulting season, like a dynamo, he was able to bring forth endless swathes of thick, dark fur, which swept across the kitchen floor like tumbleweed across a prairie. And when it came to matters of the heart, he didn't restrict his affections to the postman's leg. When one of the village bitches came in heat, Poops was as horny as Harold the Horny Hunter – who, as all *Blackadder* fans will know, had an enormous horn. My parents tried to keep him confined to barracks for those few days, but he howled and whined and tried to chew his way through the bottom of the gate, so my father eventually succumbed, opened the gate, and sent him on his way with a quiet 'and the best of British luck to you.'

You might be wondering about the name. It's easily

enough explained. He came as part of a pair, and my brother, four years older than me, was tasked with their naming. Linking, as is the way with four-year-olds, two alien concepts on the basis of their quasi-homophony, he proudly announced that they would be called 'Nincompoops' and 'Nincome Tax'.

Poops and Tax they remained.

But while Poops was soft and generous and could be trusted to treat me with appropriate gentleness, Tax's rough-and-tumble modus operandi got a bit much, so he was farmed out to a home whose inhabitants were less susceptible to the terrors of an overly enthusiastic puppy. Familiar with Poops's rambunctiousness, I sometimes wondered just how energetic Tax could have been for Poops to be the less rowdy of the two.

Eventually, as it tends to, the time came.

By the age of twelve my understanding of death had developed since Harpo, and, generally unobservant though I was about many things, even I could tell something was up. Nothing was said, but I noticed a gradual withdrawal in Poops, a slowing down, a shrinking. The cuddles I liked to give him when I got home from school were less willingly received, the bound in his gait diminished, his hitherto undimmable eagerness subdued. I have a memory of seeing him walking across the lawn, the pain clear in his every move, and in some obscure way knowing there wasn't long left.

My mother picked me up from school one day with her serious face on, prepared, no doubt, to cope with my devastation. It was a delicate situation. She knew how devoted I was to Poops.

There was a short silence, speaking volumes. She prepared me for the worst in time-honoured fashion.

'I've got a bit of bad news.'

I might have nodded.

'It's about Poops.'

No tears. No devastation. I merely turned and said, in a knowing, world-weary voice, 'Had him put down, have you?'

And that was that. I stared out of the window all the way home, upset beyond endurance but desperate to show how much I understood about the world, and equally desperate not to show anyone how much it meant to me.

THE BASSOONS IN MY LIFE

1,100

Subject provided by Jonathan Burton

An orchestra contains multitudes. Violinists – pale, sensitive flowers eating cheese sandwiches out of Tupperware; horn players – cocky, bold, no stranger to the bottle; double bassists – large, avuncular types, phlegmatic, used to being taken for granted; percussionists – people who, as per the old joke, hang around musicians; harpists – fey and ladylike and inevitably driving a Volvo; trumpeters – curry and beer with a side order of beer and curry.

Stereotypes, all of them. Unkind, unfair and inaccurate.

Mostly. Maybe.

And then there are the woodwinds. Flutes, oboes, clarinets, bassoons.

You know the bassoon. Yes you do, even if you're not musical. I promise. It's the comedy one. It plays the riff in Perry Como's 'Magic Moments'; in *The Sorcerer's Apprentice*, by Paul Dukas – you know, the Mickey Mouse one in *Fantasia* – the bassoons are the ones who kick off the whole sorry episode, a trio of them rumty-tumty-ing away with jaunty and utterly misplaced confidence; and watch any *Carry On* film and there the bassoon will be on the soundtrack, resident pratfall accompanist at your service (along, naturally, with the descending *waa-waa-waa-waaaaa* of a comedy trombone).

Oh the japes, oh the merriment, oh how we laughed.

I blame composers. They can't help themselves. They know, cognitively, what the bassoon can do. They listen to the quality of its sound when played lyrically – a unique blend of warm, mellifluous* and plaintive; they are aware of its range: from the depths, where the sound has a gruff edge and the potential for menace, to the heights, where the strained, mournful voice can express perhaps better than any other instrument the loneliness and torment of the human soul.

And then they write 'rumty-tumty, here comes Charles Hawtrey, and Jim Dale's about to put his foot in a bucket' anyway.

But here's the thing. You won't hear a bassoonist complaining. No matter how put upon, how betrayed by the vagaries of the instrument, how frustrated with the reed (you should hear bassoonists on the subject of reeds – or, rather, you shouldn't), there will be little more than a slight shrug of one shoulder, a waggle of the bocal,† and then they'll have another go. It's an approach to life forced upon them by the particular qualities of the instrument. You can prepare all you like, minimising the risk of disaster as far as possible, and then a key will stop working, or a reed will fail, or there will be a terrifying and exposed solo for which you must, absolutely must, be given a broad, accommodating upbeat, preferably accompanied by a generous smile

* Word provided by Linda Trill.

† That's the curved metal bit that joins mouth to instrument.

of sympathy and encouragement, and the conductor will acknowledge it by ignoring you completely and giving an imperceptible waggle in the general direction of the cellos instead.

Such is life.

The bassoons, make no mistake, are the linchpin of the woodwind section, the rock upon which success is founded. We can all thrill to the smooth melodious outpourings of a clarinet, the fluttering charm of a flute, the plangent skirl of an oboe, but where would they be without the bassoons? Yeah, that's right. Nowhere.

You just try building a woodwind chord on an out-of-tune second bassoon; you just try playing anything in the orchestral repertoire without a reliable principal bassoon, the proverbial 'safe pair of hands'; you just try playing Brahms's First, Third or Fourth symphonies* with a dodgy or weedy contrabassoon.

You just try it.† Go on, I dare you.

Bassoonists aren't showy types. They are, for the most part, quiet, undemonstrative, phlegmatic, not naturally disposed to pushing themselves centre stage. You're unlikely to see a bassoonist set their instrument to one side, spring to the front of the stage and attempt to break the world record for the number of botafogos‡ executed in thirty seconds. Bassoon solos are less common in orchestral music than solos for any of its woodwindy colleagues, and

* In the Second Symphony he went with a tuba for that lower-end oomph.

† More anaphora. Blame Bernard Hughes.

‡ Word provided by Louise Shield. It's a dance move named after a neighbourhood in Rio de Janeiro, as any watcher of *Strictly Come Dancing* will already know.

while Vivaldi wrote enough concertos for the instrument to keep even the most fanatical bassoon enthusiast* satisfied for a few months, the imbalance between that and the number of violin concertos he wrote is indicative of the prevailing ratio in the repertoire as a whole. The bassoon is, mostly, an engine-room instrument: quietly doing the job, getting on with it without any fuss – don't mind us, we'll be fine.

Which isn't to say they don't enjoy their moments in the limelight. The orchestral bassoon solo, when it does turn up, is a thing to be savoured. Three precipitous bars in the last movement of Beethoven's Fourth Symphony (often taken too fast by headstrong conductors, to the chagrin of the poor bassoonist who has to negotiate twenty-five notes in the twinkling of an eye, for which the instrument isn't really designed); Ravel's *Piano Concerto* (the whole piece is a woodwinder's nightmare – Maurice, old chum, what were you thinking?); and perhaps the most famous of all, the beginning of Stravinsky's *Rite of Spring* (modern bassoonists, familiar with its pitfalls, often make it seem easier than it actually is).

A personal favourite is the extended solo in the first movement of Sibelius's Fifth Symphony, against a backdrop of scrabbling and scurrying strings, like insects in a horror movie. It's marked *patetico*, which on the one hand brings to mind Eeyore's self-reproachful 'pathetic, that's what it is – pathetic', but is also the perfect word for the haunting desolation Sibelius conjures, as is his wont, with the meagrest of musical materials. It's the perfect antidote to rumty-tumty.

---

* Word supplied by Marc Dooley.

Finally, if you want to see a bassoonist blanch, mention Tchaikovsky's Sixth Symphony – four descending notes of bassoony doom, marked (completely unfeasibly – Pyotr Ilyich, old chum, what were you thinking?) *pppppp*.* Standard procedure is to hand this treacherous corner to the bass clarinet, an instrument for which those levels of quasi-silence come more naturally. In extremis, the player will simply hum the notes down their bocal, a sleight of mouth designed to hoodwink the listener into thinking you have magical powers, and which, more than anything, sums up the most admirable qualities of these most underappreciated of musicians.

Just don't ask them to play the rumty-tumty bits.

* Non-musicians: *p* means quiet, *pp* means very quiet, *ppp* means as quiet as you dare – I'm sure you can work it out from there.

JACK HARGREAVES

1,000

Subject provided by Scott Pack

A benign, friendly man, standing in a shed, talking to camera. White beard, glasses, flat cap. Behind him, tools hang in a way that tells you this is a real shed, not a studio. Next to him, what looks like a metal shepherd's crook.

The voice is low and gentle, rich with gravelly warmth.

'That yard of curly iron bar is a symbol of a dying culture, one of the rich, small cultures which are giving way, all the way from the Amazonians to the Eskimos, giving way . . . '

At this point you feel a thought has entered his head unbidden. He's deciding whether to give it voice.

'. . . before a tide of . . . '

And now a note of contempt undermines the geniality.

'. . . denim and plastic and microchips and sparking plugs and frozen snacks.'

The disdain with which he says 'frozen snacks'. I like that.

To me, he was the old one – white hair, white beard, pipe in mouth, a quiet avuncular smile at the ready as he explained how to put a ship in a bottle or how to boil water without heat or how to make a pear cut itself in half.* The other presenters of *How* – an informative children's programme which will be at least half familiar to anyone who grew up in the 1970s – were various shades of eager,† but somehow the old one with the beard and the pipe drew you in without reaching out and trying to grab you. He just talked, knowing you'd listen. To a child, he had the air of a grandfather, the type who would take you to one side at Christmas and show you a trick with three matchsticks, a feather and a threepenny bit, and then tell you an interesting fact about the Saxons.

He did it for adults, too, on the programmes *Out of Town* and *Old Country*, talking every week for twenty-five years without script or notes, as informally as if you were sitting with him in the Nadger's Arms over a pint of Old Scrofular. He talked about fishing and goats and cider-making and walking sticks and paraffin lamps and dray horses and fishing rods and cart-building and blacksmiths and wheelwrights and a thousand other things of the countryside – a world that became increasingly unfamiliar during the run of the shows from the 1960s to the 1980s, and is utterly alien now.

How boring it could have been in the wrong hands: an unwanted lecture delivered either with too much effort – all flappy hands and overexcitement – or in a stiff, droning monotone, a series of facts underpinned by tedious sentimentality at the loss of a bygone age and bitterness at the ways of the modern world.

* Fold the ship, take the water to where the air is thin, and drop the pear from height onto a knife.

† In case, like me, you struggle to remember their names, they were Fred Dinenage, Bunty James and Jon Miller. You're welcome.

But Hargreaves avoided that, communicating merely love for the countryside and deep knowledge of its ways and traditions. And his understated method of delivery took the camera out of the equation.

'I just took no notice of it. People try so hard, don't they? They stare at the camera all the time, always rehearse until they get it right. But when you talk to one another, you don't get it right, do you? So I didn't bother.'

He was being disingenuous, of course. That easy manner, the comfort with the camera, the way he had of telling a story as if remembering it as he went along, the absence of annoying tics, you knows, I means and umms – they had nothing to do with not bothering, and everything to do with professionalism. And if it seemed as though he was talking directly to you, it was not just his naturally engaging personality – although that helped – but technique, learned early in his career and entrenched through years of experience. His gentle musings were underpinned by a wide knowledge of history and geography and folklore and life in general, all worn as lightly as his trademark battered hat.

So that was Jack Hargreaves. A countryman through and through, fascinated with the ways of the past and the countryside, and helping generations of viewers to understand it, appreciate it, see it more clearly.

Except it wasn't. Not completely.

Because the same Jack Hargreaves, who walked the pony up the lane and knew how to tickle a trout and which way a hare would run when chased by hounds, who yarned about gipsies and blacksmiths and gamekeepers – that gentle old Jack Hargreaves, before he started appearing in the country's sitting rooms in the early 1960s, had already had a wide-ranging career.

Early ambitions to be a vet were thwarted by the collapse of the wool trade, meaning his father could no longer support his studies. Ever adaptable, Jack quickly found work as an advertising copywriter, and then as an astute radio producer, responsible for over eighty shows a week as head of Universal Programmes Productions with the Independent Broadcasting Company. The war years saw him rise quickly through the ranks of the Royal Artillery, before officer training at Sandhurst and a role on Field Marshal Montgomery's staff as part of the propaganda team for the Allies in the lead-up to D-Day. And in the 1950s he was a successful journalist – editor of legendary magazines *Liliput* and *Picture Post* – as well as director of communications for the National Farmers Union, before making the switch to television as presenter, programme maker and assistant programme controller.

No country bumpkin he. On the contrary, despite his countryman image, he was as cosmopolitan as any townie. The Jack Hargreaves of pipe and pint and fishing tackle was in part a self-invention, the public face of a shrewd man who knew what people liked. And if he was frustrated by throwaway culture, by the growing divide between humans and the natural world, he was merely decades ahead of his time.

A SCAR

900

Subject provided by Giles Wade

Scars would tell their stories, if they could. Stories of pain and trauma, long distant but never fully healed.

I have two of note, both relatively mundane. When I was ten, a mole on my chest threatened to go rogue, so they lopped it off with, as it transpired, spectacular incompetence. There's no associated pain or trauma, just an unnecessary blemish.

My other notable scar has a slightly more exciting provenance. The year after the mole, at the climax of a particularly tense game of cricket, I dropped a crucial catch. Had I held on to it, I would have been carried off the ground on the shoulders of my teammates. There might have been some sort of celebratory feast in my honour, a plaque, even a public holiday.* As it was, I was taken to the sick room, blood dripping from the webbing between the fourth and little fingers of my left hand. The game was won in my absence – pretty much the story of my sporting childhood – and if that all feels a bit Charlie Brown, then that's about

* Can a man not dream?

right. Allow your heart to bleed just a bit for that lonely eleven-year-old. Thanks.

I could spin either of those stories out to fill the requested 900 words, but really there's little more to them than what I've just told you, so I'll tell a different one. It starts with Goethe and ends with a limpet.

I've always wanted to be a polymath. It sounds like a crazy, freewheeling way to live. What shall I do today? I have so many talents! Perhaps some poetry in the morning, then a spot of post-lunch taphonomy,* then I'll write a cantata with my tea and crumpets before a merry evening of mayhem at the drawing board designing my latest cathedral and a touch of exploratory astronomy before bed.

Get good at loads of things and you might just become famous. And if you get famous enough, people start naming things after you.

That's exactly what happened to Johann Wolfgang von Goethe. Go to Germany and look about the place. Goethe schools, Goethe squares, Goethe streets, theatres, hotels, parks and museums. Less visible is goethite, an iron-bearing hydroxide mineral of the diaspore group found in soil and other low-temperature environments.† That such a substance should be named after a writer might seem random, but among the lad Johann's many interests was mineralogy – as I said, get famous enough and they start naming things after you.

---

* Word provided by Terry O'Connor. It's the study of how things decay and become fossilised.

† Thanks, Wikipedia.

Goethite is a fascinating substance. It's the main component of rust, and has long been used as brown-ochre paint pigment. Its relevance to this subject, though, lies in its strength. What you do is you take several million goethite nanofibres, embed them in a chitin base, and voilà! You have a substance with five times the tensile strength of spider's silk – not quite in the realm of carbon nanotubes,* but not far off. Handy if you're a gastropod wanting to scrape algae off rocks.

Hello, *Patella vulgata*, the common limpet.

You know limpets. If you've ever been at a rocky seashore you've seen them clinging to rocks. And if you've ever tried to pick one up, you'll know their routine. At the first touch they hunker down, sucking themselves against the rock with their muscular foot with such tenacity that, short of prising them off with a crowbar, you're not going to budge them. Once attached, they settle in for the long haul, rotating their shell, grinding it against the rock, and leaving an indentation in the shape of their body. This tight fit protects them from dehydration at low tide.

This much I knew. And I suppose I'd assumed they just stayed there, subsisting on, oh I don't know, bits of rock or candyfloss or crab pasties.

But of course they don't just stay there. What they do, once covered in water, is go roaming, rippling the aforementioned foot to propel themselves, and scraping algal slime off the rocks as they go with their goethite-strengthened teeth. The teeth reside in their radula, a ribbon-like organ which works like a conveyor belt, replacing the teeth as they wear

* Words provided by Matthew Longhurst.

out and moving the new ones to the front line. And whenever I read something like that I find myself wanting to jump up and shout, 'LISTEN, EVERYONE! NATURE! IT'S . . . I MEAN, JUST . . . LOOK AT IT!'

And then I remember that the limpet is, however distantly, our cousin, as indeed are the protists* off which they feed, and my head explodes just a bit. If you're not looking at nature in a permanent state of astonishment and awe, then something has gone seriously amiss. Which, I'm afraid, it has.

And the point of this limpety discursion?

Well, my favourite bit of the whole thing is that the limpet, rather than plonking itself where it lands at each change of the tide, is deeply territorial, always returning to its own indentation. And that indentation is called its 'home scar'. So while the scar might be traumatic for the rock, for the limpet it represents comfort, safety and homecoming. Which is just a lovely thing, and goes to show that not all scars are painful and traumatic.

Unless you're a rock.

* Word provided by John Bevan.

A BRIEF HISTORY OF THE KEIGHLEY AND WORTH VALLEY RAILWAY

800

Subject provided by Anna Whitaker

'Daddy! My daddy!'

Words guaranteed to bring a tear to the eye of anyone who has ever seen *The Railway Children*, and a blindingly obvious way to start this piece.

But I did it anyway.

I could have started with the Brontës, I suppose. Inextricably linked with the history of the area, the sisters were railway enthusiasts and investors in the North Midland Railway Co.* But by the time the line was built they had all died – the link is tangential at best.

The Railway Children, though, is at the heart of the line's enduring success. Released in 1970, two years after the reopening of the line, the film brought a boost in tourism that hasn't relented in the intervening fifty years. A decade earlier, the picture was bleak, the post-war decline of the

* An investment doomed to yield scant return, thanks to the volatility of the boom-and-bust economy surrounding the burgeoning railway industry.

railways resulting in the line's closure in 1961 as part of Dr Beeching's infamous cuts.

Almost immediately the Keighley and Worth Valley Railway Preservation Society was formed with the intention of buying it and opening it to the public, not just as a pleasure ride for tourists, but as a properly functioning part of the national railway network. It's thanks to them that the first ninety-five years of the line's history have been preserved and built on.

A railway between Hebden Bridge and Keighley was first mooted in 1845, at the height of Railway Mania. An advert was placed in the *Railway Times*, looking for £350,000 of subscription for the Manchester, Hebden Bridge and Keighley Junction Railway, running through Haworth and with a branch to Oakworth. This was never built, but in 1861, a scheme was launched which would lead, within six years, to the opening of the Keighley and Worth Valley Railway.

It was funded on the subscription model. The Worth Valley was a thriving area, and wealthy mill owners were keen to join the railway revolution, so 3,314 shares sold quickly, worth £310 each. The necessary Act of Parliament was passed the following year, and tenders were invited. Bradford man John Metcalfe (whose quote of £21,940. 7 s. 4 d. was the second cheapest) was chosen. Construction would take a year, they thought. This, predictably enough with the benefit of hindsight, was a woeful underestimate, as was the financial forecast. Three years after the cutting of the first sod in February 1864, and at a cost of £111,422, the line opened.

The construction wasn't without incident: quicksand oozed into the newly cut tunnel at Ingrow, and the remedial action caused severe damage to Wesley Place Methodist Church above; a storm shortly before the planned opening date washed away the embankment at Damems and caused a landslip at Haworth Station; a cow trampled all over the plans of two surveyors and destroyed their theodolite.

The dangers of construction are many, varied and unpredictable.

Despite the delays and extra costs, the line was an immediate success, and its popularity grew and grew through the end of the nineteenth century and into the twentieth. Six weekday services and two on Sundays in 1867 became twenty-two and six by the turn of the century. The next three decades were the heyday, thanks in no small part to the interest in the Brontës.

And then came the decline, exacerbated by service reductions in World War II, and accelerated by post-war competition from local buses and a drop in freight traffic.

Dr Beeching's work, unpopular and unwelcome as it was, was sadly inevitable.

We love a steam train. Never mind the dirt, the smell, the (whisper it softly) inefficiency – we love the romance of them, the nostalgia for an imaginary Better Time.

As you leave Keighley, you're already aware of something special – a 1:56 gradient, simple enough for a car, but quite a big deal for a steam locomotive trying to get traction on metal rails while pulling heavy carriages. And while it climbs, it turns sharply to the right, through ninety degrees before you know it. Then up through Ingrow, Damems (the smallest station in the UK), Oakworth, Haworth and finally Oxenhope – five miles and twenty-five minutes of pure nostalgia.

On the day of the grand opening in 1867, the first train, dignitaries and all, came to a standstill just over the River Worth, a victim of physics. The Little Train Who Couldn't.

But nowadays the trains definitely can, and do, thanks to the work of the people who, since 1968, have given their time and energy and expertise to keep those steam trains running so you and your family can take a journey into the past, chuff into the future, and stand on the platform of Oakworth Station and say, with tears in your eyes, 'Daddy! My daddy!'

MELANCHOLY

700

Subject provided by Laura Wright

There were four of them, back in the day. Blood, phlegm, yellow bile and black bile – Marvel superheroes manqué – the four temperaments central to Hippocrates's medical theory of humorism.* This idea – that a healthy body comprised these four fluids held in equilibrium, and that an imbalance of them was the cause of all manner of ailments – seems like quaint sciosophy† now, but it held sway for 2,000 years, only yielding to more advanced medical thinking in the seventeenth century. And the words – phlegmatic, choleric, sanguine, melancholic – remain in our vocabulary (some more than others) as describers of fundamental personality or outlook. Stolid and calm, passionate and irascible, confident and optimistic, mournful and gloomy. Pooh, Rabbit, Tigger, Eeyore.

'Black bile' (such a pungent image) is a direct translation from ancient Greek: *melaina chole*, and its description,

* Entirely unrelated, of course, to the four temperaments of music discussed earlier in the book.

† Word provided by Helen Ackroyd. It means something claiming to be knowledge but without basis in scientific fact.

given by Thomas Burton in *The Anatomy of Melancholy*, has something in common with what we would describe nowadays as depression: 'a compound mixed malady' – the implication being that its nature is not just mental, but physical and spiritual too. This certainly tallies with our modern understanding of depression as a clinical illness affecting the whole person, rather than a temporary state of mind. You could no more snap out of melancholy, in its old meaning, than you can snap out of a sprained ankle.

Once upon a time, melancholy had a certain romantic allure, an association with genius. A despondent artist in a garret, hitting the absinthe and producing purple-tinged images suffused with gloom; a pianist, noodling around minor keys, suffering for his art; the writer, wringing a sestina out of her tortured soul word by bloody word.

But words evolve, meanings change, and associations change accordingly. When Burton wrote *The Anatomy of Melancholy* in 1621, the theory of humorism was nearing the end of its time. We know more now; in 400 years no doubt we will know still more, and perhaps will look back on the state of today's medical understanding with equal bemusement.

And still, although we instinctively know what it means, the word's centre remains elusive. Susan Sontag's comparison – 'depression is melancholy minus its charms' – goes some way towards it, identifying correctly that in melancholy there is an obscure comfort, a perverse pleasure, an understanding that there is a way out but let's just swaddle ourselves in it for a few minutes more.

But there is more to it than that.

Melancholy is sad but not quite knowing why; it is 'ah well', not 'righty ho'; it is glass half empty, but the wine has a bitter depth – melancholy is not quaffable.

Melancholy is two hours to complete a five-minute task because you're constantly distracted and have to stop to look out of the window; and through the window you see the clouds, not the blue sky.

Melancholy sighs quietly, and wants you to hear. It is 'Yesterday', it is Billie Holiday singing 'Blue Moon', it is a Sibelius melody played on the cor anglais,* it is lying on the floor listening, allowing it to tweak your soul, and deep down, at some level, enjoying it, not quite wanting it to stop.

Melancholy is a slow tango by Astor Piazzolla in a small bar at three in the morning – bandoneon, violin, piano, and a long high melody with soft pulsing underneath, the last notes fading into silence and leaving a shape in the air, a feeling of loss and wistfulness to go with your empty glass and the cigarette butts in the ashtray.

Melancholy is light mizzle on a grey day, a long autumnal walk under a dull sky, mulling things over, and then, when you've gone round in literal and figurative circles long enough, and with dusk drawing in, you go to your dark house and sit at the kitchen table with a cooling cup of tea, looking at photos of one once loved, the long evening stretching ahead, full of fillable emptiness.

But you stay there just a bit longer.

---

* Words provided by Karen Mason.

THE LANGUAGE OF SWALLOWS

600

Subject provided by Andrew Ross

They come to us from far-off lands,* dipping and swooping with an elegance that belies their strength and stamina. Metal-blue backs with a satin sheen, creamy underparts, dark red around the forehead and throat; and then there's the tail, its slender forked streamers lending the bird a hint of the festive. An encounter to cheer, to thrill, to reassure us that summer, if not actually here, is at least icumen in.

And along with this brazen beauty comes the sound – a fast chattering, not all sweetness, but undercut with a slightly guttural quality. It's not unlike the sound you get, now largely and sadly lost to humanity, when you press play and fast-forward on a tape recorder at the same time. Within this twittering there might come an occasional croak, swooping slightly upwards, and then a rattle, like a briefly agitated Geiger counter. Slow it down and you find yourself in a surreal and weird sound world, not unlike an echo chamber, but along with that comes a form of enlightenment. Previously unheard phrasings and shapes become

* South Africa. Don't disturb me, I'm being poetic.

discernible, subtleties we're too slow to hear at full speed – that's our problem, not the swallow's.

It has a lot to say, the male swallow, and says it often. 'Come and mate with me' is the predominant message, but even when the bird has successfully paired off, the song continues. 'Hands off, she's mine', perhaps.

It's uplifting, that sound, enough to make me stop and look and listen. The French, pleasingly, give it the same word as for the babbling of a brook: *gazouillement*. The poet Abraham Cowley begged to differ.

> FOOLISH prater, what dost thou
> So early at my window do?
> Why thy tuneless serenade?
> . . .
> Cruel bird, thou'st ta'en away
> A dream out of my arms to-day

While I can always find a modicum of sympathy for the sleep-deprived, these words seem unnecessarily harsh. The swallow's voice might not have the deep and resonant poetry of a blackbird's, but there is beauty in it, and irrepressible good cheer. And if it lacks a melody discernible to human ears, then it's merely joining a very popular club – birdsong largely defies our attempts at musical notation, and the situation is even worse when it comes to finding equivalents using words. There is no birdsong transliteration *lingua franca* – one person's *tswit* is another's *tviiit* is another's *sweeeet* – and matching those words to the sounds we hear is notoriously difficult.

As well as the male's beguiling song, swallows of both sexes make a range of sounds, variously transliterated as *tsink, chur-chur, siflitt, twhitt, tswee-wit, flitt-flatt, feeta-feet, wid-wid, waeae-waeae, dschid-dschid, flü-flüh, dewihlik, zibist, zetch, tsä-tsä-tsä-tsä, weer-weer, hubba-hubba.*[*]

To our ears, these noises are part of the rich aural panoply of nature in spring and summer; to a swallow, they're everyday communication.

'Hello', 'Well heLLO there', 'Come here', 'Go away', 'Anyone fancy a bit?', 'Don't even think of coming any closer', 'Stay together, children!', 'I am enjoying this bout of sexual intercourse', 'Come on, eat it, it's just flies and you always say you like flies', 'Watch out – there's a human about!', 'SHIT! CAT! CAT CAT CAT CAT CAT!!!!'

And if that paragraph makes me guilty of anthropomorphising,[†] I am, on this occasion at least, backed up by research, which tells us that these, more or less, are the things that swallows tend to say to each other.

And if we derive pleasure from observing their chattering, twittering, swooping, gliding and diving, then so much the better.

---

* OK, it's possible I made that last one up.

† Spoiler: it does.

THE OUTREACH PROJECT

500

Subject provided by Kate Skeet

Unworthy thought occurs, on slip road out of Newport Pagnell services: why children?

Not against them per se, merely in context of own life, specifically today, extra-specifically in context of music workshop requiring realisation of theme 'Woodland Sounds'. Room of six-year-olds + box of percussion = inevitable, dismaying, anti-musical chaos. But important branch of orchestra's outreach programme, so part of job. Must knuckle down, quelling instinctive complaint that four years at music college and 10k hours practice not undergone to help little Timmy and pals shake cabasa in mimicry of rustling insects.

Early start no help. Ditto lack of caffeine and adequate breakfast – service-station croissant lacking requisite heft.

Loins girded.

Arrive at school, met by eager teacher of type thought extinct since Joyce Grenfell died. Apparently not. Teeth, tweed, earnest hands. She assures me children extraordinarily keen to meet me, can talk of little else. Suspect eagerness projected by Joyce (never catch her real name) on to kids. Suspicions confirmed when confronted by mayhem in hall – children charging around, giving me not even first glance. Caffeine, urgently requested, forthcoming in form of tepid Maxwell House in polystyrene cup.

Attempts to establish order only moderately successful. Holding beater in air to command silence of limited use when one half of group sitting on other half. Joyce, after initial introduction, scarpers sharpish, not to return until break time. Canny lady. Eventually enforce modicum of calm by engaging with group of four most responsible-looking children and starting quiet rhythmic tapping (*tap-tap-TAP*, *tap-tap-TAP*), which soon spreads. Joy of joys, manage to control volume with calming hand gestures. Tempted to start 'We Will Rock You' to *tap-tap-TAP* accompaniment, but fear would be over their heads and disturb delicate balance. Successfully hold attention, plan next move, hoping to channel momentary receptiveness towards rustling of stoats and drumming of woodpeckers.

Triumph, however, short-lived, as disrupter (shall call him Damien) grabs beater and, with unerring instinct, pounds away at loudest drum with total lack of rhythm. Wish to slap him, but of course can't, because prison.

Then, miracle. Smallest girl in room marches to Damien, rebukes him with firm, 'Stop that – it's horrible,' grabs stick, marches to me, hands me stick, turns to class and says, 'Now we're going to do something useful.'

Astonished to see complete compliance. Unprecedented. Wish to hug her, but of course can't, because prison.

Gather thoughts, and start ball rolling with request for names of woodland animals. Some inventive suggestions, though not convinced penguin notorious for bosky residence. Ditto unicorn.* Little matter, for children soon in element, and morning proceeds smoothly, construction of convincing woodland drama at its heart. Enthusiastic hootings, scrapings and patterings to the fore.

Culmination of morning's work: performance of 'Woodland Scene By Night', given to rapt attention of rest of school. No exaggeration to say am quite dumbfounded and moved. Cabasas genuinely atmospheric and insecty. Damien, charged with owl sounds, acquits himself with aplomb and exemplary restraint.

Maybe children not so bad after all.

* Word provided by Jane Allen.

HELLO DOG, GOODBYE DOG

400

Subject provided by Sara Dixon – with particular thanks to those fine dogs Ally, Sunshine, Eva, Pearl, Scooby and Eccles

You get them so young. Eight weeks or thereabouts. Little bundles of canine joy. Your job is to train them for their job. Guide dogs are friends and companions to their owners; they give confidence, independence and freedom. They transform lives. And it all starts with you, their first and only puppy walker.

They will, inevitably, be cute. Labrador puppies are known for that. Acknowledge it, ignore it – they're with you to learn. Discipline, responsibility. You have just under a year to teach them the basics – sit, stay, walk, but not that fast, and not that slow either, steady now – to deter them from their natural puppyish instincts – 'Hello, will you be my friend?', 'Will YOU be my friend?', 'You're my friend, aren't you? HELLO!' – and to prepare them for the next stage, when the early specialised skills you've instilled – this is a kerb, this is a stair, this is left and this is right – are entrenched and begin to be put to practical use.

You need consistency and patience. Just try telling a puppy that wants to go out into the sunshine that it can't until you say 'forward'; they need to curb their exuberance – a bouncy golden pup with an endearing look is a joy in most contexts, but a dangerous liability if it lets its owner down just when they need it most, if it stops being their eyes for just a second.

It can't be easy for them. The world is a fascinating place, full of tempting smells and that thing over there – is it another dog? IT IS ANOTHER DOG – HELLO, OTHER DOG! Oh, it's gone, but ooh, look at this, doesn't it look interesting? Hang on, I'll go and get it. Do you want it? Why don't you have it? Tell you what, I'll keep it for you. No, you can't have it – DON'T THROW IT.

But that's for other dogs. It has to be.

And then, after about a year of your care and understanding, and just when you really don't want them to, they go – on to full training, on to their owners, away and out of your life, your sadness at seeing them leave offset by the knowledge that this is how it must be. Otherwise, what's the point?

But you miss them and remember them and want them back.

And then another one comes, and you start all over again.

I DON'T KNOW WHY, I JUST DO

300

Subject provided by Richard Montagu

I don't know why I . . .

. . . whistle . . .

. . . love birds . . .

. . . hate desiccated coconut . . .

. . . find limpets so fascinating . . .

. . . do in fact like Mondays . . .

. . . take exception to being called 'Maestro' . . .

. . . feel melancholy when I think of goldfish . . .

. . . find windy days so unsettling for the soul . . .

. . . would travel to see a Kevin Pietersen cover drive . . .

. . . fail to engage adequately with the genius of Richard Wagner . . .

. . . suddenly feel the need for a bowl of gelato RIGHT NOW . . .

. . . hate portmanteau words like 'webinar', 'edutainment' and 'infomercial' with such fervour . . .

. . . well up whenever I conduct the last three minutes of Sibelius's Fifth Symphony . . .

. . . take my keys out when the front door is still 200 yards away . . .

. . . love most sports, but find ice hockey, while interesting enough to a point, somehow unengaging . . .

. . . associate steam trains with romance and glamour, when in reality they're noisy, smelly and dirty . . .

. . . find some sports commentators so annoying I have to turn the sound down whenever they're on . . .

. . . sometimes, but only sometimes, crave a cold-roast-lamb sandwich with redcurrant jelly and scrapings from the tin . . .

. . . make the same mistakes in life as I've made for thirty years, and probably will for the next thirty . . .

. . . fall for the cat's pitiful 'But you haven't fed me in 378 years – I'm LITERALLY STARVING' mewing every single time . . .

. . . always manage to kick at least one piece of furniture when all I'm trying to do is walk across a room . . .

. . . make a ridiculous *aahh* sound when I sit in a comfy sofa or take the first sip of a cup of tea . . .

. . . always run into those wotsits wandering all over the track in *Mario Kart* even though I can see them – THEY'RE RIGHT THERE . . .

. . . find the sight of Dean Martin sitting on a piano singing 'I Don't Know Why (I Just Do)' to Petula Clark slightly toe-curling . . .

. . . I just do.

GELATO

200

Subject provided by Jane Richards

Combine eggs, milk and sugar with your chosen flavouring. Heat to 85°C, chill to 4°C. Churn. Slowly.

Slowly.

You're not making ice cream. Ice cream is a different thing. This is not Mr Whippy. This is not even Ben & Jerry's.

This is gelato.

The fat content of gelato (minimum 3.5 per cent butterfat) is enshrined in Italian law. That's some serious shit, right there.

We don't want to get all chin-strokey and hipsterish about it. We eschew the word 'artisanal'. But we do want to take it seriously. Because gelato deserves seriousness.

The difference between ice cream and gelato? Gelato has less fat, less air, more flavour, richness, density.

It makes me think of hot Umbrian sunshine, a piazzetta hidden off a side street, that café nobody else knows, Piaggio scooter parked in the corner, the bored and tired waitress asking what you want – no words, just an enquiring upward nod.

Everyone has their BFF,* the one they choose almost instinctively. *Cioccolato* for me. Always. Darker than dark, smoother than smooth.

You might opt for something else – the subtlety of hazelnut, perhaps, or the pleasing blandness of vanilla.

Feel free. Just don't call it ice cream.

* Best Flavour Forever.

WHERE DO YOU GO TO, MY LOVELY?

100

Subject provided by Tessa Parikian

In my head I travel from West Norwood outwards, to cricket grounds near and far, where sport plays out to muted applause; to Costa Rica, where hummingbirds perform everyday miracles of aeronautical brilliance; to the finest hotels in the world, where waiters tend to my every need and leave a chocolate on the pillow.

In my head I fly free like a swallow to Africa and back.

And then I make a cup of tea and bring it in to you and we watch just one more episode of *Frasier*, and that, my lovely, is what life is all about.

INDEX

ACKNOWLEDGEMENTS

50

So many people, so few words. To all the book's supporters, subject providers and cheerleaders; to all at Unbound; to Anton, Cecily, Charles, Fenella, Jonathan, Laura, Oliver, Tessa (you all helped in various ways); to Scott (without whom . . .); to Simon (also without whom . . .); to everyone else I've forgotten . . .
. . . thank you.

A NOTE ON THE AUTHOR

Lev Parikian is a writer, conductor and keen birdwatcher. He is the author of *Why Do Birds Suddenly Disappear?* and *Into the Tangled Bank*. He lives in South London with his family, who are getting used to his increasing enthusiasm for nature. As a birdwatcher, his most prized sightings are a golden oriole in the Alpujarras and a black redstart at Dungeness Power Station.

@levparikian
levparikian.com

Unbound is the world's first crowdfunding publisher, established in 2011.

We believe that wonderful things can happen when you clear a path for people who share a passion. That's why we've built a platform that brings together readers and authors to crowdfund books they believe in – and give fresh ideas that don't fit the traditional mould the chance they deserve.

This book is in your hands because readers made it possible. Everyone who pledged their support is listed below. Join them by visiting unbound.com and supporting a book today.

Helen Ackroyd
Drew Adams
Geoff Adams
Christopher Adey
Aisha
Robert Aitken
Janet Alexander
Moose Allain
Jane Allen
Mark Allen
Jane Angell
Misha Anker
Anastasia Arnold
Amanda and Keith Ashby
Elizabeth Ashford
Nicola Ashton
Chris Astles
Philip Austin
Jonathan Ayling
Michelle Ayling
Ed Babar
Katharine Baird
Sharon Bakar
Alistair Bamford
David Barnett
Nicola Bates

Nigel Bates
Gareth Batterbee
Clare Beck
My darling Clarie Bell
Jack Bennett
John Best
John Bevan
Ann Bevington
Heather Binsch
Linda Blackburn
Sam Blade
Charles Bockett-Pugh
Susie Bokor
Gilly Bolton
Jeannie Borsch
Catherine Bowdler
Alexandra Bowers
Mark Bowsher
Alison Bowyer
James Boyd
Lindsay Bramley
Chris Brannick
Stephanie Bretherton
Rhodri Britton
Christine Bromsgrove
Lynne Bulmer
Guy Burkill QC
Eimear Burns
Jonathan Burton
Suzy Buttress
Janina Byrne
Stephen Byrne
Rachel Calderon
Simon Callaghan
Giles Cambray
Amanda Canning
Jo Cannon
Car722
George Carbutt
Bill Carslake
Meriel Cartwright
Alison Cawley
Susan Chadwick
Miles Chapman
R&E Charlesworth
Robert Chatley
Eleanor Chuck
Adrian Clark
Wing-Commander Clark
Brynly Clarke
Helen Clarke
Keith Clarke
Mathew Clayton
Jonathan Coe
Jennie Condell
Deb Conner
Andrew Connolly
Andrea Cook
Lesley Cookman
Percy Copley
Daniel Cornwell
Coruscation

Emma Cottrell
John Crawford
Jane Cronin
Julia Croyden
Charlotte Cunnibgham
Sharon Curtis
Saskia Daniel
Nigel Dant
Rishi Dastidar
Amanda Davidson
Chris Day
Susie Day
Sylvia de Bertodano
Iris de Carteret
Alison Deane
Samantha Deane
Miranda Denham
Scilla Di Donato
Miranda Dickinson
Angela Dickson
Rachael Dixon
Sara Dixon
George Dobell
Marc Dooley
Katy Driver
Rebekah Drury
Richard Dryer
Jessica Duchen
Sheila Dunn
David Durose
T & R Eaton
Sarah Eden
Jean Edwards
Gillian Eller
Helen M Elster Jones
Tom Elwin
June Emerson
Paul Emmett
Lissa Evans
Toby Faber
Susan Fall
Peter Fender
Natalie Fergie
Paul Ferguson
Stuart Ffoulkes
Aaron Fish
Neil Fisher
Marion Fleming
Margaret Ford
Ailsa Forsyth
Fiona Forsyth
Chris Foster
Paul Francis
Susan Fraser
Tom Frederikse
Kath Frodsham
Sarah Gabriel
Mark Galtrey
Timothy Garland
Viviane and Roger Garland
Lewis Gaston
Tom Gauterin

Abigail Gawith
Gavin Geary
Amro Gebreel
Josie George
Janet Gibson
Martha Gifford
Matthew Gilbert
Christopher Gillett
Ben Glassberg-Frost
David Goddard
Sarah Godwin
Miranda Gold
Sally Gooding
Gothiron
Chris Gould
Alan Grant
Lulu Guinness
Matthew H
Tor Hahn
Jim Hall
Sarah Hall
Christian Halstead
Lauren Hamer
Nathan Hamer
Tom Hammond
Stuart Hancock
Sydney Hansen
Andrea Harman
Susie and Mei Harries
Rachel Harrington
Shelley Harris
Tim Harwood
Paul Haseltine
Melinda Haunton
Nick Hely Hutchinson
Fiona Henderson
Rainer Hersch
Adrian Hickford
Steph Hicks
Paul Higham
Josh Hillman
John Holland
James Holloway
Antonia Honeywell
Claire Hoskins
John Howard
James Hoy
Bernard Hughes
Juliet Hughes-Rees
Alastair Hume
Lizzie Huxley-Jones
Annelies Ingrid
John & Sally Isaacs
Sebastian James
Mike Jarman
Helen Jeffries
Signe Johansen
Laurel Johnson
Outi Jokiharju
Shirley Judd
Andres Kabel
Tom Kane

Katherine Keen
Stephen Kenny
Dan Kieran
Patrick Kincaid
Shona Kinsella
Jackie Kirkham
Stephanie Kirschke
Medea Klan
Lord&Lady Knucketts
Paul La Planche
Ewan Lawrie
Liz Lawrie
Josephine Leak
Catherine Lee
Lia Leendertz
Mary Lester
Emma Lewis
Justin Lewis
Jeremy Limb
Matthew Longhurst
David and Lotte Lydon
Hugh Lydon
Jane MacArthur
Calum Macaulay
Andrew Macdonald
Andrew T Mackay
Stephen Macklow-Smith
Robert Maniura
Ruth Mann
Helen Mansfield
Elizabeth Manus
Fenella Mappin
Sarah K. Marr
Karen Mason
Quentin Maxwell-Jackson
Marie McGinley
Eileen McManus
Susan Metcalfe
Deborah Metters
Tim Milford
Roger Miller
Kelly Millington
Harry Mills
Sarah Milnes
John Mitchinson
Jon Mizler
Virginia Moffatt
Richard Montagu
Natalie Moore
Andy Moorhouse
Anna Morgan
Jonathan Morgan
Patrick Morgan
Muireann Murphy
Charles Mutter
Emma-Louisa Mutter
Peter Nall
Gwen Nathan
Carlo Navato
Karen Newman
Robert Nichols
Kalypso Nicolaidis

Jacqui Nobre
Ian Noonan
Katharine Norbury
Anne-Marie Norman
Sanchia Norman
Victoria Nowell
Clodagh O Connor
Terry O'Connor
Sharon O'Connor
Andrew Osborne
Vicky Owen
Scott Pack
Steven Pallett
Vicki Palmer
Robin Parer
Step Parikian
Jane Park
Karenza Passmore
Mary Jane Paterson
David Perchard
Costa Peristianis
Tara Persaud
Kim Peschier
Caroline Phillips
Robert Phillips
Jenny Pichierri
Nicola Pierre
David Pievsky
Jonathan Pinnock
Justin Pollard
Alex Postlethwaite
Dudley Pritchard
Laura Pritchard
Tessa Pritchard
David Prosser
Catherine Purcell
Toby Purser
Emma Pusill (Plum Duff)
Josephine Quealy
Jacqui Radford
Sophia Rahman
Lisa Rajan
Susannah Rang
Amanda Reed
Alison Rees
Phil Rees
Alex Reeve
Anna Reid
Emmanuella Reiter
Adele Reynolds
Denis Ribeiro
Jane Richards
Mat Riches
Richard Robbins
Andrew Roberts
Deb Roberts
Jane Roberts
Jenny & Tony Roberts
Alison Robinson
David Robson
Clara Rodriguez
Isabel Rogers

Andrew Ross
Daniel Ross
Peter Rowe
Alison Rowley
Gerard Rundell
Ken Saberi
Katherine Sanders
Anne Schirrmacher
Denise Schofield
Katy Scott
Peter Scott
Rachel Scott
Ros Seager
Anne Sedgwick
Iola Shaw
Philip Sheppard
Louise Shield
Debbie Shipton
Rachel Shirley
Sarah Siese
David Simpkin
Alastair Simpson
Peter Sive
Kate Skeet
Michael Slater
Rupert Smissen
Alex Smith
David Smith
Jane Smith
Lydia Smith
Martin Smith
Rose-Marie Smith
Anna & Ed Snow
Sylvia Snowden
Richard Soundy
Richard Souper
Helen Southwood
James Spackman
Maureen Kincaid Speller
Jackie Steinitz
Katherine Stephen
Andrew Steven
Sonia Stevenson
Tabatha Stirling
Alexander Stockler
Susan Strauss
Alice Stringer
Richard Studt
Sarah Sutherland
Mark Symons
Masayuki Tayama
Andrew Taylor
James Taylor
Charlotte Taylor-Page
Martin Terjan
Frances Tew
Helen Thompson
Mike Scott Thomson
Sebastian Till
Tithers
Paul Tomkins
Sarah Too

Lindsay Trevarthen
Graham Triggs
Linda Trill
Michael Trinder
Hilje van Beijnum
B. van Gendt
Veep
Mark Vent
Kerry Vevers
Salima Virji
Maria Vitale
Richard Vodden
Joanna Waddington
Giles Wade
Adele Wagstaff
Louise Wallis-Jones
Izzy Walsh
Matthew Walsh
Bryn Walters
Anthony Warrack
Sebastian Warrack
Robert Weaver
Mark Welling
Anna Whitaker
Celeste White
Chris White
John White
Seta White
Linda Wilkinson
Eley Williams
Helen Williams
Louise Williams
Nicole Wilson
Becky Wood
Charlotte Woodward
Jacqueline Woolf
Wendalynn Wordsmith
Christine Wordsworth
Laura Wright
Charles Wroth
Alice Yelf
Warren Zielinski